*International Kierkegaard
Commentary*

International Kierkegaard Commentary

Early Polemical Writings

edited by
Robert L. Perkins

MERCER UNIVERSITY PRESS

ISBN 0-86554-656-8

PT
8142
.A6
E27
1999

MUP/H489

International Kierkegaard Commentary
Early Polemical Writings
Copyright ©1999
Mercer University Press, Macon, Georgia 31210-3960 USA

The paper used in this publication meets the minimum requirements
of American National Standard for Information Sciences—
Permanence of Paper for Printed Library Materials, ANSI Z39.48-1984.

Library of Congress Cataloging-in-Publication Data

Early polemical writings / edited by Robert L. Perkins
xii+202pp. 6x9" (15x22cm.)—(International Kierkegaard Commentary ; 1)
Includes bibliographical references and index.
ISBN 0-86554-656-8 (alk. paper).
1. Kierkegaard, Søren, 1813–1855. Endnu levendes papirer.
I. Perkins, Robert L., 1930– .   II. Series.
B4376.I58   1984 vol. 1
[PT8142.A6]
839.8'18609—dc21   99-11601
                                                CIP

Contents

Acknowledgments

All the contributors to this volume would wish to make acknowledgments, but that privilege is reserved for the editor. Those whom the contributors would have named will be content to have served their friends and colleagues.

I have the privilege of thanking a number of persons at Stetson University who have supported my work in general and the *International Kierkegaard Commentary* in particular: H. Douglas Lee, president of the University, and Gary Maris, dean of the College of Arts and Sciences.

The advisory board and the volume consultant read all the contributions, offered valuable insights into the articles, and also made some recommendations for changes. Dr. Julia Watkin of the University of Tasmania continues to be particularly helpful in suggesting possible authors and tracking down obscure allusions in Kierkegaard's texts. The interest of Mercer University Press and especially the efforts of Senior Editor Edmon L. Rowell, Jr. are deeply appreciated. Princeton University Press gave permission to quote from *Early Polemical Writings* and other translations to which they hold copyright. Acknowledgment is also made to Bruce H. Kirmmse who gave permission to publish his privately held copyrighted article.

The several contributors and I also thank our families for the lost evenings and other scattered hours while we pursued these tasks. Finally, I wish to thank my wife, Sylvia Walsh, for assistance at every stage of this project and for making our life together an unutterable joy.

Robert L. Perkins

Sigla

AN   *Armed Neutrality* and *An Open Letter*. Trans. Howard V. Hong and Edna
       H. Hong. Bloomington and London: Indiana Univ. Press, 1968. (*Den
       bevæbnede Neutralitet*, written 1848–1849, publ. 1965; "Foranledigt ved
       en Yttring af Dr. Rudelbach mig betræffende," *Fædrelandet*, no. 26 [31
       January 1851].)

C   *The Crisis [and a Crisis] in the life of an Actress*. Trans. Stephen Crites.
       New York: Harper & Row, 1967. (*Krisen og en Krise i en Skuespillerindes
       Liv*, by Inter et Inter. *Fædrelandet* 188–191 [24–27 July 1848].)

CA   *The Concept of Anxiety*. Kierkegaard's Writings 8. Trans. Reidar Thomte,
       in collaboration with Albert B. Anderson. Princeton: Princeton Univ.
       Press, 1980. (*Begrebet Angest*, by Vigilius Haufniensis, ed. S. Kierke-
       gaard, 1844.)

CD   *Christian Discourses*, including *The Lilies of the Field and the Birds of the
       Air* and *Three Discourses at the Communion on Fridays*. Trans. Walter
       Lowrie. London and New York: Oxford Univ. Press, 1940. (*Christelige
       Taler*, by S. Kierkegaard, 1848; *Lilien paa Marken og Fuglen under Himlen*,
       by S. Kierkegaard, 1849; *Tre Taler ved Altergangen om Fredagen*, by S.
       Kierkegaard, 1849.)

CI   *The Concept of Irony*; "Notes on Schelling's Berlin Lectures." Kierke-
NSBL gaard's Writings 2. Trans. Howard V. Hong and Edna H. Hong. Prince-
       ton: Princeton Univ. Press, 1989. (*Om Begrebet Ironi*, by S. A. Kierke-
       gaard, 1841.)

COR *The Corsair Affair*. Kierkegaard's Writings 13. Trans. Howard V. Hong
       and Edna H. Hong. Princeton: Princeton Univ. Press, 1982.

CUP,1 *Concluding Unscientific Postscript*. Two volumes. Kierkegaard's Writings
CUP,2 12:1-2. Trans. Howard V. Hong and Edna H. Hong. Princeton:
       Princeton Univ. Press, 1992. (*Afsluttende uvidenskabelig Efterskrift*, by
       Johannes Climacus, ed. S. Kierkegaard, 1846.)

EO,1 *Either/Or*. Two volumes. Kierkegaard's Writings 3 and 4. Trans.
EO,2 Howard V. Hong and Edna H. Hong. Princeton: Princeton Univ. Press,
       1987. (*Enten/Eller* I-II, ed. Victor Eremita, 1843.)

EPW *Early Polemical Writings*. Kierkegaard's Writings 1. Trans. Julia Watkin.
FPOSL Princeton: Princeton Univ. Press, 1990.

EUD *Eighteen Upbuilding Discourses*. Kierkegaard's Writings 5. Trans. Howard
V. Hong and Edna H. Hong. Princeton: Princeton Univ. Press, 1990.
(*Atten opbyggelige taler*, by S. Kierkegaard, 1843–1845.)

FPOSL *From the Papers of One Still Living*. See EPW.

FSE *For Self-Examination* and *Judge for Yourself!* Kierkegaard's Writings 21.
JFY Trans. Howard V. Hong and Edna H. Hong. Princeton: Princeton Univ.
Press, 1990. (*Til Selvprøvelse*, by S. Kierkegaard, 1851, and *Dømmer Selv!*
by S. Kierkegaard, 1852.)

FT *Fear and Trembling* and *Repetition*. Kierkegaard's Writings 6. Trans.
R Howard V. Hong and Edna H. Hong. Princeton: Princeton Univ. Press,
1983. (*Frygt og Bæven*, by Johannes de Silentio, 1843, and *Gjentagelsen*,
by Constantin Constantius, 1843.)

JC "Johannes Climacus or *De omnibus dubitandum est*." See PF JC.

JFY *Judge for Yourself!* See FSE.

JP *Søren Kierkegaard's Journals and Papers*. Ed. and trans. Howard V. Hong
and Edna H. Hong, assisted by Gregor Malantschuk. Bloomington and
London: Indiana Univ. Press, (1) 1967; (2) 1970; (3-4) 1975; (5-7) 1978.
(From *Søren Kierkegaards Papier* I-XI³ and XII-XIII, 2nd ed., and *Breve
og Akstykker vedrørende Søren Kierkegaard*, ed. Niels Thulstrup, I-II,
1953–1954.)

JSK *The Journals of Søren Kierkegaard*. Trans. Alexander Dru. London and
New York: Oxford Univ. Press, 1938. (From *Søren Kierkegaards Papirer*
I-XI³ in 18 volumes, 1909–1936.)

KAUC *Kierkegaard's Attack upon "Christendom,"* 1854–1855. Trans. Walter Lowrie. Princeton: Princeton Univ. Press, 1944. (*Bladartikler* I-XXI, by S. Kierkegaard, *Fædrelandet*, 1854–1855; *Dette skal siges; saa være det da sagt*, by
S. Kierkegaard, 1855; *Øieblikket*, by S. Kierkegaard, 1-9, 1855; 10, 1881;
Hvad Christus dømmer om officiel Christendom, by S. Kierkegaard, 1855.)

LD *Letters and Documents*. Kierkegaard's Writings 25. Trans. Hendrik
Rosenmeier. Princeton: Princeton Univ. Press, 1978.

LY *The Last Years*. Trans. Ronald C. Smith. New York: Harper & Row,
1965. (From *Søren Kierkegaards Papirer* XI¹-XI².)

NSBL "Notes on Schilling's Berlin Lectures." See CI.

OAR *On Authority and Revelation, The Book on Adler.* Trans. Walter Lowrie. Princeton: Princeton Univ. Press, 1955. (*Bogen om Adler*, written 1846–1847, unpublished, Søren Kierkegaards *Papirer* VII² 235; VIII² B 1-27.)

P *Prefaces: Light Reading for Certain Classes as the Occasion May Require.* Trans. William McDonald. Tallahassee: Florida State University Press, 1989. (*Forord: Morskabslæsning for Enkelte Stænder efter Tid or Leilighed*, by Nicolaus Notabene, 1844.)

PC *Practice in Christianity.* Kierkegaard's Writings 20. Trans. Howard V. Hong and Edna H. Hong. Princeton: Princeton Univ. Press, 1991. (*Indøvelse i Christendom*, by Anti-Climacus, ed. S. Kierkegaard, 1850.)

PF *Philosophical Fragments* and *Johannes Climacus.* Kierkegaard's Writings
JC 7. Trans. Howard V. Hong and Edna H. Hong. Princeton: Princeton Univ. Press, 1985. (*Philosophiske Smuler*, by Johannes Climacus, ed. S. Kierkegaard, 1844. "Johannes Climacus eller *De omnibus dubitandum est*," written 1842–1843, unpublished, *Søren Kierkegaards Papirer* IV C 1.)

PV *The Point of View Etc., including The Point of View for My Work as an Author, Two Notes about "The Individual," and On My Work as an Author.* Trans. Walter Lowrie. London/New York/Toronto: Oxford University Press, 1939. (*Synspunktet for min Forfatter-Virksomhed*, by S. Kierkegaard, posthumously publ. 1859; *Om min Forfatter-Virksomhed*, by S. Kierke-gaard, 1851.)

R *Repetition.* See FT, R.

SLW *Stages on Life's Way.* Kierkegaard's Writings 11. Trans. Howard V. Hong and Edna H. Hong. Princeton: Princeton Univ. Press, 1988. (*Stadier paa Livets Vej*, ed. Hilarius Bogbinder 1845.)

SUD *The Sickness unto Death.* Kierkegaard's Writings 19. Trans. Howard V. Hong and Edna H. Hong. Princeton: Princeton Univ. Press, 1980. (*Syg-dommen til Døden*, by Anti-Climacus, ed. S. Kierkegaard, 1849.)

TA *Two Ages: The Present Age and the Age of Revolution. A Literary Review.* Kierkegaard's Writings 14. Trans. Howard V. and Edna H. Hong. Princeton: Princeton Univ. Press, 1978. (*En literair Anmeldelse. To Tidsal-dre*, by S. Kierkegaard, 1846.)

TDIO *Three Discourses on Imagined Occasions.* Kierkegaard's Writings 10. Trans. Howard V. Hong and Edna H. Hong. Princeton: Princeton University Press, 1993. (*Tre Taler ved tænkte Leiligheder*, by S. Kierkegaard, 1845.)

UDVS *Upbuilding Discourses in Various Spirits.* Kierkegaard's Writings 15. Trans. Howard V. Hong and Edna H. Hong. Princeton: Princeton University Press, 1993. (*Obyggelige Taler i forskjellig Aand,* 1847.)

WA *Without Authority,* trans. Howard V. Hong and Edna H. Hong. Princeton: Princeton University Press, 1997. (*Lilien paa Marken og Fuglen under Himlen,* 1849; *Tvende ethisk-religieuske Smaa Afhandler,* 1849; *Upperstepræsten, Tolderen, synderinden, tre Taler ved Altergangen om Fredagen,* 1849; *En Opbyggerig Tale,* 1850; *To Taler ved Altergangen om Fredagen,* 1851.)

WL *Works of Love.* Trans. Howard V. and Edna H. Hong. New York: Harper & Row, 1962. (*Kjerlighedens Gjerninger,* 1847.)

Introduction

This collection is the first focused effort to bring modern research techniques to bear on Kierkegaard's earliest political writings and literary efforts, gathered in the first volume of Kierkegaard's Writings under the title *Early Polemical Writings*. Some of the pieces, the speech at the Student Union, "Our Journalistic Literature," and the rather strident, though silly, play, *The Battle between the Old and the New Soap-Cellars*, were not published during Kierkegaard's lifetime. That the analytic capacities and philosophic sophistication of the mature Kierkegaard is not present is, of course, no surprise. Rather, these first writings show the young student already at work on many of the issues that will occupy him throughout his short life and perhaps experimenting with projected self-images and writing styles. Some of the critical standpoints so early enunciated will remain relatively unchanged, sometimes with no credit to himself: his conventional views of women and his suspicion of the political process. His critique of idealist philosophy is already quite apparent to any careful reader. The religious is almost entirely absent, except for a contrast between "a purely human" and the "true Christian conviction" (EPW, 76-77). His capacity to transmute his considerable learning into fresh and original literary works is also apparent even in the unfinished, unpolished, and incoherent play. This collection of literary efforts in Kierkegaard's Writings is in every way a series of voyages of self-discovery, laden with significance for the later production.

Still, Kierkegaard could only start like all other fledgling authors: with his first publication. It was an experimental, silly aesthetic piece, one he never included in his public comments about his "authorship." This newspaper article, analyzed and critiqued by Julia Watkin, is a harbinger of unhappy things to come, for his mature views of gender relations never significantly depart from the basic stereotypical views indicated in this newspaper article. There is a rather significant difference in tone between these early ironic reflections and his mature views expressed in *Either/Or* and *Stages on Life's Way* which more or less phenomenologically describe the position of woman in contemporary society without the biting, even sarcastic, irony. Unfortunately, his concept of the "universally human" so characteristic and important in his contribution to the development of social, political, philosophical, and theological thought, never quite overcomes the demeaning biases towards women almost universally held at the time and reflected so harshly in this article.

The pieces that followed were also experimental and light-hearted for the most part, though serious undertones begin to be expressed, usually in an outrageous irony that was little appreciated at the time. His first brush with the press (commented upon in the present volume by me) provoked an understanding of Kierkegaard as a political conservative that has lasted to the present day. However, I suggest that if one simply stops being mesmerized by the early liberal critique of Kierkegaard, and asks new questions, one obtains surprising new insights into the issues, insights that cast long shadows throughout Kierkegaard's relation to the press and bourgeois society. It is just possible that the politically conservative young Kierkegaard raises philosophic questions about the nature of political discourse and its relation to the media in general that today seem obvious and fundamentally important. His running controversy with the press was not just about contemporary liberal politics and practice. For instance, I do not note in my article the rather odd circumstance that though this series of polemical articles is reputably a conservative critique of liberal politics and the liberal press, the conservatives did not come to his defense or publish his offending and offensive—that is, offensive to the liberal press—student address. That deafening silence suggests that they may have realized that his views were not really malleable to their politics and purposes, and that they wisely decided not to encourage his attentions to the logical quality of their own arguments in the political debates of the time. The conservatives may have been warned off because Kierkegaard had already explicitly said in the Student Union address that he would have extended his critique to the conservative press had time permitted (EPW, 52), dropping the hint that he would gladly do so if he were asked or challenged. Whatever the case, Kierkegaard never engaged the conservative press in the manner that he criticized the liberal press in this series of articles, or was the excuse of shortness of time just a lame rationalization for the one-sidedness of his student address? But one can only wonder why the conservative press did not print the address which, to judge from the response in the liberal press, caused so much discomfort to the liberal press and provoked a long self-justificatory polemic.

Kierkegaard's first "book," *From the Papers of One Still Living*, shows the first unmistakable inklings of the serious existential dimension of his thought, almost as if he did not know himself quite what to make of it. The book is an experiment in literary criticism, and along the way Kierkegaard discovers some elements of his later existential philosophy while showing off his critical mastery of recent Danish literature. The next four articles in this collection attempt to unravel this somewhat incoherent, yet fascinating and important, first work. It is a book-length review of Hans Christian Andersen's novel, *Only a Fiddler*. Andersen was better known at the time as a novelist than as an author of children's fairy tales, and his novels were widely read in Denmark and in translation. Thus, *From the Papers of One Still Living* is a first book about an already established author. Kierkegaard was a student who had not earned a degree, but he was well enough known in Copenhagen for Andersen to be concerned about a review that Kierkegaard promised when they casually met.

Richard Summers analyzes the complex problems of the relation of metaphysics to literature and ethics, showing the first traces of Kierkegaard's lifelong emphasis upon the ethical. Summers establishes the connections of *From the Papers of One Still Living* with Thomasine Gyllembourg and Paul Martin Møller in the early development of Kierkegaard's thought. Though Gyllembourg is a representative of an older generation, Kierkegaard's appeal to her production shows her importance for the development of Danish literature as well as for his own thinking. Kierkegaard responds to her robust acceptance of historical reality which she requires her heroes and heroines to confront and overcome. In contrast with the realism and strength of the characters in Gyllembourg's novels, the principal weakness in Andersen's novel is, as Kierkegaard sees it, that Andersen cannot transmute his own suffering of existence into a literary work and his characters are overcome by time, place, and events. The result is that his characters are not well developed, are sentimental, and carry their feelings on their shoulders. Andersen's failure warns Kierkegaard that he, as an author, must manage to transform his own sufferings, pain, and regret into a realistic appraisal of historical actuality and present his readers with a life-view that will aid them in their own life-development. These last terms Kierkegaard owes more to Møller's ideal of personal integration and harmony than to Gyllembourg.

Bruce H. Kirmmse focuses the complex and tense, at least from Andersen's side, ambiguity between the two men that began in earnest with the publication of Kierkegaard's *From the Papers of One Still Living*. Although the book is ostensibly a review of Andersen's novel, *Only a Fiddler*, one can only imagine his puzzlement over the title and resentment at much of the content. Subsequently throughout his life, Andersen said one thing and then another about his personal views of the book and Kierkegaard himself. Kirmmse examines it all. Andersen appears, however, to have attempted to settle accounts in his preferred genre, in the tale that Kirmmse translates at the beginning of his article. Yet, Kirmmse's view of multiple causes of the fairy tale is controversial among Andersen scholars, whom he cites and critiques. Kirmmse's article offers a prime example of the reasons for the ancient, widespread, and tenacious interpretation of Kierkegaard as a hypersensitive, morose, spiritually proud, and judgmental misanthrope. Who could doubt the testimony of a respected novelist and beloved writer of children's fairy tales? Andersen had the last word, but it is not certain that his skin was thicker than Kierkegaard's. Kierkegaard, at least, never commented further upon Andersen in public.

Grethe Kjær notes how long and how intensely Kierkegaard was preoccupied with Gyllembourg's works. *A Story of Everyday Life* occupies Kierkegaard primarily in *From the Papers*, and her *Two Ages* was the focus of his *En Literair Anmeldelse*, published in Kierkegaard's Writings under the title *Two Ages*. Kjær's article is as much biographical as literary-critical and interprets both Gyllembourg's work and Kierkegaard's reflection on it. Though all her writings were published anonymously, Countess Gyllembourg was one of the most widely read authors of the times. Her ambiguous relation to the more conservative circles in which she moved is evident in her frank recognition of the rights of the passions. Strong moral principles and her own experience of a one-sided marriage prevent her from indulging them. Her work shows considerable psychological insight, but she avoids sentimentality by her frank realism. Interestingly, the major protagonists of her novels are all women, a fact perhaps lost on Kierkegaard.

George Pattison presents a wide-ranging study of the history of the myth of the Wandering Jew, and this essay will enter the literary bibliographies as a major study of the Wandering Jew.

Pattison takes on a difficult task, for the Wandering Jew is not explicitly mentioned in the text of *From the Papers of One Still Living*. Yet we do know from Kierkegaard's journals that he was thinking of the theme of the Wandering Jew at the time of the composition of this book. Pattison claims, and I think shows, that the figure is behind Kierkegaard's response to Andersen's novel, *Only a Fiddler*. The central female protagonist, Naomi, is the figure for the non-Danish, the exotic, the outside, but her difference is based not just on her Jewishness, though that is important, but also upon the fact that "she was more a partisan of Young Germany" (EPW, 94). Naomi's homelessness and wandering mirrors both the alienation of the Wandering Jew and the literary movement. The contrast between the Danish *hygge* (comfort, coziness) and the absence and loss of place experienced by both the wandering Naomi and the stay-at-home hero of the book, Christian, mirror each other. Both are victims; neither has a place nor can make one. Both reflect the negative view of historical actuality so apparent in romanticism and Young Germany. Pattison shows the theme of the Wandering Jew as central and vital to the early Kierkegaard, far beyond the Andersen book to which it serves as important hermeneutical background.

The two concluding essays in this volume reflect upon the ironic comedy, *The Battle between the Old and the New Soap-Cellars*, which Kierkegaard left unfinished, unpolished, and unappealing to all but the most dogged scholar. The unimportance of the piece appears to be all the more obvious, when one realizes that though a lot of labor was expended upon it; it remained a private exercise, uncommunicated to any, and it was never performed. It is also to this day the most unread exercise of Kierkegaard's youth.

David Cain is not the "solitary reader" of this essay, but he has lingered lovingly upon every line perhaps more than anyone else recently, with the exception of David Law whose essay follows, and Cain's care has paid off in an evocative essay that matches Kierkegaard's suggestibility in the play itself. The most direct benefit for many of us is the critical and explanatory summary upon which Cain hangs his critical and interpretative comments. Cain's examination of the play reveals many of the turns of thought and phrase that will become prominent features of the authorship. Rather like Johannes Climacus, who in the *Postscript* finds that every move he anticipates is accomplished as soon as he conceives it, Cain finds that many of the themes, viewpoints, fundamental concepts, and critical personae that will loom large in the subsequent authorship are already here in the play awaiting development and completion. Cain's article is then a strong argument for the unity of the authorship. Whereas Kjær's article provides some of the local color and literary background for the book on Andersen and *Two Ages*, Cain shows us the refracted reaction of the young student to the leading intellectual lights in the political arena and the university. As unpolished as the text is, it shows us a literary genius experimenting, perhaps fantasizing himself as dramatist.

David Law takes a completely different approach to the play, for he discusses at length the literary sources of *The Battle between the Old and the New Soap-Cellars* after duly noting the acerbic criticisms of Hegelianism in the play. There are dozens of literary allusions in the play, and Law tracks them all down to the editions Kierkegaard used, noting even his errors. Because of several parallels between two scenes in Kierkegaard's play and Goethe's *Faust*, Law argues that the former is an intentional parody of the latter, and that in turn makes Willibald in *Soap-Cellars* a parody of Faust. Whereas Faust turns to Mephistopheles for help to overcome his despair, Willibald turns to Hegelianism, a turn that focuses the local debate over the importance of Hegelianism as a central theme of the play. E. T. A. Hoffmann and Friedrich Schiller are also exploited to develop some action scenes, but perhaps Joseph von Eichendorff's satire, *Viel Lärmen über Nichts*, is more important than either. I drop all these names here (and Law's exhaustive study examines the relation of many more to *Soap-Cellars*) to suggest that just as *From the Papers of One Still Living* displayed the young Kierkegaard's mastery of Danish literature, *Soap-Cellars* demonstrates, for us at least, his extensive knowledge of contemporary German literature. This literary experiment more importantly suggests that Kierkegaard is developing the aesthetic powers that will make him a master of the use of literature for philosophic purposes.

This volume of essays is offered to our readers, who by criticism and better thinking we invite to become our teachers.

Robert L. Perkins

1

Serious Jest?
Kierkegaard as Young Polemicist in "Defense" of Women

Julia Watkin

In Kierkegaard's earliest writings of 1834–1836, one encounters an ironic newspaper polemic that seems to mock the issues of equality and freedom. In all four articles, Kierkegaard apparently ignores the significance of movements towards women's emancipation and freedom of the press, pouring ridicule on the educational activity of Johan Ludvig Heiberg, and the political activity of Johannes Hage and Orla Lehmann.

The reader is naturally concerned to know why the young Kierkegaard indulges himself in witty polemic concerning serious issues, and in this paper I would like to examine Kierkegaard's attitude, particularly in the context of his very first article, December 1834, "Another Defense of Woman's Great Abilities." This piece clearly concerns the issue of equality as well as freedom, and yet it seems more flagrant than the articles of 1836 where Kierkegaard displays, relatively speaking, a greater seriousness of intention.[1] Here, Kierkegaard does not seem at all interested in making contact with the subject of women's position in society. Instead, he seems to be penning an exercise in wit rather than wisdom, with women as the target of his irony.[2] One may also

---

[1]Although one may be tempted to agree with Johannes Hage, that Kierkegaard's tactic of "mockery and witticisms" is no substitute for sober data and "discussions about reality," in the press articles Kierkegaard at least makes contact with Hage and Lehmann and one can detect traces of the conservatism of his earlier paper to the Student Association. See EPW, xvii-xxiii.

[2]One might perhaps view the article as an illustration in wit of Poul Martin Møller's frequent comment at that period that Kierkegaard's polemical nature was

view Kierkegaard as adding insult to injury, since another theology student, Peter Engel Lind, had already, in the same month, written an ironic piece, "In Defense of Woman's Higher Origin."[3] Thus, there seem good grounds for labelling Kierkegaard, without further ado, "male chauvinist."

Yet how does Kierkegaard himself explain the article when he comes to speak about the intention of his authorship? At first it looks as if we must answer this by saying that he totally ignores it. It is clear from *Concluding Unscientific Postscript* and *The Point of View for My Work as an Author* that Kierkegaard regards his authorship as starting with *Either/Or* (CUP, 1:251, 625, PV, 5, 10).[4] At one point, however, Kierkegaard does indicate that he includes his article on women. In his Journals for 1846, when he is working on a draft of his "First and Last Declaration" for *Concluding Unscientific Postscript*, he declares himself to be the author of his first three pseudonymous articles (CUP, 2:109). Later, in his Journals for 1848, he even mentions the article by name, recalling its title as "Another Defense of Women's Emancipation" (JP, 6:6202 translation revised).[5]

One good reason for the exclusion of material prior to *Either-Or* is, of course, that newspaper articles and reviews are not "author-

---

"appalling" (JP, 6:6888, 6889). Yet one must note that Kierkegaard, despite this, also associates his polemical nature with a basic seriousness of purpose that started from the age of ten (JP, 5:5961).

[3]It is not clear whether Kierkegaard's article is directly connected with Lind's. They had been friends at school, and one may suspect some form of direct link in the matter of publishing the two articles. Certainly it was important for young would-be authors to get a foot in J. L. Heiberg's literary circle through his paper "Kjøbenhavns flyvende Post," and this must have been already motivation enough for both of them. See here, EPW, xv-xvi, esp. xvin.36, and 3-5, 131-33.

[4]Thus, Kierkegaard's first four newspaper articles, his review of Hans Christian Andersen's *Only a Fiddler* (1837), and his doctoral dissertation are not counted as part of the authorship.

[5]H. P. Barfod, *Af Søren Kierkegaards Efterladte Papirer*, ed. H. P. Barfod and H. Gottsched (Copenhagen: C. A. Reitzels Forlag, 1869–1881) 1848:132 and 1844–1846:866-69, ascribes a pseudonymous article from 1835 to S.K.: "Emancipation from the Burden of Duty," but this is clearly not Kierkegaard's "Ogsaa et Forsvar for Qvindernes Emancipation [*sic*]," judging from Kierkegaard's journal entry, from the style of the article, and the fact that Barfod also uncritically ascribes Lind's article to Kierkegaard.

ship" in the strict book-writing sense of the term,[6] while a doctoral dissertation is linked with the acquiring of a degree. Also, by dating his authorship from *Either-Or*, Kierkegaard may be doing no more than operating with a technical definition, the point at which, as author, he has a definite maieutic purpose with what he writes. One might suspect, however, that by the 1840s it was embarrassing for Kierkegaard to have to date his authorship from such a frivolous piece.[7] Having said this though, the fact that he writes his article the way he does is not without interest, since it indicates the beginnings of an approach to the subject of equality and freedom that is decisively different from that of the practical social reformers of the nineteenth century.

What has provoked both Lind's and Kierkegaard's articles is Heiberg's prospectus for a course of lectures, an introduction to philosophy, to be held in the spring of 1833.[8] What is unusual about the prospectus is that he invites both men and women to attend. Even though he makes it clear that he thinks men "usually have a sharper and more consistent reason," and "a greater capacity for dialectic," women are viewed as having "a surer, more infallible feeling for immediately grasping truth." Thus, Heiberg regards the capacities of men and women as being equally "effective for knowledge" and invites the educated and cultured of both sexes to his lectures.[9] Heiberg did not, of course, find the idea of

---

[6]As Kierkegaard lets us know (JP, 5:5873, 5877), when he plans to stop being an author and communicate with the public through reviews instead.

[7]The point of the article is not women or their liberation, but, as Teddy Petersen points out, *Kierkegaards polemiske debut* (Denmark: Odense Universitetsforlag, 1977) 28, rather the writing of an article for Heiberg's paper.

[8]At the Military Academy. See Johan Ludvig Heiberg, *Om Philosophiens Betydning for den nuværende Tid* (Copenhagen: C. A. Reitzels Forlag, 1833) 53. See also EPW, 230-32n.15.

[9]One may wonder with Henning Fenger, "Kierkegaard, P. E. Lind og 'Johan Gordon,' " Kierkegaardiana VII (1968): 7-18, why Heiberg accepted the articles on women when their point of departure is his proposed course. One reason may be that, since so few signed up and the course was cancelled, Heiberg is using young writing talent to ironize indirectly over the lack of interest. In fact, sixteen signed up, two of whom were women, while two of the men later crossed their names off the list. See Morten Borup, *Johan Ludvig Heiberg* (Copenhagen: Gyldendal, 1947–1949) 2:212.

women's participation in philosophy lectures comic because he was used to the society of cultured women.[10] He had also spent the years 1819–1821 studying in postrevolution Paris.[11] Yet it was a time when "respectable" women ventured out in a man's world with caution, often, as was the case with Kamma Rahbek, as cultural hostess in the home in relation to a man's position (EPW, xv). The activity of single women might meet with opposition,[12] and if women were to make a breakthrough on their own account, they must not only expect to educate themselves to a great extent, they must also be prepared to start out in the world of literature under male pseudonyms, or anonymously.[13] Heiberg, and philosophy

---

[10]E.g., Kamma Rahbek, wife of writer and literary critic Knud Lyne Rahbek; his mother author Thomasine Gyllembourg, and his wife actress Johanne Luise Heiberg.

[11]Kierkegaard, especially, lacked the experience of a home with educated women, even though he encountered cultured women in the homes of others. Kierkegaard's mother could read, but not write, and did only housework. His elder sisters had been expected to do housework too, even rough work normally done by servants, and when education was made available to them, the girls in the family could expect a very limited amount by the standard of the boys, who were sent to the Borgerdydskole with the prospect of a university education. See: Grethe Kjær, *Barndommens ulykkelige Elsker* (Copenhagen: C. A. Reitzels Forlag, 1986) 20-22, Valdemar Ammundsen, *Søren Kierkegaards Ungdom* (Copenhagen: Universitetsbogtrykkeriet, J. H. Schultz A/S, 1912) chap. 2, Sejer Kühle, *Søren Kierkegaard*, Barndom og ungdom (Copenhagen: Aschehoug Dansk Forlag, 1950) chaps. 2 and 3, T. H. Croxall, *Glimpses and Impressions of Kierkegaard* (London: James Nisbet, 1959) 50-51. It must be noted, though, that Henriette Lund was sent to school (as opposed to home tutoring) through Kierkegaard's influence (Croxall, 58).

[12]As did Charlotte Dorothea Biel (1731–1788), author, translator, and playwright, who met with fierce opposition from her father who tried to stop her from reading. See Mette Winge, *Skriverjomfruen* (Denmark: Samleren, 1988) 17, 23, 39-41, 292.

[13]In Britain, the Brontë sisters, Charlotte (1816–1855), Emily (1818–1848) and Anne (1820–1849), began with *Poems by Currer, Ellis and Acton Bell*, 1846; Mary Anne Evans (1819–1880) wrote as George Eliot. In Denmark, Heiberg's mother, Thomasine Gyllembourg-Ehrensvärd (1773–1856), was the anonymous author of a number of books and plays. See EPW, 230n.10, and "Fru Gyllembourgs litterære Testament" to her son, in *Breve fra og til Johan Ludvig Heiberg*, anonymously published for Johanne Luise Heiberg by Andræ & Kriger (Copenhagen: C. A. Reitzels Forlag, 1862) 217-22.

professor Frederik Sibbern,[14] were thus exceptional in seeing women as capable of understanding philosophy, let alone
encouraging them to come to lectures,[15] while Lind and Kierkegaard here represent the norm of finding it comic that anyone
should think women capable of following philosophy lectures.[16]

Yet the 1830s was a period of political disturbance in Europe
with movements towards freedom and equality (EPW, viii-ix, xv).
Therefore we may expect to find in the articles of Lind and Kierkegaard allusions to the subject of women's liberation. If we look at
Lind's article,[17] however, there is hardly anything. Lind's irony
reveals a man who sees woman in general terms, chiefly as a being
interested in fashion, in the making of pretty things, and useful in
the kitchen. However, apart from knowledge of the enormity of
the Heiberg philosophy prospectus, Lind implies knowledge of
discrimination against women in history[18] and notes one other
concrete item from the world of women, namely the trousers (and
lifestyle) of author George Sand, Baronne Dudevant,[19] notorious
even outside France in her young days for her bold assumption of
man's dress and lifestyle. Through clothes, novels and the
proclamation of free love, she revealed the hypocrisy of different

---

[14]Frederik Christian Sibbern (1785–1872), professor of philosophy at Copenhagen University from 1813.

[15]Men might not be keen on women taking posts as teachers in the women's
"institutes" or schools either, even though the subjects would, of course, be those
considered suitable for women. A contemporary of Kierkegaard's, pastor's wife
Eline Boisen, tells us that she wanted to teach at such a school, but her fiancé
refused to allow it. See *Men størst er kærligheden, Eline Boisens erindringer fra midten
af forrige århundrede*, ed. Anna, Elin, Gudrun, and Jutta Bojsen-Møller and Birgitte
Haarder (Denmark: Gyldendal, 1985) 100-101.

[16]See, e.g., Nikolaj Fogtmann (1788–1851), bishop of Aalborg. His reaction to
the written prospectus was: "They must be some damn fine ladies able to understand them [the lectures], if they will 'grace the gathering with their presence.' "
Poul Martin Møller (1794–1838) (EPW, xivn.26) was of the opinion that "all female
poets have been intellectual deformities or monstrosities (Sappho, Mad. Dacier,
Mad. Staël Mrs. Brun)." See Teddy Petersen, *Kierkegaards polemiske debut*, 21, 24.

[17]"In Defense of Woman's Higher Origin," EPW, 131-33.

[18]"[L]ater times and a large part of the present treat woman as a useful chattel.
. . . man . . . believed . . . he had a right to command woman as his lawful
property." EPW, 131-32.

[19]Armadine Lucile Aurore Dupin, Baronne Dudevant (1804–1876).

rules of behavior for men and women, appearing as a forerunner in the movement towards women's liberation.

Kierkegaard in his follow-up article[20] ignores George Sand's trousers,[21] and his defence of woman's abilities differs from Lind's in having concrete reference to women and their situation in history and in alluding to contemporary women.[22] Especially prominent is a direct mention of France and the socialistic Saint-Simonist movement.[23] Thus we can note that Kierkegaard avoids reference to George Sand, to individual women's efforts towards liberation, yet he makes fun of a community movement, the Saint-Simonists with their emphasis on social equality for both sexes. I would here like to look at both movements in more detail, because I think they have something important to say to us about Kierkegaard's attitude to women and their emancipation.

First, even if we regard Kierkegaard's mention of the Saint-Simonist movement merely as a literary substitute for Lind's allusion to George Sand, we still have to face the fact that he rejected women's emancipation, both as Judge William and as himself.[24]

---

[20]"Another Defense of Woman's Great Abilities," EPW, 3-5.

[21]Kierkegaard may have avoided the subject because Lind had exhausted all that could be safely said about her without shocking readers' sensibilities too much. George Sand was currently putting her theory of free love into practice in a whirlwind affair (1833–1834) with Alfred de Musset.

[22]He refers to the limitations imposed on women in the East, in Islam and Christianity, and to the persecutions of women for witchcraft. He makes mention of women's current activity as lay medical helpers, while there seem to be allusions to the writings of Thomasine Gyllembourg, Hanna Irgens's poetry, Christine Rosen's cookery book, and to Mariane Stub's paintings. See EPW, 3-5 and 229-30nn.6, 10, 11, 12, and 14.

[23]After Claude-Henri de Rouvroy, Comte de Saint-Simon (1760–1825), French social philosopher who advocated socialism.

[24]Gregor Malantschuk, *The Controversial Kierkegaard*, trans. Howard Hong and Edna Hong (Ontario: Wilfred Laurier University Press, 1980) 47-48, argues that Kierkegaard's own view of men and women coincides with that of Judge William. Birgit Bertung, "Yes, a Woman *Can* Exist," *Kierkegaard Poet of Existence*, Kierkegaard Conferences I (Copenhagen: C. A. Reitzels Forlag, 1989) 7-18, disagrees with Malantschuk, however, concluding from the writings of Judge William and the other pseudonyms that Kierkegaard is ironizing over the domination of women by men to which women give their assent. See also, Bertung, *Om Kierkegaard, kvinder og kærlighed—en studie i Søren Kierkegaards kvindesyn* (Copenhagen: C. A. Reitzels Forlag, 1987) 52-61. My own view inclines to Malantschuk rather than

Judge William makes it clear to us that although he thinks "woman is certainly just as good as man," he hates the thought of women's emancipation (SLW, 124; EO, 2:22, 311-13).[25] Kierkegaard makes some positive comment about women in his Journals, but he tells us that "the emancipation of women" is "the invention of the devil" (JP, 4:4992). In *Works of Love*, Kierkegaard, while he castigates the inequality of pagan caste systems, is still specifically against women's emancipation: "fatuous people have fatuously been busy about making it obvious in a worldly way that the woman should be established in equal rights with the man—Christianity has never required or desired this." Woman's freedom lies in choosing the husband who is to be her master (WL, 69, 138-39).[26]

When it comes to concrete efforts towards women's emancipation in the North, Kierkegaard demonstrates clearly his lack of sympathy for the individuals concerned. The first instance concerns Fredrika Bremer (1801–1865), the Finnish-born naturalized Swedish author and traveller, who started the Swedish suffragette movement. When she visited Copenhagen in 1848, she visited and made friends of several cultural notabilities, for example, Hans Andersen and Hans Martensen, yet when she requested Kierkegaard to call upon her for the purpose of discussing "life's stages," she received a polite refusal. While it is true Kierkegaard found her ensuing comments about him in her book, *Life in the North* (1849), unflattering and is reacting to these,[27] his own comments in his Journals also clearly indicate a lack of understanding and disapproval of women who publicly take an active intellectual interest in theology and other subjects (LD, letters 201, 203, and 204; JP 6:6493, 6475, 6636).[28]

Bertung here.

[25]References to an emancipated woman perhaps being against marriage, and an allusion to an article about identical clothing for women and men may possibly be aimed at George Sand, EO, 2:53, 312.

[26]One can note here, the influence of the New Testament on Kierkegaard: Eph. 5:22; Col. 3:18; 1 Pet. 3:1.

[27]*Søren Kierkegaards Papirer*, ed. P. A. Heiberg, V. Kuhr, E. Torsting, and N. Thulstrup, (Copenhagen: Gyldendal, 1968–1970) X,1 658, 412.

[28]It should be noted that Rosenmeier is incorrect (LD, 483) to translate the Danish as meaning that Bremer had had sexual intercourse with famous people.

Another object of Kierkegaard's disapproval is Mathilde Fibiger (1830–1872), sister of the Ilia Fibiger who did pioneer work in nursing and childcare.[29] Unlike her sister, Mathilde was more interested in social theory than practice, and she was driven by a desire for personal freedom to seek an independent status. She became a teacher in a family on Lolland where she was to write a book published through Heiberg that caused a sensation, namely, *Clara Raphael, Twelve Letters*.[30] Mathilde also possessed a strong patriotic sense, and, like many others, she had been inspired by the national political awakening of 1848. Yet the new constitution of June 5 gave the vote to men, not to women, whose position was thus unchanged. While this seemed unjust to many men and women strongly committed to democracy, it was Mathilde Fibiger who put the problem of women into words. Clara Raphael is a young, talented woman, fighting against social and ecclesiastical narrowmindedness. She asserts that each woman has a right to full, personal development in accordance with personal ideals, and the book ends with the prospect of Clara achieving this with the help

Kierkegaard was annoyed that she had described him as "utilgængelig" (inaccessible), and he vents his irritation in his journals by using an ambiguous phrase, "legemlig Omgang," to refer to her habit of visiting and being visited by notables. In particular, he regards as shocking the fact that Bremer visited Martensen daily to discuss theology and had been allowed to read a prepublication copy of Martensen's *Christian Dogmatics*. Respectable single women in Kierkegaard's time did not do this kind of visiting. See Elisabeth Hude, *Fredrika Bremer og hendes venskab med H.C. Andersen og andre danske* (Copenhagen: G. E. C. Gad, 1972) 153-73. Martensen's *Den christelige Dogmatik*, appeared in the July of 1849. Bremer's own venture into theology, *Morgonväkter Några Ord i Anledning af "Strauss och Evangelierne": Trosbekännelse* (Sweden, 1842), was rather unorthodox, while her *Hertha eller En Själs Historia* (Sweden, 1856), in which she defends woman's right to independent development, met with harsh criticism.

[29]Ilia was a volunteer nurse during the cholera epidemic of 1853, something educated women did not do. However, she was such a success that after the epidemic she was offered a place as senior nurse (*Overvaagekone*) at Frederiks Hospital, where she later came to have Kierkegaard as one of her patients. She gave up her work at the hospital in order to take personal care of the children of the poor, something that was to inspire others to found children's homes, just as her example caused other educated ladies to go into nursing. Although she wrote a number of books, her significance lies in her social work.

[30]Mathilde Fibiger, *Clara Raphael, Tolv Breve*, udgivne af J. L. Heiberg (Copenhagen: C. A. Reitzel, 1851). The book came out in December 1850.

of a husband in a platonic marriage. For a while, Mathilde found herself at the center of social life in Copenhagen. The book was discussed for several months in cultured circles, with warm partisans for and against it.[31] Mathilde tried to elaborate further on her views in a book entitled *What Is Emancipation?* (1851), in which she explains that she is not campaigning for the vote or better employment possibilities for women, but for liberation in personal development. This second work attracted little attention however,[32] while her plan to speak at a public gathering was resisted by her family. For the remainder of her life she lived in acute poverty on poorly paid jobs[33] until she secured a position as the first woman telegraphist. Although this helped her situation, she died at the age of 41 as a result of her previous privations, thus demonstrating how difficult it was for women who wished to live independently outside the traditional roles assigned to them.

In an unpublished review of *Clara Raphael* in his Journals of 1850 (JP 6:6709), Kierkegaard shows both his lack of sympathy with women's emancipation in general and with Mathilde Fibiger as Clara Raphael in particular. He assumes that the character in the book is merely seeking a way in which to "be original," views Clara's conception of women's emancipation as "exceedingly abstract," and is ironic and negative, especially about the heroine's

---

[31]Heiberg, who had supported the publication of the book and written its preface, refrained from getting involved in the hot debate. This seems to have been due to his wife's annoyance at Heiberg's too-enthusiastic feelings for Mathilde. In 1851 Johanne Luise Heiberg wrote an article on *Qvinde-Emancipation* (the emancipation of women) in which she accuses liberated women of offending natural femininity by "wanting to be men." See Klaus P. Mortensen: *Thomasines oprør* (Copenhagen: Gad, 1986) 126-27, and Morten Borup, *Johan Ludvig Heiberg,* 3:147-51.

[32]The debate surrounding Mathilde Fibiger's book thus had no lasting effect. Fredrika Bremer's *Hertha* and the Norwegian novel *Amtmandens døttre,* Norway, 1854–1855 (author Camilla Collett, 1813–1895) were to cause a greater stir. *Amtmandens døttre* contains sharp criticism of marriage viewed as "woman's sole vocation." From 1872 Camilla Collett was a leading figure in the fight for women's rights that took hold in Scandinavia at that time. The thrust of her work was the attempt to produce a different conception of women's place in society.

[33]E.g., she did casual jobs sewing and painting china. For a time she tried to be a private teacher again, but found that she could not bear the loss of her independent existence.

renunciation of the world for the sake of her ideas about personal
freedom. For Kierkegaard, Clara wrongly confuses the aesthetic
and the religious,[34] but in his concentration upon the book's
demerits, he fails to see the validity of the protest Mathilde makes
through Clara: Mathilde's Clara clearly lives in a "man's world" in
which women generally are deprived of the intellectual opportuni-
ties offered to men, are kept in a subordinate position and referred
to "trivial work."[35]

Clearly, in both the case of Bremer and of Fibiger, there are
personal factors that must be taken into consideration when
examining Kierkegaard's reaction, not least the women's connection with Martensen and Heiberg and Kierkegaard's attitude to
these men. One must also remember that Bremer and Fibiger, however well read and well tutored privately, lacked the university
education that would place them on a level with men in the
academic sphere.[36]

Once one has made allowance for this, however, one can detect
a matured continuation of the basic attitude so flippantly endorsed
in Kierkegaard's youthful article on women: Women must not
want or expect temporal emancipation, but ought to keep within

[34]See also *Clara Raphael*, esp. 88, on Clara's promise. Birgit Bertung ("Yes, a
Woman *Can* Exist," 15-16) argues that the force of Kierkegaard's criticism is aimed
at the fact that Clara Raphael "relates inconsistently to her idea": she marries yet
does not marry, while Kierkegaard is not antifeminist but is against her trying to
become herself through a collective cause, namely, that of feminism. While one
can agree that Kierkegaard attacks the "Protestant monastery" (Clara's platonic
marriage) as inconsistent, and also agree that Kierkegaard is not antifeminist (if
this means antiwomen), he is clearly against the emancipation of women, even in
the period when it clearly was not a "collective cause," but a matter of individual
protest.

[35]*Clara Raphael*, 20-21, 25, 43, 44, 53-55.

[36]Martensen seems to have regarded Bremer's interest in his *Dogmatics* as a
useful test of the ability of his work to attract not only theologians and other
scholars, but also "cultured members of the community." His tone towards her
in his autobiography is decidedly condescending, not least about her attempts to
work out her own theological position (in fact she asked particularly awkward
questions). See Hans Lassen Martensen, *Af mit Levnet* (Copenhagen: Gyldendalske
Boghandels Forlag, F. Hegel & Son, 1882–1883) 2:134-35. Elisabeth Hude, *Fredrika
Bremer*, 155-61.

their proper bounds.[37] This seems a harsh ruling by modern standards, yet we are being unfair to Kierkegaard if we dismiss him without considering his outlook here in relation to the rest of his thought, especially since this sheds light on his attitude to movements towards emancipation.

First, it must be noted that Kierkegaard considers that although there is a fundamental equality between men and women before God, there are fundamental differences between the sexes. In his writings over the years, a picture emerges of woman as a being more spontaneous and authentically herself than man, as instinctive, sensitive, imaginative and self-sacrificing. She is seen as making temporality, in the form of home, husband and children, the center and goal of her existence, and as relating intellectually to the religious through the man.[38]

Man, on the other hand, is seen as more intellectually oriented than woman with an interest in questions beyond temporality. He is able to face conflict, but since he identifies his life with what he does and achieves, he is also involved in selfish competition and

---

[37]One needs to note here that many women were against women's liberation in concrete terms. Friend of Hans Christian Andersen and Fredrika Bremer, Henriette (Jette) Wulff mentions *Clara Raphael* in a letter to Andersen in 1851: "You wrote to me last time about Clara Raphael, of whom I have had enough in merely hearing that she wants women's emancipation, that old nonsense! Scandinavian women have the most beautiful freedom they could wish, are the confidant and adviser of man, his consoler and helper, respected and honored by him! . . . It often seems to me that we women are freer than the men who are bound—to a position, a country, a job, and the like. When I see women who want to be members of parliament and clergy, I have to laugh, for they are wanting first to be bound by oath to a place." Elisabeth Hude, *Fredrika Bremer*, 175.

[38]It ought also to be noted that Kierkegaard (both under his own name and as his pseudonyms) tends to use *Qvindagtig* (effeminate), and the harsher term *Fruentimmeragtig* (womanish), to indicate negative characteristics in men. In his use of these terms Kierkegaard implies, among other things, that woman is self-loving, demands immediate justification and success, runs away from, or collapses in the face of, trouble, is emotional and shrieks about things, coddles herself and whimpers, talks rather than acts, and is illogical concerning her explanations about things. It is also implied that she is childish and lets her imagination range too freely. See, e.g., *Qvindagtig*: TDIO, 81; SLW, 53, 262, 291; UDVS, 40; WL, 171; CD, 74; PC, 117; *Fruentimmeragtig*: CUP, 1:11, 239, 266, 296, 443; OAR, 54n.; SUD, 111; PC, 117; KAUC, 176. (The English translators have not always translated these terms correctly.)

triviality in the world outside the home. Although viewed as stronger and intellectually superior to woman, he needs the inspiration of either a woman or an idea to motivate his life.

It follows from this that men and women, since fundamentally different, have special distinct tasks in life, and each sex must therefore stick to the range of tasks appropriate to that sex. In the temporal world, woman is not to be temporally equal to the man. Man is to maintain a position of responsible mastery over woman, and woman is to be silent and submissive regarding matters outside the home, where she is viewed as the superior power.[39]

Kierkegaard, however, does not exclude the thought that men and women may have each other's characteristics, while his idea of a truly religious person is of one having a masculine intellectuality and feminine submissiveness (SUD, 49; JP, 4:5006). Yet despite this recognition, and despite his emphasis on fundamental Christian equality, Kierkegaard refuses women temporal equality, including political equality, on the grounds that there are fundamental differences of nature (JP, 4:5006).[40]

The second thing one needs to note about Kierkegaard's attitude to women's emancipation though, is that it is linked to his negative attitude to "numbers," to humanity in the mass. "A man," says Kierkegaard in his Journals for 1849 (JP 4:4992), "already even as a lad is demoralized by having to be like the others, and as a youth, to say nothing of the adult, is completely demoralized by learning how things go in practical life, in actuality. This very knowledge is the ruination of him. If girls were brought up in the same way—then good night to the whole human race." Because woman is granted "distance from life" for a period, she retains her individuality, is "a bit closer to ideality." In this context, emancipation "is the invention of the devil" because it tends towards the

---

[39]For Kierkegaard's description of men and women see especially JP, 4:4987-5008 and pp. 771-75, also Gregor Malantschuk, *The Controversial Kierkegaard*, 37-61.

[40]This type of argument can be seen also in the writings of C. S. Lewis, e.g., who argues for the headship of man on biblical grounds, and on the empirical grounds that one must have one final court of appeal in an argument (the man). He also adds the argument that man is needed to control woman, because she will instinctively fight for her young. See especially *Mere Christianity* (London: Collins Fontana, 1955) 99-100. Cf. JP, 2:1823, JP, 4:4998.

same upbringing the men receive. In other words, men have to be involved in the dirty practicalities of life, including the horrid business of voting, but there is no need to drag women into it too.[41]

With this we can now turn to Kierkegaard's attitude towards socialistic movements involving women's emancipation. In his article on women, the young Kierkegaard refers jokingly to "the Saint-Simonists" (EPW, 4), but for the members of the movement the conditions of the working class poor were anything but a joke. Although there was a lack of coherency in Saint-Simon's ideas, the movement developed a positive, utilitarian humanism that emphasized material needs in relation to a religion free of theological dogma. Work was to be treated as a holy duty by all, but the emphasis was on each individual developing a thoroughgoing neighbor love. The Saint-Simonist standpoint can be summed up in a precept from Saint-Simon's book *New Christianity* (1825): that the whole of society ought to strive towards the amelioration of the moral and physical existence of the poorest class. Society ought to organize itself in the way best adapted for attaining this end.

Despite an account of the movement in *The Copenhagen Post* of 1830,[42] it was not clear to people exactly what it stood for.[43] While

---

[41]It is interesting to note here, that Kierkegaard, while believing there are basic natural differences between men and women, also clearly recognizes the formative effect of knowledge, here practical knowledge, on an individual's development.

[42]*The Copenhagen Post* of 1830 (*Kjøbenhavnsposten* 290, 9 December 1830, 968 and 291; 10 December 1830, 970-72) regards the Saint-Simonists as a political and religious sect, as idealistic and well-intentioned, even noble, since they want to do something positive for the poor, but it also views it as naive and unrealistic. The chief criticism made is that the movement wants to start its new society from scratch, as if this were possible, while their desire for communism (*Ejendomsfælledsskab*) is found ridiculous since the rich will hardly want to part with their wealth. The paper notes that the movement seems to accept the need for a leader, but that leadership and ownership is based on personal ability. It also tells us that the rich seem to enjoy going to listen at the Saint-Simonist meetings in Paris, but do not join the movement, which, in the paper's view, is harmless as long as the poor do not attend the meetings in large numbers, when these might become a source of social unrest. It is also mentioned that the movement wants to procure for ladies the same rights as the men, so that a man and his wife form one civic individual. This, the paper treats as slightly comic, as something interesting for the ladies who are presented with a picture of an attractive future in which they

some features of the movement's theory were plain, how theory was to function in practice was especially doubtful.[44] There was no agreement on how reform was to be carried out. One view saw man and (liberated) woman as a unit taking joint charge of functions in the state, but internal disagreements and eccentricity burdened the movement. Certain religious elements awaited in vain the advent of a female Messiah[45] until the movement petered out in 1831.

Although naive and unrealistic, the Saint-Simonist movement was one of the first to make a link between discrimination against women and the capitalistic, class-ridden society. Kierkegaard, however, in his article, links the effort to "place women on a totally equal footing with the men" (EPW, 4), with his comic mention of a woman as goddess of reason in the French Revolution. Unlike Lind, Kierkegaard shows, as we have seen, a greater awareness of what women—even specific women—are doing in society, and while ironizing about women at Heiberg's lectures, he at least does not insinuate that woman's place is in the kitchen.[46] Yet he here fails to be interested in, let alone understand, what the Saint-Simonists were trying to do. In *The Concept of Irony*, however, Kierkegaard does make his one serious allusion to the movement, and there he makes it clear that he regards it as "wanting to deify actuality" (CI, 328), while the context of the comment suggests that

---

might hope to become pastors. The movement was at its strongest in 1830 but had collapsed by November 1831.

[43]Bishop Fogtmann thought the Saint-Simonists were a group of philanthropists or theophilanthropists, who might succeed in making France more religious. Army Captain Anton Frederik Tscherning (1795–1874, officer and politician, in exile in Paris 1835) thought the movement was political and slightly comic. Teddy Petersen, *Kierkegaards polemiske debut*, 26-27.

[44]It was clear that the movement opposed Christianity's idealizing of the spirit at the expense of the flesh. It was also clear that all material needs and sex were emphasized, while the position of women in the family, in politics and religion, was to be altered radically, thus liberating them from unfair discrimination.

[45]The movement also viewed God as masculine and feminine, thus foreshadowing elements of twentieth century women's theology.

[46]Later he is to write positively about the work of Thomasine Gyllembourg and Johanne Luise Heiberg See FPOSL, TA, and C.

the Saint-Simonists' emphasis on actuality was not the "appropriate" one.

Clearly, in the light of Kierkegaard's belief in fundamental differences between men and women and his rejection of women's emancipation, one inappropriate emphasis must be Saint-Simon's attempt to achieve equality for men and women within the temporal order. Yet, as the later Kierkegaard's view shows us, there is another source of inappropriateness, namely that Saint-Simon is trying to "realize complete equality in the medium of worldliness . . . in the medium the very nature of which implies differences, and to realize it in a worldly way, that is, by positing differences" (PV, 107).[47] While Kierkegaard does not deny the crowd (*Mængde*) competency in deciding "temporal, earthly, worldly matters" (PV, 110), Saint-Simon's movement is seen as doomed because he is trying to do the impossible: he is trying to achieve equality in the medium of diversity after drawing attention to the differences. Kierkegaard in *The Point of View*, makes a sharp distinction between religion and politics (PV, 107), and in *Works of Love*, he has specifically stated that Christianity does not take distinctions away. Instead, the individual, whether king or tramp, is to "lift himself up above" the distinctions in the loving of the neighbor. Equality is, in Kierkegaard's view, already "secured by each individual's equal kinship with and relationship to God in Christ" (WL, 69-90), and since such an outlook calls for personal exercise in this radical idea of equality, it might well also have a concrete reforming effect in the temporal world.

The point at issue then, between Kierkegaard and Saint-Simon and other practical reformers, is, first and foremost, what equality is and which distinctions are intrinsically unalterable. Kierkegaard is horrified by the social discrimination within pagan caste systems (WL, 69), but he fails to understand discrimination as a phenomenon in a Christian culture, not least because he draws restrictive conclusions from his position that there are fundamental differences between the sexes. As Malantschuk points out,[48] Kierkegaard "has not said much about the particular external tasks man and

---

[47]Cf. *Søren Kierkegaards Papirer*, IX B 10, pp. 309-11.
[48]*The Controversial Kierkegaard*, 61.

woman can have over and beyond the traditional ones,"[49] but this is precisely something that Kierkegaard needs to clarify, for while Kierkegaard denies that women have equal rights with men (WL, 139) and speaks glowingly of domestic womanhood, he allows women the right to have at least some tasks outside the home.[50]

Kierkegaard, as we have seen earlier, recognized that upbringing, education, was a factor in the question of how men and women developed, but he does not seem to understand how far his picture of woman is based on a culturally conditioned situation;[51] therefore he is unable to deal satisfactorily with the still unresolved question of whether there are fundamental differences between the sexes concerning personality and intellectuality.[52] Secondly, Kierkegaard was well aware of the problems concerning temporal equality and its achievement,[53] but he believed that the problem could be solved only by starting from equality as a fundamental standpoint and confronting the question of differences by accepting them in their relative, temporal, character. Unfortunately, as people like the Saint-Simonists saw, this was a standpoint that

---

[49]Malantschuk seems to think that the tasks can always be arrived at deductively from Kierkegaard's view of "the psychical and spiritual differences between the sexes." *The Controversial Kierkegaard*, 61. (Malantschuk's meaning here is unclearly translated from the Danish.)

[50]E.g., actress Johanne Luise Heiberg, C.

[51]See here, Sylvia Walsh, "On 'Feminine' and 'Masculine' Forms of Despair," International Kierkegaard Commentary 19: 121-34, esp. 134; also in *Feminist Readings of Kierkegaard*, ed. Céline Léon and Sylvia Walsh (University Park PA: Penn State University Press, 1997).

[52]Kierkegaard operates with a rather questionable model in which there are clear fundamental differences between the sexes. Even as late as 1854, when he strongly attacked the Protestant emphasis on marriage as the godly life, we find him identifying men and women with their sexuality and referring to woman's role as childbearer. In JP, 4:5008, Kierkegaard tells us that Christianity cannot change the natural qualifications of men and women, so that "sometimes it would be the woman, sometimes the man, who bore the child," yet this goes dangerously in the direction of identifying person with sexuality, taking for granted that marriage and childbearing is an inevitable part of female existence.

[53]Aldous Huxley, writing in 1958, points out the difficulties of eliminating social inequalities caused by poverty and sickness. He gives practical examples that well illustrate Kierkegaard's skepticism. See *Brave New World Revisited* (New York: Harper & Row Perennial Library, 1989) esp. chaps. 1 and 2.

could easily lead to a "laissez faire" attitude regarding a practical attack on social problems and thus prevent the elimination of grossly unjust forms of discrimination. While Kierkegaard is right that one can never eliminate all inequalities, this is no reason for not eliminating the ones that can be eliminated.[54]

Yet Kierkegaard's approach is strong in that he starts from the individual rather than from the social order of things and seems to concentrate more radically than Saint-Simon on the individual's ethical-religious basis. Instead of trying to draw up some utopian blueprint of the successful society in which freedom and equality are to function in a problem-free manner, he starts from a claim to equality and freedom for every individual in a dynamic love relation to God and fellow human beings. Long before Hitler's Germany, Kierkegaard understood the dangers surrounding the "reformer," which is why he tellingly comments, in his *Book on Adler*,[55] on the need for individual ethical and ethical-religious effort if social reform is to be made possible.

What, though, is the individual's reforming idea to be? Kierkegaard at Gilleleie is clear about the need for the individual to have an idea or an ideal for which to live, and that this must be religiously based (JP, 5:5100). Judge William[56] sees marriage as the obligatory life-idea for both men and women,[57] yet develops to an

---

[54]We may, perhaps, detect conflict in Kierkegaard's thought, arising from his sharp distinction between the temporal and the eternal and his allocation of politics to temporality. He states that it is religion that "seeks to explain and transfigure and thereby exalt the earthly to heaven" and that it is "only religion that can, with the help of eternity, carry human equality to the utmost limit" (PV, 107, 108). One cannot realize equality in the medium of worldliness (PV, 107), but is it impossible to have a godly politics removing unjust inequalities? On the one hand Kierkegaard seems to imply such an impossibility and the need to resort to the category of spiritual equality, on the other there is the suggestion that the community can make decisions and change temporal conditions.

[55]Søren Kierkegaards Papirer, VII,2 B 235, p. 49n.: "Every reformation that does not pay attention to the fact that basically it is each individual who is to be reformed is in fact an illusion."

[56]One can note that Kierkegaard's aesthete A considers that, "As a bride, woman has fulfilled her destiny" (EO, 1:157).

[57]There is a "duty" to marry and marriage is the highest telos of existence for the Judge, since marriage provides the possibility of uniting earthly and spiritual love in community life. Not to marry is even to "cross out the whole of earthly

acknowledgement that there is a higher state, namely the religious as totally spiritual altruistic love (SLW, 107, 169, 175-77).

Thus, marriage, as an idea for which to live, even in Judge William's thought, is definitely not the whole purpose of existence, and Kierkegaard in the writings of his last years cannot help but move with the logic of his argument that the self-denying life of religiousness is the highest life, such that absolute spiritual ideality is to anticipate the life of heaven by not marrying.[58] As Judge William considering ideality he could speak glowingly about marriage. As himself, situated in a society where marriage was treated as the godly norm and ideal and the single person as an unsatisfactory deviant, Kierkegaard went to the attack when he came to stress Christian ideality in his last years.[59]

There is thus movement in Kierkegaard's thought, but woman seems always to remain in the same place. She is superior passive inspiration, one of the two powers able to save wayward man (JP, 2:1157, 1832; JP, 4:5003), but she needs him as culmination point and as source of intellectual ethical-religious superiority (JP, 4:4989, 5007, p. 583).[60] Kierkegaard stops here, but his thought would seem to take us further, since if it is granted that the individual has ethical choice and the self as a task in relation to the social whole (EO, 2:168-69, 214-15, 259, 262-63), then there can be no intrinsic fixed limit, based on sexual difference, concerning how the individual is to understand his or her particular task in society. This must be something that has to develop within the context of the person's relationship to God and neighbor. This is particularly

---

life," and the men are condemned for wanting emancipation when they make a decision not to marry. See CUP, 1:254; cf. JP, 5: 5634; EO, 2:62, 245, 250, 302; SLW, 101-102, 106-107.

[58]Again we can detect biblical influence on Kierkegaard from New Testament thought that there is no marriage in heaven, Matt. 22:29-32.

[59]See here my article, "The Logic of Søren Kierkegaard's Misogyny 1854–1855," *Kierkegaardiana* 15 (1991): 82-92; also in *Feminist Readings of Kierkegaard*.

[60]This line of thought would seem to inspire Anti-Climacus's comment, SUD, 50 ft., that "in most cases the woman actually relates to God only through the man." This thought also appears in JP, 4:5007 and 5008, where it is clear that while women have an advantage over men concerning the emotional element of devotion to God, they are dependent on male intellectual superiority concerning the intellectual, dialectical, element.

indicated by Kierkegaard's shift of emphasis from ideality temporally defined (marriage) to ideality eternally defined (renunciation). Thus, when he tells us the individual must choose, even though he has man in mind, he opens the door of possibility for woman too—not just the door leading to the philosophy lectures, but the door to women's emancipation.

2

Power, Politics, and Media Critique:
Kierkegaard's First Brush with the Press

Robert L. Perkins

During his lifetime Kierkegaard was embroiled with the public press on four occasions: (1) the series of newspaper articles that opened his career; (2) the *Corsair* affair;[1] (3) "An Open Letter Prompted by a Reference to me by Dr. Rudelbach"; and (4) the attack on the people's church in the last year and a half of his life. His relation to the press is indeed complex, but here I shall examine only his earliest perceptions and interactions. The history of the times is tightly interwoven with the philosophic issues that Kierkegaard raises. Thus, first, a bit of history.

The press had been under strict censorship since 1799 when Frederick VI tightened the press laws in response to the publication of liberalizing ideas inspired by the French Revolution. Two prominent journalists had to leave Denmark immediately, and as a result a generation-long period of passivity ensued.[2] At the behest of Metternich[3] and in response to recent political developments in Slesvig-Holstein, Frederick VI reluctantly called four Provincial Consultative Assemblies in 1831 which he finally convened, with all deliberate speed, in 1834. Though advisory only, the assemblies raised questions regarding the financial policies of

---

[1]The major study of the *Corsair* is *International Kierkegaard Commentary: The Corsair Affair*, ed. Robert L. Perkins (Macon GA: Mercer University Press, 1990.

[2]On the political passivity of the early decades of the century, see Teddy Petersen, *Kierkegaards polemiske debut* (Odense DK: Odense Universitetsforlag, 1977) 55ff.

[3]Denmark had been on the losing side in the Napoleonic wars and was subject to many penalties and injunctions in the Treaty of Vienna. For a brief review, see Palle Lauring, *A History of the Kingdom of Denmark* (Copenhagen: Høst og Søn, 1960) 176-221.

the government which were then reported in the press. The King responded with legislative proposals for the most restrictive censorship ever considered in Denmark.[4] There was a public uproar, and a petition containing 572 signatures of the leading intellectuals, politicians, and business leaders was presented to the King. At the same time, an association, "The Society for the Proper Use of the Freedom of the Press," was formed that further strengthened the opposition to the proposed legislation and the institution of absolute monarchy.

The society's principal concern was the issue of press freedom, but the subject of the "proper use" of the press, that is, its responsibility, accuracy, and objectivity or fairness (today parts of the ethics of journalism), was not discussed. The leading lights of the time, including Kierkegaard, supported the freedom of the press (EPW, 48), but, unfortunately, only one person raised the question of the intellectual integrity and the political and social responsibility of the press itself, and that person was Kierkegaard.[5]

While the press was struggling for its right to exist, most would find the issue of the epistemological responsibility of the press to print the truth and not self-serving ideology to be a question of secondary importance. Kierkegaard soon found an occasion to raise the principled questions of the self-image of the press, of its veracity and regard for facts, and the integrity and/or easy conscience the press had about its own authority and use in the political arena. The fact that Kierkegaard's critique of the press is presented in humorous and ironic ways does not detract from the importance of the issues he raises.

Kierkegaard thought that the government had acted unwisely and repressively in the recent past about several matters: the trial of Professor David, the founder and editor of *Fædrelandet* (hereaf-

---

[4]Christian Kirchoff-Larsen, *Den danske Presses Historie, 1827–1866*, 3 vols. (Kjøbenhavn: Berlingske Forlag, 1962) 3:80-89; Petersen, *debut*, 57-58; Watkin's introduction, EPW, ix-xii.

[5]For a brief review of the history of criticism of the press in the early nineteenth century see Stephen Best and Douglas Kellner, "Modernity, Mass Society, and the Media: Reflections on the *Corsair* Affair," in *International Kierkegaard Commentary: The Corsair Affair*, 23-31.

ter, *The Fatherland*),[6] the threat of stricter censorship that would include the denial of any appeal process for accused journalists, and the prohibition of publication of the subsequent proceedings of the Roskilde Consultative Assembly (EPW, 45-46). In these matters Kierkegaard sides with the liberals against the crown in spite of his reservations about the press. Because of these criticisms of the crown, it is difficult to understand why Kierkegaard, though he was a conservative for most of his life, has ever been thought to be a defender of absolute monarchy.

With that brief background, I shall now turn to the long exchange between Kierkegaard, Orla Lehmann, and Johannes Hage about the press.

Kierkegaard's Critique of the Liberal Press

During this period the student union was very much a center of debate about the major issues, both political and cultural, of the time. Johannes Ostermann, a student, gave a lecture, "Our Most Recent Journalistic Literature," (EPW, 189-99) on 14 November 1835 at the union, and it was subsequently published in *The Fatherland* on 22 January 1836. Kierkegaard presented his reply, "Our Journalistic Literature" (EPW, 35-52; JP, 5:5116), on 28 November 1835, but, and this fact may be very important, it was not published until the first edition of his journals and papers included it. Without a hard copy the critics could only base their remarks upon ill-recalled ideas or second or third hand recollections, which were, no doubt, biased, defensive, and self-serving. The rule that journalists should check and recheck (we call it "independent confirmation") their sources was not followed. Without a hard copy, the detail of Kierkegaard's address was selectively remembered and commented upon. This journalistic lapse has been the source of much misunderstanding of Kierkegaard to the present day.

Ostermann based his lecture on the apparently widely held view that the press is primarily responsible for raising the political issues of the time. Kierkegaard, on the other hand, argues that it

---

[6]For Ostermann's comment, EPW, 192-94. Bruce Kirmmse, *Kierkegaard in Golden Age Denmark* (Bloomington: Indiana University Press, 1990), 47-49.

"has not been so active as it is convenient to believe" (EPW, 52). This is the major bone of contention between Kierkegaard and the other commentators on the liberal press: he challenges the widespread view of the press as the initiator of the recent political events. To support this contention, Kierkegaard examines the issues of the liberal newspaper, "*Kjøbenhavnsposten* (hereafter, the *Copenhagen Post*) from 1829 to 1834.[7] It is apparent that he is alive to the important issues discussed in the contemporary press: Slesvig-Holstein, the Provincial Consultative Assemblies, the national economy, the continuation of the theological dispute between N.F.S. Grundtvig and H.N. Clausen,[8] and the freedom of the press. Contrary to Ostermann, Kierkegaard claims that the government, not the press, is the "active agent" in the calling of the Consultative Assemblies (EPW, 40). Still, we cannot but wonder why Kierkegaard raises this very minor historical issue against Ostermann. A smaller tempest in a smaller teapot is difficult to imagine, unless a fundamental conceptual issue is at stake.

Kierkegaard was interested in the facts themselves, the content of the newspapers, what was actually printed. His examination of the *Copenhagen Post* shows that Ostermann's recall of the history of the press, though apparently widely accepted at the time, was not based upon an examination of the newspapers themselves. Ostermann did not do his homework. Rather he served the press's uncritical self-congratulation by suggesting that it had the power to create and guide political discussion. Though Kierkegaard's lecture has been criticized since its presentation as a defense of the establishment, no one has challenged his examination of the newspapers or suggested that his review of the evidence is incorrect or slanted. Good research technique is not, one hopes, the captive of ideological statements, and Kierkegaard did his homework. He addresses only one issue: the creation of a false perception of the power of the press. The lecture is not a conservative ideological statement, but rather a call for critical and truthful historical recapitulation.

---

[7]EPW, 42-46. Petersen, *debut*, 46-47.
[8]Kirmmse, *Kierkegaard in Golden Age Denmark*, 200-20.

Kierkegaard claims that the July Revolution of 1830 in France and the calling of the Provincial Consultative Assemblies had been far more important in initiating the political movements than the Danish press which only reported these events; it did not instigate them. After all, by the liberal account, the press had been in a period of passivity. However, he recognizes that more recently it is difficult to trace the give and take between the press, the crown, and other centers of activity, and that the press may now indeed be an actor in the political debate (EPW, 45-46). He recognizes but neither endorses nor criticizes this change.

In developing his criticism of the press, Kierkegaard makes several allusions that may help us understand the issues between him and the liberal account of the importance of the press. His principal criticism of the press is that it is a "bustling busyness" and is characterized by a "formal striving." With a disregard for "a cheerful atmosphere," the age prefers "symmetrical beauty" and "conventional" relations, or as we would say, abstract class designations such as "peasant" or "citizen" rather than "sincere social relations." In an unsuccessful effort at dark humor, he compares this formalism to Fichte's effort "to construct systems" by "sharpness of mind" to Robespierre's effort to do it with the help of the guillotine (EPW, 46). These allusions are less than clear, and so we must follow up on these clues in order to understand his obscure and heavy or frivolous irony.

Fichte attempted to overcome the Kantian thing-in-itself by making the ego the source of all certainty in knowledge. The ego formalizes the nonego according to its own immanent categories. As a result there is no basis to claim the existence of a residual unknown beyond the ego and its categories. Turning to morality, Fichte found that our experience suggests an infinite moral ideal. Unfortunately, strive though we may, we are less successful morally than metaphysically. The result is that we are all condemned to an infinite moral striving.[9]

---

[9]Frederick Neuhouser, *Fichte's Theory of Subjectivity* (Cambridge: Cambridge University Press, 1990) 50-51. George J. Seidel, *Fichte's "Wissenschaftslehre" of 1794: A Commentary on Part One* (West Lafayette IN: Purdue University Press, 1993) 113-15.

The press, Kierkegaard's ironic jab suggests, is a parody of Fichte's ego, for it too posits everything into its own pattern and categories. Unfortunately, the press constantly vacillates between the centrifugal and the centripetal, for it has neither a consistent nor a complete political platform that encompasses the issues of the society. By contrast, political accountability compels the state to develop policies, though perhaps not always good ones, and this task requires the state to move with slow deliberation in its processes. The press, having neither political responsibility nor accountability, buffets and cajoles, first in one direction and then in another, those who must make decisions and act (EPW, 49). It reflects on the activities, foibles, and crimes of others. The press persists in a fit of "bustling busyness" and urges us ever toward an undefined moral and political rectitude.

Turning to Kierkegaard's other clue, Robespierre's resort to the guillotine, let us recall the ideals of the revolution, "Liberty, Equality and Fraternity." These words were sloganized ideals, but they had no concrete political content. The use of the guillotine showed how empty the professed revolutionary ideals were and also demonstrated the determination of Robespierre to impose his will upon his fellows at any cost to them.

Compared to Fichte's philosophic efforts and Robespierre's political fanaticism, the press is a mere "bustling busyness" but like Fichte, it shapes reality into its self-defined categories, and like Robespierre, it permits no opposition. In contrast to such bustling busyness, "Authentic action goes hand in hand with calm circumspection" (EPW, 48).

Kierkegaard links authentic action with the issue of social change, which he views as reformative rather than revolutionary. Kierkegaard makes the same two-edged critique of both the liberals and the reactionaries: a leap backward and a leap forward are equally wrong, "because a natural development does not proceed by leaps, and life's earnestness will ironize over every such experiment even if it succeeds momentarily" (EPW, 47). His rejection of the metaphor of leaping as a model of political change does not mean that he rejects social change, either liberal or conservative, but only that he rejects discontinuous, authoritarian, and top-down, dictated change, any sort of great leap forward or backward. This passage suggests that Kierkegaard is, at this time, neither a reactionary conservative nor a radical liberal, but a moderate urging a "natural development," whatever that imprecise term may mean.

This openness to change and the ability to see two sides of a controversy also suggest that Kierkegaard was not the uncritical conservative some have thought and others continue to think he was. He twice requests that he be considered, in a phrase reminiscent of Hegel, a *réflecteur*, that is, one who thinks, contemplates or observes.[10] This self-characterization suggests that Kierkegaard has already rejected an active political life in favor of that of public commentator and critic, that he had already found a likely expression for his polemical nature. Most importantly, he explicitly rejects the dichotomizing mentality that categorizes persons into one of two camps, either liberal or conservative, for that is to forget "the countless number of shadings that must occur" (EPW, 38).[11]

As a *réflecteur* Kierkegaard attempts to make distinctions and to offer a critique of some of the objectionable features of the modern press. In this first encounter with the press, Kierkegaard develops a critique of a practice that will remain an important category throughout his life: the use of anonymity (EPW, 51). He argues that anonymity is "a secret court," and fairness requires that one be able to face his accuser. If the accused proves himself innocent, then the anonymous accuser deserves to be branded a liar, a result made impossible by the anonymity itself, thus compounding the unfairness. This critique will remain a staple in Kierkegaard's views of the press.[12]

---

[10]EPW, 38, 52. Thulstrup is of the opinion that Kierkegaard knew something of the *Philosophy of Right* at this time, even if indirectly. See Niels Thulstrup, *Kierkegaard's Relation to Hegel*, trans. George L. Stengren (Princeton NJ: Princeton University Press, 1980) 24-85 and passim. For Hegel's insight that philosophy is an afterthought, see *Hegel's Philosophy of Right*, trans. T. M. Knox (Oxford UK: Oxford University Press, 1958) 12-13. To compare Kierkegaard's and Hegel's views of the press, see Hegel, *Right*, 204-208.

[11]Kierkegaard did not forget his concern for the "countless shadings" when he became the author of *Either/Or* and other works, for he presents many shadings of the aesthetic, the ethical, and the religious in this and subsequent works.

[12]COR, xviii, 178. See Nerina Jansen, "The Individual versus The Public" in *Kierkegaard Commentary: The Corsair Affair*, 1-22, esp. 8-9, 11, 19.

One is puzzled by the lack of attention this first encounter with the press has received and the widespread misunderstanding of it when it was discussed. His critique of the crown on the issue of the freedom of the press separates him forever from the charge of being an apologist for the absolute monarchy. The only justifying circumstance for the misunderstanding of Kierkegaard's critique of the popular perception that the press was the instigator of the contemporary political situation is that the lecture was just that, a lecture. It was not publicly circulated and commented upon in a reflective and responsible manner at the time. Perhaps Kierkegaard thought it too aesthetically lighthearted for publication, or perhaps no one wanted to print it because it challenged what common sense knew to be true, but whatever the case, the discussion of it in the bustling press rooms and coffee shops lost sight of, or perhaps never really perceived, the philosophic and methodological questions Kierkegaard raised about the examination of sources, truth, and the necessity of interrogating one's self-justifying and flattering assumptions. Unfortunately, that does not excuse those who have uncritically repeated the original misunderstanding of this lecture as conservative apologetic.

Kierkegaard and the Liberal Spokesmen: Lehmann and Hage

Two prominent spokesmen of the liberal movement, Orla Lehmann and Johannes Hage,[13] replied to Kierkegaard's lecture as if Kierkegaard had given an unqualified defense of absolutism. That is difficult to understand, for on all important matters regarding the freedom of the press, Kierkegaard sided with the liberals.[14] Lehmann was a gifted orator and publicist, while Hage mixed scientific exactness in economics with a capacity for personal nastiness. Lehmann, ever the politician, was the more conciliatory. Kierkegaard replied to each response and had the last word to boot. Let us briefly consider the extended exchange.

---

[13]See Kirmmse, *Kierkegaard in Golden Age Denmark*, 49-63.

[14]For a rather critical view of Kierkegaard's activities and a more sympathetic treatment of Lehmann and Hage see Petersen, *debut*, 103-12. See also EPW, xiv-xxiii.

Lehmann wrote a five-part series on the press, the first of which is "Press Freedom Affair" (EPW, 134-41). Lehmann's loose style and florid oratory appeared to Kierkegaard to be misleading, and it brought forth an ironic response. I shall not summarize Lehmann's article but comment only on those items that provoked Kierkegaard. There is no defense for Kierkegaard's irony, and it needs none. Socratically he raised fundamental questions about truth, myth, and the interpretation of history by the use of an irony that seemed nit-picking to those on the receiving end.

In his reply to Lehmann, "The Morning Observations in *Kjøbenhavnsposten* Number 43" (EPW, 6-11), Kierkegaard raises two objections, the matter of truth and the creation of historical myth, and in each case he shifts the issue from historical and contextual concerns to the philosophic. It is easy to see that Kierkegaard has a lot of fun at the expense of the liberals, but a philosophic reading shows that he raises issues that became central in his later thought and are still important today. His ironic effort should be Socratically read: the commonplace and obvious should be questioned (Plato, *Apology*, 20-23 C) and pat answers should be ironized (Plato, *Euthyphro* et al.). Kierkegaard raises and attempts to answer at least these questions: Does the press discover the truth and report it? What is the relation of a "liberal" or a "conservative" to the truth? How seriously does the press report its own errors? To whom is the press responsible?

Regarding the matter of truth, Lehmann dismissed the press's errors with the offhanded comment that, after all, the press is only a human production: "Here below where everything is imperfect, how could *this* alone be perfect" (EPW, 139)? This quotation indicates how seriously Lehmann took the question of truth and with what ease he excuses errors in the press, including his own. This uncritical excuse provoked Kierkegaard's irony and humor, for it glosses over or diminishes the importance of the question of truth. Kierkegaard understood, even if Lehmann did not, that every piece of misinformation is a deep betrayal of the public trust the press demands as well as a betrayal of the high-mindedness, fairness, and objectivity the press presumes and claims on its own behalf. Though Kierkegaard's irony is directed against the liberal press, his argument is not intended to support conservative positions (EPW, 52). Rather, he raises the question whether one can believe what one reads in the press, the issue of the veracity and integrity of the press and media. To what standard of truth should/must the media be held? To be sure, at the time this question was new, even a new kind of question about the ethics of communication, but it is very important in late capitalist societies.

Kierkegaard catches Lehmann in the act of creating a historical myth in his summary of the history of Denmark's recent past. Lehmann reveals his bourgeois, urban, and ideological prejudices when he suggests that the past, beginning in 1799, was "sentimental-idyllic" (EPW, 137), while the present age represents the "dawn of the life and freedom of the people" (EPW, 136). These remarkably vague phrases (one can hardly call them categories) serve the liberals as a self-congratulatory characterization of their activity in the recent past. To appeal to an example Kierkegaard did not use, one can only wonder how the landless peasants, whose situation throughout the period Lehmann refers to grew constantly more desperate, could have conceived of their past as "sentimental-idyllic." Lehmann's unconscious political prejudices, based narrowly in his urban experience, limit whatever skills he had in historical analysis.[15]

Lehmann attempts to give a psychological explanation of the past, an explanation prescient of the concepts of alienation and mystification. He claims that the recent past was an escapist effort to suppress the memory of the disastrous consequences of the Napoleonic wars. Romantic poetry and an emphasis upon the atomic family kept people "warm" and "cozy," and able to "amuse themselves." Lehmann exemplifies the modern trivialization of poetry when he characterizes it as "sentimental baubles" and attributes the recovery of Danish self-consciousness and "courage" to the changes in politics initiated by the press (EPW, 135). While

---

[15]No one could claim that Kierkegaard's class consciousness was any less urban and bourgeois than Lehmann's. For discussions of the state of agriculture see B. J. Hovde, *Scandinavian Countries, 1720–1865: The Rise of the Middle Class* (Boston: Chapman and Grimes, 1943) 276-302; for a recent history of Danish agriculture see Erling Olsen, *Danmarks okonomiske historie siden 1750* (Copenhagen: G. E. C. Gads Forlag, 1962) 24-93; and for a good general social history of this period see Hans Chr. Johansen, *En Samfundorganisation in opbrud 1700–1870*. Dansk social historie, bd. 4. (Copenhagen: Gyldendal, 1979).

the press was "politically passive" (EPW, x-xi) the literary revival was active in reviving the spirit of the people. With its emphasis upon land and people, Danish romanticism, inaudibly and certainly unintentionally, suggested the transfer of the loyalties of the cultural elite from the crown to other foci and also laid the foundations of the nationalism that the liberals exploited in their critique of the crown and later in the fateful conflict with Germany over Schleswig-Holstein. Neither Lehmann nor Hage understood this.

In addition to the question of truth and the issue of self-justificatory explanation in historical thought, Kierkegaard also raises the question of corporate responsibility. The objects of his criticism were no doubt enraged by the picayune comic disproportionality when he ironically asked who, if anyone, is responsible for the mistakes of the press. The question has to do with "corrections." Kierkegaard notices that, unlike the other contemporary papers, the *Copenhagen Post* groups all errors, printer's and author's alike, in one box without distinction. Of course, printer's errors are usually trivial and distinguishable from those of authors, but that is not the issue. Kierkegaard ironically suggests that the editors, by the use of only one correction box, hide the authors' errors among those of the compositors in order to use them "as a shield" (EPW, 8 n**). Kierkegaard's mocking innuendo suggests that this avoidance mechanism borders on irresponsibility and/or anonymity.

Kierkegaard raises issues that were not appreciated or even understood at the time. The questions of truth, responsibility, and objectivity, the invention of historical myths, and the claim of impartiality and objectivity that a partisan press claims on its own behalf are still problematic not only in the printed media but throughout all the media in late capitalist societies. Kierkegaard, using an aesthetic and ironic mode, sounds an early warning about some of the complex power relations between politics, a public matter, and the press, which is at best a capitalist corporation, or at worst an ideological mouthpiece. He does not present these issues in jargon recognizable by modern social science or media critique. However, just like Socrates (Plato, *Apology*, 21-22), Kierkegaard uses irony and discerning conceptual analysis to elucidate what is hidden in many minute details.

At this point, Johannes Hage published an article, "On the Polemic in the *Flying Post*," in *The Fatherland* on 4 March 1836

(EPW, 142-48). The central feature of Hage's article is a thorough analysis of the economic situation of the country which conflicts with the crown's view as reported in the *Flying Post*. However, before he begins the economic analysis, Hage makes a number of derogatory comments about Kierkegaard's previous article.

Hage's remarks are highly personal and contain only hypothetical psychological observations about the size of Kierkegaard's ego, his lack of the love of truth, and the motivation of his criticisms of Lehmann. There is a complete contrast of personality types and interests between Hage and Kierkegaard, the former apparently lacking the humor, elasticity, and irony of the latter. Kierkegaard, on the other hand, has little interest in the controversy regarding the condition of the national deficit, the matter of prime importance to Hage. No doubt both were hypersensitive to criticism of themselves or the issues they held to be important.

Hage is deeply angered by Kierkegaard's criticism of a "deformity of form" found in Lehmann's article, his unfortunate choice of a few words, and Kierkegaard's "petty hunt to find phrases that in some way or other should be stated more precisely" (EPW, 142). Hage appears to take the worse part, actually defending vague writing and an imprecise and deficient vocabulary. His comment has to be one of the most remarkably silly pieces of writing in the history of journalism. Can anyone doubt that the young ironic *réflecteur* smiled?

On the issue of truth, referring to Kierkegaard's article, Hage writes: "But it also uses other weapons in seeking to amuse [the newspaper's] readers with witticisms without caring whether or not the truth suffers on that account" (EPW, 142), for "wit and dialectical skill when these are not matched by a love of truth serve only to glorify one's own little self" (EPW, 144). That is true enough. Unfortunately, however, Hage uses neither wit, irony, humor, nor dialectical skill in his critique of Kierkegaard. He confuses these with invective.

Hage writes of Lehmann's reading of the past that he "has not blamed the past in general; he has presented only its lack of interest in common affairs, and presented it as something that must of necessity follow from the course of events." Hage seems to be utterly unaware of the implications of this claim to historical necessity. Another problem of the past, i.e., history as remembrance of things past, is that it may "weaken the vigor with which we are going to meet the future" (EPW, 143). He seems oblivious to the possibility that we may not intelligently respond to the present or the future if we misunderstand the past.

However, much more is at stake than Hage's moralizing invective and obtuseness about the nature and importance of historical knowledge: Hage undercuts the very possibility of politics itself by demeaning the character of Kierkegaard and asserting that he has no love for the truth. To deny the integrity and decency of one's opponent destroys the necessary condition of conversation and politics. Disagree as we will politically, we must believe in each other's honesty and integrity or civilization becomes impossible. In his ironic reply, "On the Polemic of the *Fatherland*" (EPW, 12-23), Kierkegaard writes,

> When in a dispute the point is reached where the opponent says: I cannot understand you, although I have the best intentions—then that ends the dispute. . . . But when instead [Hage] starts to attack the character of the person he is speaking to, accuses him of being a wilful sophist etc., then it can at most provoke a smile on the lips of the opponent, because the whole thing is nothing other than a comic despair. So in our no. 76 we have not permitted ourselves one single attack on the opponent's character. (EPW, 22)

Although Kierkegaard does not literally attack anyone's character in his article, he does ironize their activities and beliefs. But that is exactly the difference. It is one thing to criticize another person's poor writing or to ironize his or her point of view or opinions, but it is entirely different to demean another's character or motivation. This is the fundamental *sine qua non* of politics and the point Hage missed. He indulged all sorts of private rages and frustrations on Kierkegaard from the highest intellectual principle: the love of truth.

Kierkegaard flatly denies Hage's charge that he "shamelessly stabbed" the editor of the *Copenhagen Post* in the back (EPW, 19J). On the contrary, Kierkegaard asserts that the editor, Andreas P. Liunge, has too much integrity to yield to "the demands of the times" (EPW, 20). He maintains that Liunge is "too good" to preside over the "reforming endeavor that goes through a number of articles" authored by a "motley militia" (EPW, 22). The issue is that as publisher Liunge is still legally responsible under the press laws for all that appears in the paper. Kierkegaard says no more here than in the previous article where he focused the issue of the legal responsibility of the editor (EPW, 10) or the "author" using "the compositor as a shield" (EPW, 8**).

Hage claims that Kierkegaard has no regard for the truth because he rejected Lehmann's interpretation of the recent past. Apparently this view of history was widely held among the liberals who, if Hage is typical, did not recognize the political bias in their reading of history. Kierkegaard, on the other hand, catches them red-handed remembering the past as if it leads inevitably to their position. He, at least, is aware that the remembered past has its political uses while his critics apparently are not. In their own eyes at least, they report things "as they actually happened" implying that if you disagree with their interpretation of history, you have no love for the truth. In order to defend himself against Hage's charge Kierkegaard has to criticize Lehmann's views again.

In his second critique of Lehmann's view that the past was "sentimental-idyllic" Kierkegaard points out that recently, during Christian VII's and Frederick VI's time, the country faced real problems and overcame them. During their reigns, in addition to the reform in agriculture that permitted the peasants to buy their land, there were numerous disasters such as the mercantile war with England and the battle of Copenhagen harbor (1801), the treachery of France and Russia in the Treaty of Tilsit with the consequent bombardment of Copenhagen and the loss of the naval forces along with the destruction of the shipyards by the English (1807), Napoleon's "occupation" of Jutland and Funen, the loss of Norway, the loss of the maritime fleet, and the national bankruptcy. Without rehearsing the above litany which everyone knew, if for no other reason than that Lehmann had previously reported it, Kierkegaard cannot understand how anyone, apart from political bias, could say that this past had been "sentimental-idyllic" (EPW, 136) or that there had been a lack of interest in public affairs (EPW, 141). Kierkegaard urges that it is "psychologically inconsistent" to characterize an age that can survive such disasters as "sentimental-idyllic" (EPW, 18).

Yet in the midst of the multiple disasters there occurred the most remarkable event in Denmark's cultural history: the Golden

Age of Danish literature. If Lehmann had said that the literature was "sentimental-idyllic," Kierkegaard would, perhaps, have had no quarrel with him at all. But a characterization of literature and a characterization of an era, the political history of Denmark since 1799 and the military disasters resulting from the Napoleonic wars, are not the same things. This is a simple conceptual distinction, but one unfortunately lost on Lehmann and Hage. Whether or not they accurately understood the past, they are guilty of the simplest kind of logical mistake, the confusion of whole and part or of selecting/ suppressing evidence.

Kierkegaard then challenges the liberal politicians to achieve the greatness in politics that the Golden Age achieved in literature. Not only does Kierkegaard refuse to accept the characterization of the previous era as "sentimental-idyllic," he takes their great achievements in literature as the standard for success for the age that prides itself upon political reform. It is also important to note that Kierkegaard does not defend absolute monarchy. In a passage that sounds almost like a farewell to politics, he encourages political activity: "One age cannot do everything, and if our age can take it as far in political intelligence as that time [did] in aesthetics, then it can lie down in the grave in peace" (EPW, 19). In spite of the military and economic losses in the Napoleonic wars and additional diplomatic losses at the Congress of Vienna, Denmark still existed. He understands that as a considerable political achievement, and he sets that as the standard by which the liberals and others as well should measure their successes or lack thereof.

Kierkegaard was considerably educated by this experience with Hage, and his irony is sharpened by the public tutorial he received. Kierkegaard's ironic tenacity is apparent, but his first brush with the press was not complete.

In the *Copenhagen Post* (31 March 1836) Lehmann published a short conciliatory note, "Reply to Mr. B. of the *Flying Post*" (EPW, 152-59), modifying his position by dropping the offending expression, "sentimental-idyllic," but now maintaining that the literary age was not one of politics but rather a "period of enfeeblement" (EPW, 154). Since Kierkegaard's attack was a matter of second order questions about sustaining historical claims, the identification of category mistakes, the defense of the foundations of political discourse, the question of the creation of political myths, and the issue of legal responsibility, it is obvious that Lehmann cannot grasp the conceptual issues at all: He suggests that the controversy be ended, for, after all, much of it is merely "a matter of taste about which everyone must be permitted to have his own opinion" (EPW, 156).

Kierkegaard is also willing to let the matter go away, but not by backing down from his position. In his reply, "To Mr. Orla Lehmann" (EPW, 24-34), Kierkegaard rejects the allegation that his criticisms are matters of taste; rather he claims to have pointed out "logical confusions" in the liberal position (EPW, 27). Further, he argues that if the distinction between logical distinctions and taste is blurred, then the possibility of meaning anything at all will be negated. If in fact the principle of taste is the test, then it is only a matter of taste that Hage is offended, that Lehmann complains, that others found his attack "shameless," that they prefer liberalism, and that the king prefers monarchy, the more absolute the better (EPW, 27). Judged by his own principle, Lehmann's criticism of the monarchy and Hage's criticism of the royal financial statements and Kierkegaard are merely subjectivism, and on that basis, Hage has no reason to call into question either Kierkegaard's intelligence or his bona fides (EPW, 32-33). The worst that can be said is that a person has poor taste, but that is usually more a matter of cultivation than character. However, argued and principled differences of interpretation of a matter are one thing; a mouthing of tasteful or tasteless opinions renders the matter trite and irrational.

From this contrast between Lehmann and Kierkegaard, it is apparent that the latter has an understanding of the political as founded in open communication and rational argument. Politics is a matter that must be founded in the meaning of our very selves, who and what we are, rather than in an unjustified taste. After all, it is not too far from unjustified taste to unjustified political claims—at least according to Lehmann. Is it the case that those who have the reputation for political wisdom still lack it (Plato, *Apology*, 22)?

The self-serving confusions in the liberal view of history are just as confusing as the reduction of all political difference to a matter of taste. Kierkegaard raises the question when the "time of enfeeblement" began. Lehmann's first article said it began in 1799, but in his last article he said it began during the period 1807–1827. Hage says that it was "a number of years ago" that the unhappy times began. Obviously, the liberals have neither a precise theory of decline nor of recovery by which they construe the facts (EPW, 29-30). They admit that the present reformers are not so vigorous as "previously," a comparison, but a comparison to what (EPW, 157, 30)? Kierkegaard again finds that the liberal analysis of history creates nothing but puzzlement or irony.

These various disputes were more than an episode in the biography of a young aesthete. The articles are not just "humoristic;" rather they are Socratically ironic. No one would claim that Kierkegaard had at this time developed as secure a sense of history as he demanded of the journalists and politicians. Still he thinks that he has shown that they do not have a viable theory of history, which should include a criterion of acceptable evidence, a logically coherent concept of historical causation that maintains the difference between necessity and action, an understanding of political argument that does not reduce it to "matters of taste" that end in subjectivism, a respect for the opponent's integrity and honesty which is the basis of all politics, a recognition of the power of the press to create myths by reshaping events into its own categories, and a respect for precise language, which is the most powerful capacity we have to express our meanings. Unfortunately, the journalists and politicians did not take up Kierkegaard's challenge to redefine their position through a historical and philosophical ordering of their political insights by any of these criteria.

Given this early tutorial, it is not surprising that Kierkegaard's view of the press and politics is essentially negative throughout his life.[16]

As obnoxious a gadfly as Kierkegaard showed himself to be in these articles, there is no question of his intellectual victory over his opponents. Because these issues do not appear in his writings in the familiar categories used in modern historical, sociological, and media analysis, his critique has been largely invisible. He

---

[16]On the press see JP, 2:2148, 2173-74. On his lifelong ruminations on politics and politicians, as well as the events of 1848 and after see JP, 5:4060-4242. Again, I call attention to Watkin's introduction to this exchange (EPW, xiv-xxiii).

raised issues that were not at all appreciated or perhaps even understood at the time or even today. The issue of truth and myth making is still a subtle issue in dealing with the media. Much of our public discourse has been reduced to a cynical manipulation of popular historical myths and beloved symbols. Some of these myths we have inherited and some are recent inventions of cynical power brokers and promulgated by a beguiled and beguiling media corps. The question of legal responsibility for corporate acts, raised almost in passing by Kierkegaard with regard to Liunge, is still problematic not only in the press but also in the wider areas of corporate ethics. Kierkegaard perceived, at least to a greater degree than his contemporaries in Copenhagen, the complex power relations between the media and politics.

These confrontations in the student union and the press, though primarily focused on political and social issues, also helped Kierkegaard to shape himself, to become a person. By distinguishing himself from the busyness of everyday politics and claiming the privileged status of the *réflecteur*, he came to realize both the importance and the severe limits of both practice, on the one hand, and observation, criticism, and irony, on the other. To make a conceptual distinction is not to choose a vocation, but Kierkegaard's claim to be a *réflecteur* is more than a mere resignation from active political life. Positively, he has marked out the life of the mind as his form of life, though the full content of that form of life is still undetermined. From our vantage point we can recognize even in this first brush with the press the irony, humor, and intellectual penetration that characterize his authorship, the birth of his disdain for politics, his immense capacity for careful conceptual analysis, and his tenacity once he has decided that a stand must be taken. By reading these documents we cannot determine for what he will stand and what will be the content of the life of his mind, but we have discovered some hints.

3

Aesthetics, Ethics, and Reality:
A *Study of* From the Papers of One Still Living

Richard M. Summers

Despite the fact that Kierkegaard excluded it from his author-ship proper, *From the Papers of One Still Living*, his first work, still amply repays attention.[1] It not only marks an important stage in his early development, but also already contains a number of the ideas that were to become major themes of his subsequent author-ship, in particular the critique of Romanticism, the stress on per-sonal responsibility, the contrasting of the aesthetic and ethical atti-tudes to life and, not least, the device of pseudonymity since, as the flyleaf declares, *From the Papers of One Still Living* was "pub-lished against his will by S. Kjerkegaard."

One of the most interesting aspects of the work, however, is the way that it uses aesthetic categories in the form of a critique of the contemporary novel to investigate more fundamental questions about attitudes to life. For the underlying concern of *From the Papers of One Still Living* is with ways of relating to reality, which is of course something the novel is particularly well placed to explore. From this angle Kierkegaard's criticism of Andersen and championing of Thomasine Gyllembourg take on a wider signifi-cance. Here reference can also be made to Merete Jørgensen's use-ful distinction between two kinds of literary critical texts in Kierke-gaard, those that are "aesthetic" in his sense, comprising the texts penned by the aesthetic pseudonyms (primarily the aesthete A in

---

[1] In Kierkegaard scholarship recognition of the significance of this work has been increasing. For a recent major treatment of *From the Papers of One Still Living*, which emphasizes its place in the development of Kierkegaard's aesthetics, see Sylvia Walsh, *Living Poetically: Kierkegaard's Existential Aesthetics* (University Park PA: Penn State University Press, 1994) 23-41.

Either/Or), and those which are more ethically orientated and primarily concerned with the view of life expressed in the literary work.[2] *From the Papers of One Still Living* belongs very definitely to the latter group.

From the Papers of One Still Living is, as its subtitle states, a study of Andersen as a novelist "with continual reference to his latest work: *Only a Fiddler*."[3] But for Kierkegaard this provides an opportunity for a critique of what he sees as a dominant contemporary attitude to reality.[4] Taking a novel to explore a social trend was something he was, of course, to do again in the later work, *Two Ages*, where Thomasine Gyllembourg again figures importantly: it is her novel of that title which there furnishes the starting point for a critique of the age. This wider context of *From the Papers of One Still Living* is indicated at the outset. Kierkegaard begins by describing the modern desire to forget the long and painful process of historical development that has been required to reach the present stage of world history, and begin anew. He finds this rejection of historical reality particularly apparent in the obsession of the age with politics, where it is expressed either in "youthful arrogance too confident of powers untried in life" or in an inability to accept a particular position in the state and "share the burden of history, which is light and beneficent for the reasonable" (EPW, 63). In both its forms this attitude is guilty of "an attack on the given actuality; its watchword is: Forget the actual" (EPW, 64). The present political and social systems, which are the result of centuries of development must, according to this view, if they cannot be simply ignored, give way, like the primeval forests of old, "before the plough of culture at the dawn of enlightenment" (EPW, 64). In place of the rich variety brought forth by historical differences the "few pure examples of normal people" could sire "with an appalling monotony, a whole brood of select abstract *Cosmopolit-Gesichter* [cosmopolitan faces]" (EPW, 64). According to Kierkegaard, the driving force behind this whole

---

[2]Merete Jørgensen, *Kierkegaard som kritiker* (Copenhagen: Gyldendal, 1978) 11.

[3]*Only a Fiddler* (*Kun en Spillemand*), published in 1837, was Andersen's third novel. The two previous ones were *Improvisatoren* (*The Improvisatore*) and *O.T.*, published in 1835 and 1836 respectively.

[4]Cf. Walsh, *Living Poetically*, 27-30.

approach to reality, this desire to begin anew from nothing, is distrust (EPW, 64), the distrust here being the refusal to accept as good what has been handed down.

After this analysis of the contemporary condition, Kierkegaard turns his attention to the novel and short-story literature of the time, singling out Thomasine Gyllembourg's *Everyday Stories* for the life-view[5] they contain. This life-view he praises for its "joy in life," its "battle-won confidence in the world," its "confidence that the spring of the poetry of life has not gone dry in the world," its "confidence in people," that there is to be found in them "if one will only seek properly, a fullness, a divine spark, which, carefully tended, can make the whole of life glow," and, finally, its demonstration of how the demands and aspirations of youth are congruent with life's achievements. All this, Kierkegaard writes, "gives these stories an evangelistic tinge that inevitably must assure them great importance . . . and make their reading a truly upbuilding study" (EPW, 65-66). In contrast to the polemical "forget the actual" of the political trend, which was represented particularly by the writers of the Young Germany school, this life-view accepts reality in full awareness of its imperfections and finds its task there.

Armed with this perspective Kierkegaard embarks on his critique of Andersen as novelist. The fault he highlights is lack of detachment, but the underlying problem, from which this defect springs, is Andersen's attitude to life, which is one of discontentedness. This triumphs over his art. Instead of dealing with them creatively, Andersen lets the unresolved tensions of his own life overflow into his work, with the result that the "whole mob of depressing reflections about life," which are Andersen's own, submerges his characters. As Kierkegaard puts it, "the same joyless battle Andersen himself fights in life now repeats itself in his poetry," so that this poetry cannot achieve autonomy but is "immediately overwhelmed . . . by the prosaic" and his fiction "weighs one down like actuality" (EPW, 75). It is therefore impossible to get a satisfying total impression of Andersen's novels; his works do not form coherent wholes. Instead of providing an

---

[5]The hyphen in "life-view" follows the Danish *Livs-Anskuelse*.

aesthetically autonomous treatment of reality, Andersen's novels give only his own reality volatilized into fiction (EPW, 75).

What Andersen lacks as an author, according to Kierkegaard, is an epic development. By this he means a "deep and earnest embracing of a given actuality" (EPW, 71). It is a matter of achieving a certain attitude to reality, so as to get a grip on it. This is essential to the novelist, and it is where Andersen fails. What is particularly significant here is the relationship Kierkegaard is establishing between aesthetic and ethical criteria. The epic stage implies a particular relation to reality, the attainment of which is a task of personal development. But Andersen is an undeveloped personality, that is, "a possibility of a personality, wrapped up in . . . a web of arbitrary moods . . . who, in order to become a personality, needs a strong life-development" (EPW, 70).[6] Here Andersen has not been helped by the age he is living in, "the so-called political period" which, Kierkegaard suggests, will have the effect on "a temperament such as the Andersenian" (EPW, 71) of making him even more turned in on himself, his "original elegiac mood" tending to degenerate into "a certain gloom and bitterness against the world" (EPW, 73) which then comes out in his novels and tends to submerge them.

In this situation, what Andersen needs both as a writer and as a human being, in Kierkegaard's opinion, is a life-view. This he defines as "the transubstantiation of experience . . . an unshakable certainty in oneself won from all experience" (EPW, 76). This last phrase emphasizes that an element of personal appropriation is required. As to how such a life-view comes into being, Kierkegaard speaks of "a moment in which a strange light spreads over life without one's therefore even remotely needing to have understood all possible particulars . . . a moment . . . when . . . life is understood backward through the idea" (EPW, 77-78).[7]

---

[6]The way that for Kierkegaard a life-development was an indispensable requirement for the novelist, alongside the life-view, has been underlined by Sylvia Walsh. See Walsh, *Living Poetically*, 30, 32-35.

[7]Sylvia Walsh has drawn attention to the similarity between Kierkegaard's description of the coming into being of a life-view, and Heiberg's account of how he became converted to Hegelianism. See Walsh, *Living Poetically*, 37-38.

A life-view of this kind is not a merely theoretical notion, but a coherent, unifying view of reality as a whole, which gives consistency to personal life and also provides an organizing principle for the novelist,[8] enabling him to structure his material and making for a certain objectivity. As Kierkegaard puts it, the role a life-view plays in the novel is as a kind of "providence," giving it its deeper unity and freeing it from being arbitrary or purposeless (EPW, 81). Where a life-view is lacking, the novel either tries to insinuate some theory (the case of doctrinaire novels) or else becomes bogged down in a finite and inessential relationship with the author's flesh and blood (as in subjective novels) (EPW, 81). Kierkegaard sees these as in fact two expressions of the same thing—doctrinaire novels also stand in a casual relationship to personality, since their authors acquiesce in propositions "that they have not yet sufficiently experienced" (EPW, 82). The requirement that the novelist have a life-view does not therefore mean that he should express some theory of life of his own in his novels but, quite the contrary, that he should approach his material in complete freedom from subjective bias and preconceived ideas since these will inevitably distort his perspective and prevent him attaining the objectivity towards his subject matter which is essential if his novel is to have an autonomous aesthetic existence. To achieve this objectivity, however, this freedom from subjective distortions, the novelist has to tackle the source of these distortions, which is his personality. Kierkegaard therefore demands that the novelist must first and foremost "win a competent personality," and goes on to declare that it is only this "dead and transfigured personality" that should and can produce, not the "many angled, worldly, palpable one" (EPW, 82). That the attainment of such a personality is difficult is shown by the fact that in many otherwise good novels a "residue" of the author's finite personality remains as a third person, volunteering his opinions at the wrong moment. A defect that is apparent in aesthetic terms, as a fault in the work, thus be-

---

[8]The close relationship between these two aspects of the life-view has been pointed out by George Connell, *To Be One Thing: Personal Unity in Kierkegaard's Thought* (Macon GA: Mercer University Press, 1985) 27.

trays an ethical failure in personal development on the part of the author.

It is this weakness that Kierkegaard finds exemplified in Andersen, whom he classifies as one of those authors "who give an unpoetic surplus of their own merely phenomenological personality" (EPW, 82). That is to say Andersen lets his own experience and opinions flow untransformed into his artistic creations. And the reason for this, according to Kierkegaard, is inadequacy in his life. It is because Andersen himself "has not lived to the first power with poetic clarity" that "the poetic to the second power has not achieved greater consolidation in the whole" (EPW, 83-84).

Moving on to a criticism in detail of *Only a Fiddler* Kierkegaard shows how the consequences of Andersen's lack of a life-view are apparent in specific features of the novel. Kierkegaard arranges his criticisms under a number of headings, the most important of which in the present context is what he terms Andersen's "superstition as a surrogate for genuine poetry" (EPW, 87). By this he means the excessive power he thinks Andersen attributes to negative circumstances, even trivial ones, to affect his heroes, extending in the case of Christian, the male protagonist of the novel, to the power to crush true genius, which Kierkegaard sees as blatant special pleading. He regards it as intended that we should see Christian as a true genius, which he refuses to do. For Kierkegaard, genius "is not a rush candle that goes out in a puff of air but a conflagration that the storm only incites" (EPW, 88), and the figure that Andersen portrays is consequently "not a genius in his struggle but rather a sniveler who is declared to be a genius, and the only thing he has in common with a genius is that he suffers a few trifling adversities . . . " (EPW, 88). Kierkegaard sees Andersen's attempt as novelist to weight the scales and make the novel confirm his own preconceptions as the source of two other defects. These are the ways Andersen lets his basic mood, which is dissatisfaction with the world, intervene in the presentation of detail (EPW, 89-90) and the relationship he has to his fictional characters, whom he appears at times to consider as real individuals, treating them as clients he has an interest in and wishes to push forward in the world (EPW, 90).

Finally Kierkegaard takes up the question of the poetic truth of the novel, of whether, that is to say, Christian is successfully portrayed as a genius by the author and whether "sufficient factors are then procured to bring about his ruination" (EPW, 95).[9] His conclusion is that neither condition is satisfied. He homes in on that passage at the beginning of chapter seven of *Only a Fiddler* where Andersen considers Christian's destiny in the terms of two possibilities, that either he will become an exceptional artist or else a wretched, confused being, a pathetic fiddler playing in wretched inns, and declares that the deciding factor will be the environment in which he develops. It is this conception according to which genius is made dependent on favorable circumstances for its flowering, which he calls Andersen's "passivity theory" (EPW, 96), that Kierkegaard objects to so strongly. Going through the novel he finds no signs of the genius in the way Christian is portrayed. Above all Christian lacks the pride which is the essential hallmark of genius. Instead all he has is vanity (EPW, 99).

Scholars have tended to see the attitude to the genius as the explanation for Kierkegaard's treatment of Andersen in *From the Papers of One Still Living*. This was the view taken by Brandes, who argued in his pioneering study of Kierkegaard, published in 1877, that the conception of genius he found in *Only a Fiddler* affected Kierkegaard personally by challenging his "courage to go out and confront life" with its contention that genius required care, a loving environment and a certain tepid warmth to bear fruit, and that without that support it would inevitably perish.[10] Elias Bredsdorff in a study of Andersen and Kierkegaard supports Brandes's view and rejects Frithiof Brandt's theory[11] that *From the Papers of One Still Living* was an act of revenge by Kierkegaard for his portrayal as the parrot in Andersen's *Lykkens Kalosker* (The Galoshes of Fortune), published on 19 May 1838.[12] That there is a

[9]It should be noted that Kierkegaard does not rule out the possibility of an individual succumbing in the novel, but he stipulates that it must then be a poetic truth (EPW, 83). By this he means that the negative outcome must be aesthetically justified in the development of the novel, not simply imposed by the novelist.

[10]Georg Brandes, *Samlede Skrifter* II (Copenhagen: Gyldendalske Boghandels Forlag, 1899) 273.

[11]See Frithiof Brandt, *Den unge Søren Kierkegaard* (Copenhagen: Levin & Munksgaards Forlag, 1929) 125-53.

[12]Bredsdorff refers to Topsøe-Jensen's dismissal of that hypothesis. See Elias Bredsdorff, "H C Andersen og Søren Kierkegaard," *Anderseniana* 3. række III

definite connection between Kierkegaard's reaction to *Only a Fiddler* and his view of what is involved in being a genius seems to be borne out by a later journal entry, where he writes:

> Even if I proved nothing else by writing *Either/Or*, I proved that in Danish literature a book can be written without needing the warm jacket of sympathy, without needing the incentive of antici- pation, that one can work even though the stream is against him, that one can work hard without seeming to, that one can private- ly concentrate while practically every bungling student dares look upon him as a loafer. Even if the book itself were devoid of meaning, the making of it would still be the pithiest epigram I have written over the maundering philosophic age in which I live. (JP, 5:5614)

Although the context here is *Either/Or* the sentiments expressed suggest that in relation to Christian Kierkegaard saw himself as the "one still living," the genius who succeeded despite the opposition, and that this was the immediate personal reference of the title of *From the Papers of One Still Living*.

As a literary response, however, to see *Only a Fiddler* as being primarily about the fate of a genius is a somewhat limited reading. In concentrating exclusively on Christian it completely overlooks the other main character, Naomi, yet it is one of the special features of this novel that it has not one but two protagonists, who are treated more or less equally, a fact that can be easily estab- lished by simply adding up the amount of space devoted to each, as Sven Møller Kristensen does.[13] In *From the Papers of One Still Living*, however, Naomi receives no more than a brief mention in passing, the part of the novel devoted primarily to her being dis- missed as "bits and pieces of Andersen's reminiscences smuggled into Naomi's diary" (EPW, 100). When she is taken into account, though, Christian's fate appears in a slightly different light, his weakness of character being counterbalanced by her strength of will. On this level the novel can be read, as in Sven Møller Kristensen's interpretation, as illustrating "the contrast between tameness and freedom . . . taming and liberation, weakness and

---

(Odense: H C Andersens Hus, 1981) 235.

[13]Sven Møller Kristensen, *Den dobbelte Eros* (Copenhagen: Gyldendal, 1966) 172-73.

strength," which is brought out in particular in the symbolism of wild and tame birds, with the stork playing the role of a kind of leitmotiv in the novel.[14] In Christian we see the combination of artistic talent and a weak personality, while Naomi attempts to shape her life according to her will. Christian's failure is more immediately obvious, but it is questionable whether Naomi is really more successful. She certainly pays a heavy price for what freedom she gains. In Kierkegaard's categories they could both be seen as examples of attempts to live poetically which come to grief in their different ways. It is surely clear, though, to an unbiased reading, that we are not meant to identify with Christian, for his failings, particularly his vanity and his blindness to the world around him, are presented too clearly to allow that, and Andersen's sympathies seem if anything to lie more with Naomi.

Even critics sympathetic to Andersen, however, would agree with Kierkegaard's point about his digressions in *Only a Fiddler*,[15] the way he brings in feelings and reflections which, while important to him, are often of doubtful relevance to the story. The substance of Kierkegaard's criticism, though, concerns Andersen's lack of a life-view and the effect this has on the success of the novel. According to Kierkegaard a novel of the kind Andersen is writing—and he explicitly allows that this is not the only kind of novel as his remarks about Blicher and the unity born of mood show (EPW, 69, 79)—should be a coherent whole, with an organizing principle running through it, informing and coordinating the various parts. This, as we have seen, is the role the life-view plays. For Kierkegaard an example of such a life-view constituting the organic unity of a novel was provided by Goethe's *Wilhelm Meister*, where he admired "the capacious governance which pervades the whole work, the entire Fichtean moral world order . . . which is inherent in the whole book" (JP, 2:1455).

The criterion that the novel should form an organic totality is of course an idealist one. There is no need, however, to look to a reading of Hegel's *Aesthetics* to account for this in Kierkegaard's

---

[14]Kristensen, *Den dobbelte Eros*, 174.

[15]E.g., Johan de Mylius, *Myte og roman: H. C. Andersens romaner mellem romantik og realisme* (Copenhagen: Gyldendal, 1981) 123.

case. The source is likely to have been much closer to home, for an attraction to Goethe's classicism was an important feature of Danish Romanticism, associated in particular with Oehlenschläger. This outlook was shared by Poul Møller, whom the evidence suggests was the most important direct influence on the *Papers of One Still Living*. It has been pointed out, for example, that Møller complained in 1835 that much of contemporary Danish literature was written without a life-view at its base,[16] but this is not the only point in the work where his influence can be discerned. In a major essay reviewing Thomasine Gyllembourg's novel *Extremerne* (The Extremes), but also setting out his own critical views, which was published in the *Maanedsskrift for Litteratur* (Literary Monthly) in 1836, Poul Møller introduces several of the major themes that Kierkegaard develops in his criticism of Andersen. Again there is the admiration for Goethe, whom Møller extols for his "poetic freedom of spirit," his ability to conceal his prosaic sympathy for human concerns behind his poetic creations.[17] This comment relates to Møller's identification, earlier in his essay, of two possible failures on the part of the writer, one of which was to show too little interest in the ordinary life of the mass of people while the other was to allow his "prosaic interests" to have too great an influence on his poetic creation.[18] "That sympathy with the other interests of life, which is the condition for true poetry" should not, according to Møller, be manifested in such a way that the poet's political views or social involvement are directly apparent, a point which seems to anticipate Kierkegaard's criticism of doctrinaire novels. The requirement for harmony too, which Kierkegaard expresses in his demand that the novel be a coherent whole, is likewise underlined by Møller, who sees it as one of the merits of Thomasine Gyllembourg's work, though elsewhere he finds it to be less and less frequent. And where it is lacking the poet's creation is inevitably "pieced together from heterogeneous elements."[19]

---

[16]In a review in *Dansk Litteraturtidende*, see W. Glyn Jones, "Søren Kierkegaard and Poul Martin Møller," *Modern Language Review* 60 (1965): 81.

[17]Poul Møller, *Efterladte Skrifter*, vol. 6, 2nd ed. (Copenhagen: C A Reitzel, 1850) 56.

[18]Møller, *Efterladte Skrifter*, 6:54.

[19]Møller, *Efterladte Skrifter*, 6:60.

More important, even, for *From the Papers* than these aesthetic influences is the connection Poul Møller makes in his review between the quality of a writer's work and the quality of his life. "The true poet," he writes, "must first and foremost be a true human being."[20] He returns to this principle later, explaining it as follows. "The person who belongs to the great multitude, who is wholly incapable of reconciling himself to the way the world is, and who sees nothing more in human life than chance, folly and wickedness, and that without even really believing in the reality of wickedness, who feels himself to be in conflict with himself and with the whole of reality, that person cannot possibly be a true poet."[21] The aesthetic quality of the work of literature, that is to say, stands in an essential relationship to the quality of personality of the author. This, as we have seen, was precisely the point that Kierkegaard was making in his criticism of Andersen as novelist, and it seems natural to see Poul Møller's influence here. For Møller the principle derived from his ideal of personal integration and harmony. In his application of the principle too, Kierkegaard was following Poul Møller who had little sympathy with the cultivation of the aesthetic in the productions of such younger contemporaries as Paludan-Müller and Andersen, on whose *Fodreise fra Holmens Canal til Østpynten af Amager* (Journey on Foot from Holmens Canal to Amager), published in 1829, he was particularly harsh.[22] In contrast he had a high opinion of Thomasine Gyllembourg, and in praising the harmony present in her work Møller was appealing to the Goethean ideal of the first phase of Danish Romanticism, which was his own foundation. He recognized, though, that the Goethean period in European literature was coming to its end[23] and was aware of the forces now ranged against it, as is apparent from his *Ahasverus* aphorisms.[24] It was in fact in the context of a

---

[20]Møller, *Efterladte Skrifter*, 6:56.

[21]Møller, *Efterladte Skrifter*, 6:65-66.

[22]See Vilhelm Andersen, *Poul Møller*, 3rd ed. (Copenhagen: Gyldendalske Boghandel, 1944) 344.

[23]Møller, *Efterladte Skrifter*, 6:66.

[24]See George Pattison, *Kierkegaard: The Aesthetic and the Religious: From the Magic Theatre to the Crucifixion of the Image* (Basingstoke: Macmillan, 1992) 31-32.

criticism of the "Gospel of irony" of Schlegel's *Lucinde* that Møller made his remark that a true poet had to be a true human being.

It thus seems to be clear beyond doubt that Kierkegaard in *From the Papers* was building on Poul Møller's position which, as Rubow says, in the field of criticism he never definitively formulated.[25] In fact the way this work takes up and develops ideas of Poul Møller's lends support to the theory that the "One Still Living" of the title among other things refers to Kierkegaard's relation to Poul Møller, who had died earlier that year (on 13 March 1838), as Vilhelm Andersen suggests in his study of Møller.[26]

If Kierkegaard was carrying on Poul Møller's work in criticizing Andersen, he was doing so even more in looking to Thomasine Gyllembourg as a positive counterweight. The essay in which Poul Møller set out his objections to the nihilistic tendencies of contemporary literature was, as we have seen, a review—and a very favorable one—of Thomasine Gyllembourg's novel *Extremerne*.

There was also, however, a personal factor in play here to predispose Kierkegaard towards Thomasine Gyllembourg and away from everything represented by Andersen, and that was the development he had undergone in the years immediately prior to *From the Papers of One Still Living*. Here he was part of a general trend, for while the first phase of Danish Romanticism, as represented in particular by Oehlenschläger, had been characterized by a spirit of life-affirmation and optimism, and found its ideal in German Classicism and Goethe, in the period between 1820 and 1830 the German Classical ideal of order and harmony began to come under fire as new influences from abroad made themselves felt. Byron in particular began to have an influence in Denmark where he was seen as the "poet of despair" and as such as a challenge to the dominant idealistic and Christian worldview.[27] Heine too exercised an influence in the same direction.[28] Stimulated by these influences, a new movement arose in Danish literature

---

[25]Poul Rubow, *Dansk Litterær Kritik i det Nittende Aarhundrede* (Copenhagen: Levin & Munksgaards Forlag, 1921) 66.

[26]Vilhelm Andersen, *Poul Møller*, 388.

[27]Gustav Albeck, Oluf Friis, and Peter P Rohde, *Dansk Litteratur Historie* (Copenhagen: Politikens Forlag, 1965) 2:256. Friis is the author of this section.

[28]Albeck et al., *Dansk Litteratur Historie*, 2:257.

which took up the themes of disappointment, frustration and despair expressed by contemporary European writers. Its results are seen in such works as Carl Bagger's *Min Broders Levned* (The Life of My Brother) (1835) and Paludan-Müller's early work, especially *Dandserinden* (The Dancer) (1833), which has been called the major work of Danish Byronism[29] and in which a note of pessimism predominates. Andersen's first three novels, culminating in *Only a Fiddler* also belong with this trend. By 1837-38, however, as Sven Møller Kristensen comments, the opposing movement, represented by the older writers and critics, had succeeded, at least temporarily, in stemming the tide and exorcising the evil spirits. The change is marked by Paludan-Müller's crisis, Heiberg's *Fata Morgana* and Kierkegaard's *From the Papers of One Still Living*.[30]

Kierkegaard had made his début in 1834 with the polemical, if not very distinguished, *Another Defense of Woman's Great Abilities* (EPW, 3-5) which was obviously an attempt to break free from the constraining atmosphere of his home and of theology, and get into the more exciting and prestigious contemporary literary world. That Kierkegaard was familiar with doubt, despair and irony, the mainsprings of nihilistic polemic, is attested by the very important Journal entries of the summer of 1835. In the draft letter dated 1 June 1835 (JP, 5:5092), generally taken to be addressed to Peter Wilhelm Lund but possibly fictional, he speaks of the "Faustian element" of doubt that is a stage in every intellectual development. In the slightly later "Gilleleie entry" (JP, 5:5100) he refers to "that irksome, sinister traveling companion—that irony of life," which is here seen as a force to which the individual is subject, and which in "the waters of morality" attacks in particular those who have not yet come in under "the tradewinds of virtue." Now, however, Kierkegaard has the remedy, and the Gilleleie entry concludes with a resolution to act.

From the journal entries of the immediately following period we can see that one of the forms that action took for Kierkegaard was an analysis of irony and humor as attitudes to reality. They are seen as two different stages in the development of subjectivity.

---

[29]Albeck et al., *Dansk Litteratur Historie*, 2:520.
[30]Sven Møller Kristensen, *Den dobbelte Eros*, 109.

Irony, while fundamentally polemical was, as a movement, insufficiently radical. For in irony the subject itself is kept out of the field and allowed to be absolute. Once irony is extended to the subject, however, and it comes to see itself as part of the reality it mocks, the deeper stage of humor is reached. In a journal entry of 1837 this process is described succinctly:

> Irony is first surmounted when the individual, elevated above everything and looking down from this position, is finally elevated beyond himself and from this dizzy height sees himself in his nothingness, and thereby he finds his true elevation. . . . The ironical position is essentially: *nil admirari*; but irony, when it slays itself, has *disdained* everything with humor, itself included. (JP, 2:1688)

In humor the subject has given up its illusory absoluteness, and the rejection of given reality from the standpoint of absolute demands has given way to its acceptance, with a calm acknowledgement of all its shortcomings, which the subject now sees itself as sharing, whereas formerly it would have judged them. The attitude of humor can thus be seen as fundamentally one of acceptance of the way things are. Its hallmark is an affirmation of the finite, an embracing of everyday reality in all its particularity and limitations, an attitude which borders on the religious, and for Kierkegaard the master here was Hamann. This attitude may have been further confirmed for him by the religious experience of *"indescribable joy"* of 19 May 1838 (JP, 5:5324).

It is in this context of the rediscovery of the value of the everyday that Kierkegaard's enthusiasm for Thomasine Gyllembourg can best be understood, for the outstanding feature of her stories is their interest in ordinary life, and conviction that it is here that happiness is to be found. It is this that gave them their tremendous contemporary appeal, and it also constitutes their importance in Danish literature. For in these stories, as Henning Fenger points out, Thomasine Gyllembourg succeeded in creating a modern prose fiction dealing with contemporary individuals and their problems, which was something quite new.[31] In particular her stories stand out in contrast to the literature of Romanticism

---

[31]Henning Fenger, *The Heibergs* (New York: Twayne, 1971) 142-43.

which, with its worship of the past, its fantastic subjects, and a predominantly versified form of expression, had nothing to offer the middle classes.[32] In Thomasine Gyllembourg's fiction, by contrast, people found their everyday lives and concerns dealt with.

One of the great strengths of Thomasine Gyllembourg's stories, and one of the sources of their appeal, was the fact that they were drawn from the material of her own life, a factor which needs to be taken into account in any consideration of her work. She was born Thomasine Buntzen on 9 November 1773. At home she received an excellent education and indulged in extensive novel reading, Rousseau's *La nouvelle Héloïse* and Goethe's *Werther* becoming lifelong influences.[33] In 1788 she became engaged to the fifteen years older Peter Andreas Heiberg, and on 7 August 1790, not yet seventeen, she married him. Less than eighteen months later, on 14 December 1791, their son Johan Ludvig was born. P A Heiberg, who was by then beginning to make his mark as a playwright, was also active in politics as an ardent supporter of the French Revolution. When the political climate changed he found himself on the wrong side of the Danish Crown Prince and was sentenced to permanent exile, leaving Denmark on 7 February 1800.[34] In the years leading up to that event P A Heiberg's home had been a meeting place for people sympathetic to the French Revolution, and it was here that Thomasine Heiberg met the Swedish baron Carl Frederik Gyllembourg-Ehrensvärd, who had been exiled from Sweden in 1792 for his part in the plot which resulted in the murder of King Gustaf III. For Thomasine Heiberg this was, in Fenger's words, "both *le coup de foudre* and her life's passion,"[35] and after the departure of her husband she was able to give it free reign. On 11 September 1801 she wrote to P A Heiberg and asked for her freedom. In expecting his understanding she soon found she had made a serious mistake,[36] but despite family

---

[32]Fenger, *The Heibergs*, 75.
[33]Fenger, *The Heibergs*, 30.
[34]Fenger, *The Heibergs*, 29.
[35]Fenger, *The Heibergs*, 31.
[36]The correspondence between P A Heiberg and Thomasine reveals two totally different conceptions of love, the one deriving from Condorcet, the other from Rousseau. See Fenger, *The Heibergs*, 34, and Klaus P Mortensen, *Thomasines oprør*

pressure and public gossip she held out single-mindedly for a divorce, which was granted, by the King himself, on 4 December 1801. She and Gyllembourg were married the same month. There followed some happy years, first in their country house "Ruhedal" near Ringsted and then in Copenhagen, where Oehlenschläger and Baggesen were among their regular guests, until Gyllembourg's sudden death in 1815. There were then a variety of homes until 1831 when Johan Ludvig Heiberg married Johanne Luise Pätges, and Thomasine Gyllembourg moved in with them. She lived with her son and daughter-in-law until her death in 1856.

Thomasine Gyllembourg made her literary debut at the relatively late age of 53 in her son, Johan Ludvig Heiberg's, journal *Kjøbenhavns flyvende Post* (The Copenhagen Flying Post). Her contribution took the form of a letter to the editor purporting to be from a young lieutenant in the unfortunate predicament of being refused access by her family to the girl he wished to marry. This letter appeared on 12 January 1827 and was followed by others, from the other parties involved in the affair, all of which were so realistic that many readers were taken in. These letters were later collected in the story *Familien Polonius* (The Polonius Family), published in 1834.

In order to get an impression of the *Everyday Stories* and appreciate what it was that Kierkegaard found in them there may be some value at this point in looking briefly at three stories which represent different aspects of Thomasine Gyllembourg's oeuvre. (It should be mentioned that Thomasine Gyllembourg published her work anonymously, a point which Kierkegaard always respects by referring invariably to "the author of an *Everyday Story*.")

En Hverdagshistorie (An Everyday Story), probably the most well known of the stories, appeared in 1828. Its motto could be the proverb, act in haste and repent at leisure. The hero, who is nameless, is staying at a country house in Mecklenburg where, bored by the stiffness and formality of the aristocratic company, he is predisposed to the attractions of a young and vivacious fellow countrywoman, Jette, who happens to visit. Without much thought he gets engaged to her, but it is not long before he begins to

(Copenhagen: G. E. C. Gad, 1986) 12-53.

suspect he may have made a mistake. This is confirmed when he gets back to Copenhagen and visits her home, where he is greeted by disorder and mess, and also discovers that her accomplishments are rather less than he had expected. It turns out, however, that she has a half-sister, Maja, who has been brought up in Sweden and has all the qualities Jette lacks in the way of sobriety, orderliness and neatness. As he gets to know her better he soon realizes that he is in love with Maja, and that it is her and not Jette whom he should marry. This potentially difficult situation is resolved for him when, in a parallel development, Maja's former fiancé discovers that he loves Jette instead, and she in turn willingly accepts him. Thus all can end happily.

This story illustrates some of the features of Thomasine Gyllembourg's fiction which help to explain its popular appeal. Primary among these is the realism of the setting. Then there is the concern with relationships, and particularly with the formation of the right couples. The didactic element is unmistakable in the way the signs that augur well or badly are described, and bad manners criticized. In the matter of cultivation, of course, Thomasine Gyllembourg was at one with the ideals of her son, Ludvig Heiberg, though her particular concern was the cultivation of the heart. Above all there is growth in the hero as he comes to awareness of who he is and what he really wants.

The psychological aspect is given more prominence in the slightly later story *Drøm og Virkelighed* (Dream and Reality) of 1833, which also affords a glimpse into the frequently less salubrious reality behind the respectable facade of contemporary bourgeois life. The hero Julius B is in love with a servant girl, Lise, who is expecting his child and whom he is visiting in secret when the story opens. Julius lives with a wealthy uncle, on whom he is dependent, and were it not for this uncle, he would have married Lise. Some years previously this uncle had himself been deserted by his young wife, whose sudden death now provides the occasion for him to be reunited with his daughter, Laura, who is thirteen. He wants Julius to marry Laura so that he can make him his son and heir, but Julius, on account of the relationship he is already involved in and his lack of attraction to Laura cannot agree to this. He moves out of his uncle's house and goes to live with Lise and his baby son. It is not long, however, before the incompatibility between him and Lise becomes painfully apparent. She proves to be dirty, disorganized, untidy, unable to occupy herself and to have some unpleasant personality traits. Soon Julius has to admit that all the illusion has disappeared from the relationship. With the birth of a second child the situation becomes much worse. For six years Julius endures a miserable life with Lise until one day, on his way out to visit her, he is moved by the sight of a strikingly attractive young woman who turns out to be none other than his cousin Laura, with whom he then falls in love. He is reconciled with his uncle and marries Laura shortly afterwards, despite the problem of his existing relationship. It transpires, however, that Laura has already found out about Lise, who is by this time terminally ill, and has visited her and Julius's sons disguised as a sailor. This part of the story gives rise to some moving scenes in which Laura's goodness, practical concern and readiness to forgive are powerfully contrasted with the selfishness and suspicion of the men, particularly Julius and his uncle. It is wholly thanks to Laura that the situation is brought to a good outcome. After Lise dies, Laura brings Julius's sons to live with her and their father. In this way Julius's dream is given reality. But Julius has developed. His commitment to Lise reveals his good qualities, and his loyalty to her through the suffering it has brought him has had the effect of maturing him so that he is now able to find happiness with Laura.

Dreams do not therefore have to be illusion, they can also guide us to reality and our deepest happiness, provided that we learn to read them aright. This is an important theme in another story, *Extremerne* (The Extremes), which we have already encountered as the subject of Poul Møller's review discussed above. Here the male protagonist, Rudolph Hermes, a doctor by profession, admits at the outset that he does not know what he really wants. Hermes is an idealist who has so far found reality disappointing. As the story opens, he and his friend, Philip Roller, are on their way from Copenhagen to the country home of Roller's cousin, Elise. The intention is that Hermes should get to know Elise better with a view to possible marriage, but he is not optimistic. His fears prove well founded, but before the meeting takes place, while the two friends are still on the way, they make the acquaintance of Palmer, an eccentric artist and Swedenborgian, who also lives in the area. From Palmer Hermes acquires a drawing depicting an idyllic, homely scene, which makes a deep impression on him, filling him with an intimation of happiness. This proves to be well founded, as he discovers when he meets Gabriele, Palmer's niece. It is a case of love at first sight. In Gabriele Hermes recognizes a kindred spirit, but before they can be happily united several obstacles have to be overcome and at key stages in the process the image of the house plays a part, both in dream and in reality, in guiding Hermes to his true goal. The most intractable of these obstacles is the aristocratic rigidity and prejudice of Gabriele's father, Count Granhjelm, who refuses to accept the bourgeois Hermes as a potential son-in-law. This provides Thomasine Gyllembourg with an opportunity to contrast the ideal of cultivation, for which Hermes is the spokesman, as the contemporary form of nobility, with the prejudice of the traditional aristocracy, which in the story begets its opposite, as Count Granhjelm's son Fritz is discovered to be active in revolutionary politics in Germany. Hermes and Roller, the idealist and the practical man, are also opposites, and the story ends with Hermes being vindicated, for in Gabriele reality exceeds all his hopes.

There is an element of the religious here, the human experience of love revealing a dimension of the infinite. This is another set of extremes, for at the outset Hermes expresses contempt for what he sees as the childishness of religious notions. At the end, however, he undergoes a conversion. The occasion for this is another of Palmer's artistic creations, this time an altarpiece depicting the Resurrection which, at a propitious moment, makes a deep impression on Hermes, causing him to accept in faith the Risen Christ. He then pledges his commitment to Gabriele.

If we turn back now to Kierkegaard's praise of Thomasine Gyllembourg it may be with a better appreciation of what was at stake in it. As we saw, the reason for his appeal to her stories in *From the Papers of One Still Living* was "out of consideration for the life-view contained therein" (EPW, 65), and one of the features of that life-view was its attitude to reality, an attitude which stressed its richness, its ability to satisfy our longings. Reality is not seen here as having split away from the ideal and being bound to disappoint. Rather it is the place where our hopes can be fulfilled. As Kierkegaard puts it, the stories show "the verified congruence of youth's demands and announcements with life's achievements," demonstrated not from philosophical principles (*ex mathematica pura*) but from experience (*de profundis*) (EPW, 66), and here we may instance Julius B's maturation process through the years of misery with Lise or Rudolph Hermes's doubts and agonies before the way is clear to union with Gabriele.

This serves to underline a fundamental feature of the life-view of the *Everyday Stories*, which is that it is something that has been positively acquired. If we contrast this with Kierkegaard's critique of Andersen, that fundamentally he lacks personal development, we could say that while Andersen is an example of the attitude that Kierkegaard will call the aesthetic, the *Stories*, on the other hand, spring from an ethical attitude to life. What is particularly significant here though is that the ethical purpose is achieved through the medium of literature, which gives grounds for suggesting that the *Everyday Stories* could have played a part in the development of Kierkegaard's view of how an aesthetic production could serve ethical and religious ends. The possibility seems worth mentioning, for while it has been recognized that his treatment of Andersen anticipates his critique of Romanticism, the possible influence of Thomasine Gyllembourg in a different direction has received little attention.

An ethical intention was in fact fundamental to Thomasine Gyllembourg's purpose in the *Stories*. Her basic concern was with relationships, the short story form enabling her to explore a particular situation on each occasion. This is one of the contrasts with the Romantic novel, where the theme is the hero's self-development. For Thomasine Gyllembourg self-development is achieved in love, that is, in the relation to an other, and the task is therefore to get rid of the illusions and projections which threaten this relationship. This is what the stories are about. The basic structure, as Klaus Mortensen points out,[37] is always the same: two people who love each other are confronted by various obstacles which stand in the way of their coming together. The aim is then, as we have seen in the examples discussed, to remove the obstacles by disentangling the threads of conflict, so that the right people can be united and stable families formed. For Thomasine

---

[37]See Klaus Mortensen, *Thomasines oprør*, 143.

Gyllembourg this latter is essential. As Mortensen writes: "The invariable moral goal of the *Everyday Stories* is to ensure that couples and families are formed on the right basis, which is the deep and inextinguishable love of the parties for each other."[38] In normal circumstances, however, the course of love does not run smoothly, and it is the most important concern of the *Stories* to establish why. The source of most conflicts Thomasine Gyllembourg finds in the emotional life, but emotions are the result of people's relations with their environment. From this follows the importance not only of self-knowledge but also of the ability to understand others. As Mortensen puts it: "In order to be able to love truly one must not only know oneself and one's background, one must also be able to enter into the beloved's personality and situation."[39]

If failure then to understand the other person and oneself spells disaster in love, the encouraging thing that Thomasine Gyllembourg's stories show is that these are things that can be learned. Thus the aim of the *Everyday Stories* is didactic, and the universal enemy, whether it occurs as personal oddity, blind passion or egotistical calculation, is self-absorption.[40] There was much, then, in the *Stories* that Kierkegaard could use in his own psychology. Probably this was partly what he was referring to when he later acknowledged his indebtedness to the author of an *Everyday Story* (JP, 5:5868).

If the emphasis so far has been on the ethical, and specifically on the way Kierkegaard saw in Thomasine Gyllembourg how an aesthetic production could be made to serve an ethical purpose, this should not lead us to overlook the significance of religion in the life-view of the *Stories*. It is particularly evident in the "joy in life" Kierkegaard finds in them, from which springs confidence—"confidence in the world," confidence in poetry ("that the spring of the poetry of life has not gone dry in the world") and "confidence in people, that even in their most trivial manifestations there is to be found, if one will only seek properly, a fullness, a

[38]Mortensen, *Thomasines oprør*, 143.
[39]Mortensen, *Thomasines oprør*, 145.
[40]Mortensen, *Thomasines oprør*, 145.

divine spark, which, carefully tended, can make the whole of life glow" (EPW, 65-66). Kierkegaard recognizes that this is an attitude that has been won from experience on the basis of a religious faith, albeit "the truly religious" in Thomasine Gyllembourg is sometimes replaced by "a certain well-being within the cozy walls of amiable domestic relationships" (EPW, 66). Her stories have "an evangelistic tinge," but the "joy" to which they testify has been acquired through suffering (EPW, 66). It is a joy that is the fruit of resignation, not, be it noted, the resignation of "flattened persons," brought about by external pressures, but the resignation achieved by "internal elasticity" (EPW, 67). And in this sense the stories are not limited in their appeal to older readers, but can also be helpful to the younger generation (EPW, 67-68). The reference to Kierkegaard's own recent development seems here unmistakable.

Resignation has to do with living in, and accepting, the conditions and limitations of ordinary human life which, as we have seen in the case of humor, can be a liberating experience. For this is a viewpoint which does not see limitedness as a deficiency, and enables the concerns of everyday life to be enjoyed and given their proper importance. Here there is a respect for actuality in all its richness, for people, and for the circumstances which have made them and in which they have to find their happiness.

We are thus brought back to the starting point of *From the Papers of One Still Living* and the question that is its theme, namely the relation to reality, and the two fundamental options, on the one hand willing acceptance of the finite and contingent in all its imperfection, and readiness to work with it within these limitations, on the other, rejection of the constraints of the actual in the desire to begin anew and create something not determined by the imperfections of the past. This, as we noted, Kierkegaard saw as the goal of revolutionary politics with its watchword "forget the actual" (EPW, 64). He saw the same trend reflected in contemporary literature, and from this perspective his choice of *Only a Fiddler* for his critique can be seen to have been particularly apt. For it is an important feature of that novel that both protagonists attempt to find fulfillment beyond the limits laid down for them, Christian in his musical ambitions and Naomi in a dream of personal freedom.

The view of reality obviously has implications for the view of aesthetics. Nowhere is this more the case than in Romanticism where, as Kierkegaard was to argue in the *Concept of Irony*, it was the same principle, namely irony, that was at the root of each. Here Kierkegaard explicitly makes the connection between the polemical attitude to reality expressed in the Young Germany school and the irony of Tieck and Schlegel (CI, 275). Fundamental to the ironists' attitude is polemic, the rejection of given reality for a world of the imagination, where the constraints of ordinary life do not apply. This, though, is not liberation but escapism, and it was the escapist and destructive aspects of Romantic literature, seen particularly in the breaking loose of the imagination from all ethical constraints, that Kierkegaard castigated so vigorously.

The critique of Romanticism, however, does not exhaust Kierkegaard's view of aesthetics. He also saw a positive role for it as, among other things, his enthusiasm for Thomasine Gyllembourg clearly shows. But Thomasine Gyllembourg's life-view, as we have seen, was one of acceptance of given reality "in resignation's quiet joy over life" (TA, 13). Kierkegaard was to go beyond Thomasine Gyllembourg in his own aesthetic production, in the types of experience he explored and the techniques he employed, but he retained his high opinion of her work, as his later review of her novel *Two Ages* shows, and remained faithful to the principle he found embodied in it of an aesthetic oeuvre devoted to the service of ethics. Here art is not an escape from reality, but a means to its deeper understanding. The difference between the two roles of art is also emphasized in the essential distinction Kierkegaard makes between a "Digter" (poet) and a "Forfatter" (author),[41] the latter term always being used for Thomasine Gyllembourg.

Ultimately Thomasine Gyllembourg's outlook was that of an earlier generation. In championing her in the contemporary debate, however, Kierkegaard was criticizing his age from a standpoint which also looked ahead towards the movements that were to supplant Romanticism. For one of the principal features of the attitude to art and life of the Romantic ironists was the confusion of their boundaries. The attempt to apply the freedom of the world

---

[41]On this distinction see Merete Jørgensen, *Kierkegaard som kritiker*, 131-33.

of imagination without further ado to the world of everyday life has the effect of turning life into an aesthetic phenomenon, to be judged by purely aesthetic criteria. This is the situation that Kierkegaard depicts in the "aesthetic" attitude to life. The role of an art that does not accept this situation will not therefore be to create imaginary worlds to indulge our fantasies, but rather to help us to see the actual world in a new way, to discover its hidden riches and to live our lives with greater understanding. It was this conception of aesthetics that, despite all their differences in practice, united Kierkegaard and Thomasine Gyllembourg.

4

A Rose with Thorns:
Hans Christian Andersen's Relation to Kierkegaard

Bruce H. Kirmmse

The Snail and the Rosebush

The garden was surrounded by a hedge of hazel bushes, and beyond it there were fields and meadows with cows and sheep. But in the middle of the garden there was a blossoming rose-bush, under which sat a snail which had a great deal within itself—it had itself.

"Wait until my time comes!," said the snail, "I will do something more than bring forth roses, or bear nuts, or give milk like cows and sheep."

"I expect an awful lot of you," said the rosebush. "Dare I ask when this will be?"

"I am taking my time," said the snail. "You are in such a hurry! That doesn't raise expectations."

The next year the snail lay in more or less the same place, in the sunshine under the rosebush, which brought forth buds and blossomed with roses, always fresh, always new. And the snail crept out halfway, stretched forth its feelers, and drew them back in again.

"Everything looks the same as it did last year! There has been no progress. The rosebush continues with its roses; it does not get any further!"

The summer passed by. Autumn came. The rosebush still had flowers and buds right up until the snow fell. The weather became raw and damp. The rosebush bowed down toward the ground. The snail crept underground.

Then a new year began. And the roses came forth, and the snail came forth.

"Now you are an old rosebush," it said. "You must soon die. You have given the world all that you had within yourself. I don't have time to consider the question of whether it was of any significance, but it is clear that you have not done the least for your inner development, for otherwise you would have produced something different. Can you defend this conduct? Soon you will be nothing but bare twigs! Do you understand what I am saying?"

"You terrify me," said the rosebush, "I have never thought about these things."

"No, you have of course never occupied yourself much with thinking! Have you ever explained to yourself why you blossomed and how this blossoming comes to pass? Why it is this way and not some other way?"

"No!," said the rosebush. "I blossomed out of happiness, because I couldn't do otherwise. The sun was so warm, the air was so refreshing. I drank the clear dew and the strong rain. I breathed, I lived! A strength from the earth came up into me. A strength came down from above. I sensed a happiness, always new, always great, and therefore I always had to blossom. It was my life, I couldn't do otherwise!"

"You have led a very comfortable life," said the snail.

"Indeed! Everything was given to me," said the rosebush. "But even more was given to you! You are one of these thoughtful, profound types, one of the highly gifted who will surprise the world."

"That is something to which I have given absolutely no thought," said the snail. "The world does not concern me! What do I have to do with the world? I have enough with myself and enough in myself."

"But shouldn't all of us here on the earth give the best portion of ourselves to others! Shouldn't we bring whatever we can! Indeed, I have only given roses, but you, you who received so much, what did you give to the world? What do you give to it?"

"What did I give? What do I give! I spit at it! It's just no good at all! It is of no concern to me. Bring forth roses—you cannot do anything else! Let the hazelnut bush bear nuts! Let the cows and the sheep give milk. They each have their public—I have mine within myself! I am retreating into myself, and there I will remain. The world is of no concern to me!"

And then the snail went into its house and straightened it up.

"It is so sad," said the rosebush." "Even with my best efforts I cannot creep into myself. I must always spring forth, spring forth in roses. My petals fall off and fly away on the wind! Yet, I saw one of my roses placed in a housewife's hymnal; one of my roses found a place on the breast of a lovely young girl; and one was kissed in blissful happiness by the mouth of a child. It seemed so good to me. It was a true blessing. That is what I remember, that is my life!"

And the rosebush blossomed innocently. And the snail lay about in its house. The world was of no concern to him.

And years passed.

The snail was dust in the earth. The rosebush was dust in the earth. The rose that had been preserved in the hymnal had vanished. But new rosebushes bloomed in the garden. And new snails lived in the garden. They retreated into their houses and spat. The world was of no concern to them.

Shall we read the story over again? It will not be any different.[1]

† † †

As is well known, Søren Kierkegaard's first published book, *From the Papers of One Still Living*, which came out in September 1838, was a book-length review of Hans Christian Andersen's 1837 novel *Only a Fiddler*. Most of what is generally known about Andersen's reaction to Kierkegaard's review is based on the well-known passage in Andersen's 1855 autobiography, *The Fairy Tale of My Life* [*Mit Livs Eventyr*]:

For a short time the novel *Only a Fiddler* engrossed one of the brilliant young men of our country. This was *Søren Kierkegaard*. When we met on the street he told me that he would write a review of it, and that I would surely be more satisfied with it than with earlier reviews, since, he granted, I had been misunderstood! A long time passed. He read the book again, and his initial good impression was obliterated. I must assume that the more seriously he considered the composition, the more faulty it became. When the review appeared I could not be pleased with it. It was an entire book (the first, I believe, that *Kierkegaard* wrote), and somewhat difficult to read with its heavy *Hegelian* style. It was said in jest that only *Kierkegaard* and *Andersen* had read the whole book. Its title was *From the Papers of One Still Living*. At that time this is what I got out of it: that I was no writer, but a fictitious character who had slipped out of my category, and that it would be the task of some future writer to put me back into it or to use me as a character in a work in which he would create a supplement to me! Later I better

---

[1]"Sneglen og Rosenhækken" ["The Snail and the Rosebush"], in *H. C. Andersens Samlede Skrifter* [*The Collected Writings of Hans Christian Andersen*], 2nd ed., vol. 15 (Copenhagen: C. A. Reitzels Forlag, 1880) 16-18. All translations in this essay are my own.

understood this author, who has obliged me along my way with kindness and discernment.[2]

Kierkegaard's review of Andersen's novel was anything but complimentary; he was strongly critical both of the novel and of the ethical and aesthetic stance represented by its author. Andersen's account of this incident, which was published seventeen years later, when Kierkegaard had established himself as Denmark's leading religious writer and controversialist,[3] was quite gentle and forgiving.

If we are to believe Andersen's 1855 autobiography, Kierkegaard's scathing criticism of him in *From the Papers of One Still Living* was a minor event which left no hard feelings. There is, however, always reason to be somewhat suspicious of autobiographical accounts of controversies, especially if the controversy involves a collision with someone who subsequently turned out to be an important and respected figure. In 1855 Andersen was already a world-famous and highly revered writer. Nonetheless it would not have been to his advantage for him to portray himself as having been seriously wounded by another writer who was already widely recognized as one of Denmark's greatest authors, and Andersen could quite logically have wished to avoid giving the appearance of hypersensitivity or of bearing a grudge. Thus there were good reasons for Andersen to have painted a rosier-than-true picture of his relations with Kierkegaard—*if* he had in fact been seriously aggrieved and injured by Kierkegaard's 1838 book. And there is evidence which argues against Andersen's 1855 trivialization of his collision with Kierkegaard; many of the items which cast doubt upon Andersen's interpretation of that collision are to be found in Andersen's writings and letters themselves and in the letters and memoirs of his close friends and associates. A review of some of this material may contribute to a reconsideration

---

[2]The text cited here is translated from Andersen's *Mit Livs Eventyr* [*The Fairy Tale of My Life*], ed. H. G. Topsøe-Jensen (Copenhagen: Gyldendal, 1951) 1:204.

[3]This is not only the judgment of a later generation. At his death, *Fædrelandet* [*The Fatherland*] called Kierkegaard "Denmark's greatest religious author" (*Fædrelandet*, 16th year, no. 270 [Monday, 19 November 1855]), and the Stockholm newspaper *Aftonbladet* [*The Evening News*] called him "Scandinavia's greatest religious author" (repr. in *Fædrelandet*, 16th year, no. 272 [Thursday, 21 November 1855]).

of the conventional view of Andersen's rather benign attitude toward Kierkegaard.

In his recently published (and quite private) *Almanacs* [*Almanakker*], Andersen notes that in the month preceding the publication of Kierkegaard's long-awaited review he was apparently nervous about what it would say: "Experienced mental torture [*Sjælmarter*] about Kierkegaard's not-yet-published critique."[4] A week later, when he received Kierkegaard's book, Andersen's almanac entry reads: "An atrocious letter from Wulff and immediately thereafter Kierkegaard's critique. Eduard [Collin] gave me cooling powders. Walked as if in a coma."[5]

There has long been controversy about how to interpret this entry in Andersen's almanac. Captain [later Admiral] P. F. Wulff had been Andersen's early friend and benefactor, but in the letter Andersen received from him on September 6, 1838 Wulff unfairly accused him of slander and barred him from his home. Andersen was understandably very upset with this rejection. What is unclear is how much of the reaction Andersen mentions in his almanac entry is attributable to the rejection by Wulff and how much to the scathing criticism from Kierkegaard. Andersen scholars such as Helge Topsøe-Jensen[6] and, more recently, Elias Bredsdorff[7] have argued that the letter from Wulff was the real cause of Andersen's dismay, and this view has been echoed by Julia Watkin.[8] Bredsdorff, in particular, is insistent about the unimportance of Kierke-

---

[4]*H. C. Andersens Almanakker 1833-1873* [*Hans Christian Andersen's Almanacs, 1833-1873*], ed. Helge Vang Lauridsen and Kirsten Weber (Copenhagen: Det danske Sprog- og Litteraturselskab / G. E. C. Gads Forlag, 1990) 23 (30 August 1838).

[5]Ibid., 24 (6 September 1838). Kierkegaard's *From the Papers of One Still Living* was published on 7 September 1838, so either Andersen received a copy in advance of the official publication or the date in Andersen's almanac is in error.

[6]*H. C. Andersen og Henriette Wulff. En Brevveksling* [*Hans Christian Andersen and Henriette Wulff: Correspondence*], ed. Helge Topsøe-Jensen, vol. 1, *Indledning: Breve 1826–1848* [*Introduction: Letters 1826–1848*] (Odense: Flensteds Forlag, 1959) 252.

[7]Elias Bredsdorff, "H. C. Andersen og Søren Kierkegaard" ["Hans Christian Andersen and Søren Kierkegaard"], *Anderseniana*, 3rd ser., vol. 3/4 (1981): 235-36.

[8]Julia Watkin, "Historical Introduction" to Kierkegaard's *Early Polemical Writings*, vol. 1 of *Kierkegaard's Writings* (Princeton NJ: Princeton University Press, 1990) xxv-xxvi.

gaard in this connection, citing Topsøe-Jensen's remark that Kierkegaard was at that point "still an unknown student" and concluding that there are "all possible grounds for believing that it is Wulff's letter—and not Kierkegaard's book"[9] which so affected Andersen in his almanac entry of September 6, 1838. Nonetheless, it does not have to be one or the other; that is, *both* Wulff's letter *and* Kierkegaard's book could have combined to upset Andersen, who was notoriously thin-skinned. As will be demonstrated in the present essay, the possibility that Andersen had a highly charged reaction to Kierkegaard becomes especially plausible in the light of later evidence concerning his view of Kierkegaard.

A few months later, in December 1838, Andersen received a letter from his friend B. S. Ingemann, who easily surmised Andersen's displeasure with Kierkegaard's book. Ingemann attempted to mollify Andersen by smoothing things over:

> Kierkegaard's review has depressed you, I should think. I don't see that it contains any bitterness or any desire to injure you, however. He probably intends much better by you than he has indicated. The conclusion contains hints of a friendly attitude, albeit strangely repressed. Still, it is one-sided and unreasonable to express unfavorable criticism loudly while whispering praise and appreciation in one's ear, to express disapproval in printer's ink while writing one's thanks and approval in invisible ink. I wish that he would acknowledge and rectify his error by setting forth in equal detail the things that he merely whispered in your ear and that he himself would hold his invisible ink up to the light. He owes this to your readers and to his own, as well as to you and to himself. Even though I only know him from this piece, I believe that he has the honesty to do this. And if he could do so in a clearer expository style than that which he used in the review, I believe that the half of his views which are missing would be read by many more people and would probably demonstrate that he could view you and your work in a quite different light—and without coming into contradiction

---

[9]Bredsdorff, "H. C. Andersen og Søren Kierkegaard," 236. Most of the evidence discussed in the present essay is also adduced by Bredsdorff in his own exhaustively researched article, which is a masterpiece in its way. What I argue for here, however, is a more skeptical and open reading of the entire matter, which admits the possibility, and indeed the likelihood, that Hans Christian Andersen was susceptible to mixed motives and to a wide range of feelings in the wake of his initial collision with Søren Kierkegaard.

with himself. By all means you must not allow this opposition to depress you. Every spiritual opposition is a temporary obstacle which ought only to impart more strength to the stream of life.[10]

Unlike some later Andersen scholars, Ingemann seems to sense that Andersen was indeed quite deeply hurt by Kierkegaard's critique. Andersen himself appears to confirm this impression in a letter to his friend Henriette Hanck, dated February 1, 1839, five months after the appearance of *From the Papers of One Still Living*: "It's odd. Here at home only one single voice [that is, Kierkegaard's] was raised in connection with that book [*Only a Fiddler*], and it was negative. Abroad, on the other hand, everyone is in favor of the *Fiddler* and its author."[11]

As is well known and has been widely discussed, the next year, in May 1840 (now almost two years after the appearance of Kierkegaard's review), Andersen revenged himself openly on Kierkegaard in *A Comedy in the Open Air* [*En Comoedie i det Grønne*] (1840)[12], in which he cites or paraphrases many ponderous and obscure passages from the latter's review by putting them in the mouth of a pompous and self-important philosopher-cum-hairdresser [*Haarskærer*, literally "hair cutter," perhaps in reference to philosophical hair-splitting]. The tone was one of light but sharp banter, and the target was unmistakable. (As it turned out, Kierkegaard was as thin-skinned as Andersen.)[13]

---

[10]B. S. Ingemann, letter to Hans Christian Andersen of 9 December 1838, in *Breve til Hans Christian Andersen* [*Letters to Hans Christian Andersen*], ed. C. St. A. Bille and Nicolaj Bøgh (Copenhagen: C. A. Reitzels Forlag, 1877) 293-94.

[11]Hans Christian Andersen, letter of 1 February 1839 to Henriette Hanck, in *Breve fra Hans Christian Andersen* [*Letters from Hans Christian Andersen*], ed. C. St. A. Bille and Nikolaj Bøgh, vol. 1 (Copenhagen: C. A. Reitzels Forlag, 1878) 476.

[12]*En Comoedie i det Grønne* [*A Comedy in the Open Air*], published in *H. C. Andersens Samlede Skrifter*, 2nd ed., vol. 9 (Copenhagen: C. A. Reitzels Forlag, 1878) 399-428. Relevant excerpts have been translated in Julia Watkin's edition of Kierkegaard's *Early Polemical Writings*, 202-204.

[13]Kierkegaard himself wrote a riposte to Andersen's drama, but did not publish it. See "Et Øieblik, Hr. Andersen!" ["Just a Moment, Mr. Andersen!"] in *Søren Kierkegaards Papirer* [*Søren Kierkegaard's Papers*] I-XVI, ed. P. A. Heiberg, V. Kuhr, and E. Torsting, 2nd and augmented ed. by Niels Thulstrup, index by N. J. Cappelørn (Copenhagen: Gyldendal, 1968–1978) vol. III B 1. (Available in English

Three years later, in April 1843, Andersen, who was then staying in Paris, received a letter from his good friend Signe Læssøe, who gave him a very negative description of Kierkegaard's "real" debut book, *Either/Or*, which had created a literary sensation:

> A new literary comet (I think it looks like I wrote "camel," but I mean a comet) has soared in the heavens here—a harbinger and a bringer of bad fortune. It is so demonic that one reads and reads it, puts it aside in dissatisfaction, but always takes it up again, because one can neither let it go nor hold onto it. "But what is it?," I can hear you say. It is *Either/Or* by Søren Kierkegaard.[14] You have no idea what a sensation it has caused. I think that no book has caused such a stir with the reading public since Rousseau placed his *Confessions* on the altar. After one has read it one feels disgust for the author, but one profoundly recognizes his intelligence and his talent. We women have to be especially angry with him: like the Mohammedans he assigns us to the realm of finitude, and he only values us because we give birth to, amuse, and *save* menfolk. In the first part (this is a work of 864 octavo pages) he is aesthetic, that is, evil. In the second part he is ethical, that is, a little less evil. Everyone praises the second part because it is his alter ego, the better half, which speaks. The second part only makes me the angrier with him—it is *there* that he ties women to finitude. In fact I only understand a small fraction of the book; it is altogether too philosophical. For example, he says "There is no bliss except in despair; hurry up and despair, you will find no happiness until you do." At another point he says "One's happiness can only consist in choosing oneself." What does that mean? The entire book contains a dissatisfaction with life which can only be the product of a warped life. A gifted young man ought not say: "Happy the man who dies; happier still the child who dies; happiest of all he who is never born." At first Heiberg wrote a glowing review in the *Intelligencer* [*Intelligensbladet*], but I think that his eyes have now been opened upon further reflection and re-reading. I expect

---

translation in EPW, 218-22.)

[14]It was no surprise to Andersen to learn that Kierkegaard was the pseudonymous author of *Either/Or*. Andersen had already heard about the book in a letter of 20 February 1843—the very day *Either/Or* was published—from his friend Henriette Wulff, who correctly identified the pseudonymous author as Søren Kierkegaard (in *H. C. Andersen og Henriette Wulff. En Brevveksling*, 1:315-16). So much for the ruse of pseudonymity!

a critique to appear in his newspaper in the middle of the month; therefore we did not receive anything on April 1st, when it is usually 16 quarto pages long. I am looking forward to it. He deserves rough treatment. Only someone who has contempt for everyone can express himself as he has done. Poor wretch, it is worst for him himself![15]

Andersen's reply to Signe Læssøe's letter on Kierkegaard's book is in the same hostile vein, even though he has clearly not yet read the book itself:

What you have sent me about Kierkegaard's book does not exactly excite my curiosity. It is so easy to seem ingenious when one disregards all considerations and tears to pieces one's own soul and all holy feelings! But this sort of thing has an effect. It is reasonable to assume that Heiberg has for the time being been dazzled by the philosophical brilliance![16]

At this point it is almost five years since Kierkegaard had attacked Andersen's *Only a Fiddler*. As we have seen, Andersen later claimed that that incident never left any lingering hard feelings, yet he was willing to accept at second hand Signe Læssøe's moral indignation about a book he had not read by an author he claimed to like and respect.[17]

---

[15]Letter of 7 April 1843 from Signe Læssøe to Hans Christian Andersen, in *Breve til Hans Christian Andersen*, 466-67.

[16]From a letter of 21 April 1843 by Hans Christian Andersen, then in Paris, to Signe Læssøe. The original letter is in the Danish National Archives (Rigsarkivet) (Niels Frederik Læssøe og [Margarethe Juliane] Signe Læssøes Privatarkiv, privatarkivnr. 5917, A. II); it has been published in Poul Høybye, "Om Søren Kierkegaard i H. C. Andersens Correspondence" ["On Søren Kierkegaard in Hans Christian Andersen's Correspondence"] in *Meddelelser fra Søren Kierkegaard Selskabet* [*Communications from the Søren Kierkegaard Society*], 3rd year, no. 1 (Copenhagen: Ejnar Munksgaard, March 1951) 86.

[17]Although Andersen seemed strangely willing to accept *in absentia* Signe Læssøe's negative judgment on Kierkegaard's book sight unseen, his friend and correspondent Henriette Hanck objected to Læssøe's position (which Andersen had apparently recounted to her), and in a letter of 19 May 1843 Hanck calls Læssøe's version "a nasty description of [the book], and it seems to me that it doesn't deserve it." Hanck goes on to label as "unreasonable" the sort of judgment that Læssøe has pronounced, not least because this sort of opinion is usually held by people who have not read the entire work. As we have seen, Andersen himself had already embraced Læssøe's condemnation without having read any

Three years later Kierkegaard was under attack by *The Corsair*, an attack he had at least to some extent brought upon himself. Andersen's friends Edvard and Henriette Collin informed him of Kierkegaard's difficult position with a touch of unmistakable *Schadenfreude*. They do not seem to be troubled by the possibility that Andersen might have tender feelings for Kierkegaard:

> Something in literature which stirs the greatest interest right now is *The Corsair*'s sustained attack on Søren Kierkegaard, and the poor victim is not enough of a philosopher to ignore this annoyance, but is occupied with it night and day and talks about it with everyone. He called this fate down upon his own head, however, because he attacked *The Corsair* in a remarkably affected article in *The Fatherland*.[18]

It is now almost eight years since the appearance of *From the Papers of One Still Living*.

Andersen's view of life, of art, and of religion differed sharply from Kierkegaard's, and he seems to have retained a fundamentally negative view of the latter's work. Nonetheless, Andersen is prepared to acknowledge agreement with Kierkegaard, at least with respect to what he believed to be their shared political views. In a letter of May 1846 to his friend Henriette Hanck (whom we have seen to be considerably more sympathetic toward Kierkegaard's work than was Andersen), Andersen praises the view of modern politics which he finds in Kierkegaard's recently published *A Literary Review*, noting that "[Kierkegaard] has constructed an essay on our times . . . which is so totally in agreement with my

---

of *Either/Or*! There is no evidence that Hanck's letter changed Andersen's view of Kierkegaard's work. Hanck's letter was published with the rest of her correspondence with Andersen in *H. C. Andersens Brevveksling med Henriette Hanck* [*Hans Christian Andersen's Correspondence with Henriette Hanck*], ed. Svend Larsen (Copenhagen: 1946) 594 (published as *Anderseniana* IX-XIII [1941–1946]); it is cited in Bredsdorff, "H. C. Andersen og Søren Kierkegaard," 242.

[18]Letter of 2 February 1846 by Edvard and Henriette Collin to Hans Christian Andersen, in *H. C. Andersens Brevveksling med Edvard og Henriette Collin* [*Hans Christian Andersen's Correspondence with Edvard and Henriette Collin*], ed. C. Behrend and H. Topsøe-Jensen, vol. 2 (1844–1860) (Copenhagen: Levin og Munksgaards Forlag, 1934) 59-60.

own views that I must naturally judge it to be excellent."[19] In keeping with this apparently amicable attitude to Kierkegaard, in 1848 Andersen sent him a copy of his *New Fairy Tales: Two Collections* [*Nye Eventyr. 2 Samlinger*] with the following dedication: "Dear Mr. Kirkegaard [sic]! *Either* you like my little works *Or* you don't like them. They are nonetheless sent without *Fear and Trembling*, and that is something, at any rate. Most amicably, from the author."[20] (Interestingly, Andersen here makes a wordplay on the title of *Either/Or*, the scandalous book which had made Kierkegaard famous and which we know Andersen had rejected without having troubled to read.) In the spring of 1849 Kierkegaard apparently reciprocated by sending Andersen a copy of the second printing of *Either/Or*, for which Andersen duly thanked the author in a note of May 15, 1849.[21] This is the only known contact between Andersen and Kierkegaard after the publication of *From the Papers of One Still Living* in 1838.

Between 1838 and Kierkegaard's death in 1855, Kierkegaard does appear several times in Andersen's correspondence, however. In a letter to his friend Henriette Wulff, dated October 10, 1855, Andersen writes: "Kirkegaard [sic] is very sick. They say the entire lower part of his body is paralyzed and he is in the hospital. A theologian named Thura has written a *coarse* poem against him."[22]

---

[19]Letter of 15 May 1846 from Hans Christian Andersen to Henriette Hanck, published in *H. C. Andersens Brevveksling med Henriette Hanck*, 628, and cited in Bredsdorff, "H. C. Andersen og Søren Kierkegaard," 244.

[20]Printed in *Auktionsprotokol over Søren Kierkegaards Bogsamling* [*Auctioneer's List of the Library of Søren Kierkegaard*], ed. H. P. Rohde (Copenhagen: The Royal Library, 1967) 87-88.

[21]Andersen's note is published in *Breve og Aktstykker vedrørende Søren Kierkegaard* [*Letters and Documents concerning Søren Kierkegaard*], ed. Niels Thulstrup, vol. 1 (Copenhagen: Munksgaard, 1953) 228. An English translation is available in *Kierkegaard: Letters and Documents*, Kierkegaard's Writings 25, trans. and with intro. and notes by Henrik Rosenmeier (Princeton NJ: Princeton University Press, 1978) 289.

[22]With respect to the "coarse poem" by Thura (i.e., Thurah): Theological student Christian Henrik de Thurah (1830–1898), later a pastor, was one of Kierkegaard's most outspoken opponents during the attack on the church, and is particularly remembered for his coarse poem "Riimbrev til Johannes Forføreren alias Dr. Søren Kierkegaard" ("Epistolary Verse to Johannes the Seducer, alias Dr. Søren Kierkegaard"), published in late September 1855, and which, it has been speculated, led to Kierkegaard's collapse. We know from the auction catalog of

And shortly after Kierkegaards's death, in a letter dated November 24, 1855, Andersen wrote to his friend, the choreographer August Bournonville:

> Søren Kierkegaard was buried last Sunday, following a service at the Church of Our Lady. The parties concerned had done very little. The church pews were closed, and the crowd in the aisles was unusually large. Ladies in red and blue hats were coming and going; *item*: a dog with a muzzle. At the gravesite itself there was a scandal: When the whole ceremony was over out there (that is, when Tryde had cast earth upon the casket), a son of a sister of the deceased stepped forward and denounced the fact that he had been buried in this fashion. He declared—this was the point, more or less—that Søren Kierkegaard had resigned from our society, and therefore we ought not bury him in accordance with our customs! I was not out there, but it was said to be unpleasant. The newspapers say a little about it. In *Fædrelandet*'s issue of last Thursday this nephew has published his speech along with some concluding remarks. To me, the entire affair is a distorted picture of Søren K.; I don't understand it![23]

Not long afterwards Andersen received a letter from the Swedish literary figure Frederika Bremer:

Kierkegaard's library that Kierkegaard owned a copy of Thurah's scurrilous book. The present passage is from a letter from H. C. Andersen to Henriette Wulff, dated 10 October 1855, originally published in *Breve fra Hans Christian Andersen*, 324, and repr. in *H. C. Andersen og Henriette Wulff. En Brevveksling*, vol. 2, *Breve 1849–1858* [*Letters, 1849–1858*] (Odense: Flensteds Forlag, 1959) 244.

[23]Apropos of "ladies in red and blue hats," Andersen notes two improprieties: (1) in accordance with the custom of the time, it was not proper for women (excepting family members) to be present at public funerals; and (2) their hat colors were inappropriate—apparently just as inappropriate as the presence of dogs! Tryde was Archdeacon Eggert C. Tryde of the Church of Our Lady, who had the official responsibility of presiding over Kierkegaard's burial. The nephew who stepped forward and gave a controversial speech at Kierkegaard's burial was Henrik Lund, the son of Kierkegaard's sister Petrea Severine.

The present passage is from a letter from Hans Christian Andersen to August Bournonville, dated 24 November 1855. The letter has been published in *Breve fra Hans Christian Andersen*, 329-30. Andersen sent a very similar letter to Henriette Wulff on 26 November 1855: see *H. C. Andersen og Henriette Wulff. En Brevveksling*, 2:247, and *Deres broderligt hengivne. Et udvalg af breve fra H. C. Andersen* [*Yours in Brotherly Devotion: A Selection of Letters from Hans Christian Andersen*], ed. Niels Birger Wamberg (Gyldendal: Copenhagen, 1975) 169.

God's will be done, I say, along with S. Kierkegaard. Would that we might have a sense of assurance that we are following His exhortation and carrying out His commandment to us! With respect to your Danish Simeon Stylites, he has awakened a great deal of interest, even here. Most people—myself included—know that he was *right in much and wrong in much.* He is no pure manifestation of the truth, and his sickly bitterness has certainly stood in the way of clarity and reasonableness in the judgments reached about him.[24]

This was Kierkegaard's last appearance for quite a while in Andersen's correspondence or writings. Then, in 1861, when Kierkegaard had been dead for five and a half years, Andersen travelled to Italy with his friend Edvard Collin's son, Jonas Collin the younger (1840-1905), and was continually annoyed both by the fact that Jonas had brought along as reading matter works by Kierkegaard and that the young man kept misplacing them along the way. Andersen's diary entry from Avignon of April 15, 1861 notes that Jonas Collin "forgot his Søren Kierkegaard, which was brought to him by a railway employee."[25] In a letter to Jonas Collin's parents, dated May 5, 1861, Andersen notes, in apparent annoyance, "Jonas is reading a great deal of Kierkegaard in his free time."[26] On the same day Andersen wrote much the same to Jonas Collin's father, Edvard Collin, and made his annoyance even clearer: "In his free time Jonas is reading a great deal of Kierkegaard, boiling snails, killing lizards and other animals I do not recognize—which he says is very interesting."[27] And on May 30, 1861, on the train from Leghorn to Pisa, Collin lost his bag, which, Andersen notes, "was of course an annoying event; it had been

---

[24]From a letter by Frederika Bremer to Hans Christian Andersen, dated 14 December 1855. Published in *Breve til Hans Christian Andersen,* 674.

[25]Hans Christian Andersen, *H. C. Andersens Dagbøger 1825–1875* [*Hans Christian Andersen's Diaries: 1825–1875*], vol. 5 (1861–1863), ed. Tue Gad and Kirsten Weber (Copenhagen: Gad, 1971) 27.

[26]Letter of 5 May 1861 from Hans Christian Andersen to Edvard Collin, in *H. C. Andersens Brevveksling med Edvard og Henriette Collin,* ed. C. Behrend and H. Topsøe-Jensen, vol. 3 (Copenhagen: Levin and Munksgaards Forlag, 1936) 13.

[27]From *H. C. Andersens Brevveksling med Edvard og Henriette Collin,* 3:13.

forgotten in the railway coach with his diary and the Kirkegaard [*sic*] book which had also been forgotten in Avignon."[28]

Thus, in May 1861 Andersen was in Italy with Jonas Collin, who annoyed Andersen with his continual preoccupation with Kierkegaard. This much is clear. It is clear, moreover, that it was during that month in Italy that Andersen wrote his bitter little tale "The Snail and the Rosebush" [*Sneglen og Rosenhækken*].[29]

But at this point interpretations of just what was the occasion for the tale diverge markedly. In a diary entry for May 14, 1861 Andersen writes: "Home, conversation with Jonas, who valued Viggo [Drewsen] higher than Bjørnstjerne [Bjørnson] and Clemens Petersen. He [that is, Viggo Drewsen] work[ed] on his development and had nothing to do with other people. This gave me occasion to write the story about the snail and the rosebush."[30]

Bredsdorff interprets this diary entry of Andersen quite plausibly—though in my view a bit too simplistically—as proof that "The Snail and the Rosebush" is about Viggo Drewsen (whom Andersen disdained), and that is that: "It is thus Viggo Drewsen, subsequently an amateur philosopher, who is the model for the snail."[31] Furthermore, Bredsdorff says in puzzlement: "I don't know the origin of the misunderstanding to the effect that Hans Christian Andersen's tale 'The Snail and the Rosebush' is supposed to be a concealed clash with Kierkegaard, with the snail representing Kierkegaard. . . . The theory that Andersen had Kierkegaard in mind with the snail has in fact won adherents abroad."[32]

---

[28]Andersen, *Dagbøger 1825–1875*, 5:62.

[29]Andersen's story was first published in 1862. A translation can be found at the beginning of the present essay, above.

[30]Andersen, *Dagbøger 1825–1875*, 5:49. Viggo Drewsen (1830–1888) was Jonas Collin's elder cousin, the son Adolph Drewsen (1803–1885) and Jonas Collin's aunt Ingeborg Nicoline Collin Drewsen (1804–1877); Viggo subsequently married his cousin—and Jonas Collin's sister—Henriette Louise Collin (1839–1920). Viggo Drewsen was an amateur philosopher who preached a distinctive philosophy of individualism and "development." Bjørnstjerne Bjørnson (1832–1910) was a Norwegian playwright, nationalist, and freethinker who won the Nobel prize for literature in 1903. Clemens Petersen (1834–1918) was an author and theater critic.

[31]Bredsdorff, "H. C. Andersen og Søren Kierkegaard," 249.

[32]Ibid., 248-49.

It is difficult to account for this expression of puzzlement by
the great Andersen scholar Bredsdorff about the origin of this
"misunderstanding." He must undoubtedly be familiar with the
"continuation" of *The Fairy Tale of My Life*, covering the years 1855-
1867, which was edited by the very same Jonas Collin who
accompanied Andersen to Italy in 1861 and who published it in
1877, two years after Andersen's death. In that volume, Andersen's
account of his 1861 trip to Italy with Collin is accompanied by a
lengthy note by Collin in which he explains that

> the . . . tale was "The Snail and the Rosebush." It came into being
> in the following way: One day *Andersen* discovered that I was
> reading one of *Søren Kierkegaard's* books, and this put him in a bit
> of a bad humor, because ever since *Kierkegaard* had criticized
> "Andersen as a Novelist" (*From the Papers of One Still Living*,
> 1838) Andersen had felt some bitterness toward him and did not
> really approve of the admiration I felt toward him. A remark
> which A. made about a mutual friend [that is, Viggo Drewsen]
> infuriated me, one word led to another (I was only twenty-one
> years old), and I, at any rate, said many things which I would
> not have said upon more careful consideration and which were
> completely misunderstood by *Andersen*. Our argument ended
> when A. burst into tears and went to his own room. A couple of
> hours later he came into my room, calm and happy, and said
> "Do you want to hear a fairy tale?" Then he read "The Snail and
> the Rosebush," which in the meantime he had written in its
> entirety. When Andersen writes in his "Notes on *New Fairy Tales
> and Stories*, volumes 1-3," that "'*The Snail and the Rosebush*' is one
> of the stories which stems from experience,"[33] this must be under-
> stood as meaning that a little incident had of course been the
> occasion of its appearance. But a profound misunderstanding of
> that incident had taken place, and this had to have been the case
> in order for that event to have served as the occasion. I also
> remember that when A. asked me what I thought of the fairy tale
> I answered: "Excellent! You are the rosebush, that is clear. But let
> us not argue about who is the snail." (The fairy tale was written
> the 24th of May.)[34]

---

[33]See H. C. Andersen, *Samlede Skrifter*, 2nd ed., 15:311.
[34]H. C. Andersen, *Mit Livs Eventyr. Fortsættelse (1855–1867)* [*The Fairy Tale of My Life: Continuation, 1855–1867*], ed. Jonas Collin (Copenhagen: C. A. Reitzels Forlag, 1877) 64-65. (This work was published bound together with vol. 1 of the 2nd ed. of Andersen's *Samlede Skrifter*, the same volume which contained the 1855 version of *Mit Livs Eventyr*.)

The problem is that we are *still* arguing about who is the snail. But in fact Andersen's account in his diary entry of May 14, 1861, cited above, does not necessarily have to be in conflict with Jonas Collin's account of what happened on May 24, 1861. Andersen merely states that his discussion of Viggo Drewsen with Collin served as the "occasion" [*Anledning*] for the story. This does not invalidate Collin's recollection that Andersen's continuing resentment of his preoccupation with Kierkegaard also contributed a good deal to the origin of the story, and that the tale in fact crystallized as a result of Andersen's May 24th argument with Collin about *both* Kierkegaard *and* Drewsen. In brief, it seems most plausible that the story took shape during the entire April-May 1861 period, when Andersen and Collin were in continuing disagreement about the worth and significance of both Kierkegaard and Drewsen.

The available evidence supports a theory of multiple causation. It does not support Bredsdorff's unequivocal assertion that "The Snail and the Rosebush" is entirely about Viggo Drewsen and that any attribution of its origin to Andersen's resentment of Kierkegaard is a puzzling "misunderstanding." And it is not only Collin's account, in which he and Andersen tacitly agree to allow the precise identification of the "snail" to hover in ambiguity, which encourages this theory of multiple causation. Indeed, the argument for multiple causation—for Andersen's conflation of Jonas Collin's favorites, Viggo Drewsen and Søren Kierkegaard—is placed beyond any doubt when one reads the surviving draft of a letter by Andersen to Adolph Drewsen, Viggo Drewsen's father, dated October 2, 1862:

> Both here and in his correspondence, [Jonas] is living a strange snail-like existence. . . . [Jonas] does [not] think of how pleased I would be with a little less of this Kierkegaardian framework [*Kirkegaardsk Bindings Værk*]. But I assume that the feeling runs deep in him. In him Viggo has his most devoted friend. Viggo is his ideal. Viggo is perhaps the only person he calls his friend.[35]

---

[35]From a draft of a letter from Hans Christian Andersen to Adolph Drewsen, dated 2 October 1862, printed in *H. C. Andersens Brevveksling med Jonas Collin den ældre og andre Medlemmer af det collinske Hus* [*H. C. Andersen's Correspondence with*

In his otherwise encyclopedic survey of every scrap of evidence which would link Andersen and Kierkegaard, Bredsdorff's failure to make any mention of Jonas Collin's account of the origin of the controversial little fairy tale seems inexplicable, and his neglect of the above letter by Andersen to Adolph Drewsen seems equally so. It would appear that Bredsdorff is bending every effort to uphold the veracity of Andersen's account in the 1855 edition of *The Fairy Tale of My Life*, which paints a generous and benign picture of Andersen's view of Kierkegaard, according to which Andersen soon forgot the rough treatment he had received from Kierkegaard in 1838. There are, however, reasonable and indeed compelling grounds to conclude—on the basis of a good deal of evidence— that Andersen was in fact (and quite understandably) deeply wounded by *From the Papers of One Still Living* and that he bore a smoldering resentment of Kierkegaard which lasted for at least twenty-four years (until 1862) and possibly for even longer. It does no additional harm to the reputation of a great writer, who is in any event known to have been notoriously thin-skinned, to point out that he also was (and long remained) thin-skinned in his relation to Søren Kierkegaard—a man who was himself not lacking in hypersensitivity.

Jonas Collin the Elder and Other Members of the Collin Family], ed. H. Topsøe-Jensen, with Kaj Bom and Knud Bøgh, vol. 2 (1847–1874) (Copenhagen: Einar Munks- gaard, 1945) 291.

5

Thomasine Gyllembourg, *Author of* A Story of Everyday Life

Grethe Kjær

Outside Denmark, Thomasine Gyllembourg (1773–1856) is best known as the author of the book *Two Ages*, the subject matter of Søren Kierkegaard's *A Literary Review* (1846). Yet she also figures in his *From the Papers of One Still Living* (1838), a somewhat strange review of Hans Christian Andersen's novel *Only a Fiddler*. Here, by way of introduction and giving a short characterization of their work, Kierkegaard mentions first two Danish authors (EPW, 64-69), "the author of *En Hverdags-Historie* [A Story of Everyday Life]" and "Steen Steensen Blicher" (1782–1848). Like Andersen's, Steen Steensen Blicher's works belong among Denmark's literary classics and still in our own time find enthusiastic readers. The first-mentioned and anonymous author, Thomasine Gyllembourg, is, on the other hand, as good as totally unread today, and interest in her is due particularly to the role she played as the unifying center in the home of her son, Johan Ludvig Heiberg. Thus, despite her anonymity as author, she was a well-known person in the Copenhagen of Kierkegaard's time.

Yet who was this woman, who succeeded in preserving her anonymity right up to her death, whose long life unfolded itself through all of three "ages," and whose private life was fatefully affected by the influence the spirit of an age exercises "in family life, in private relationships, in the views and opinions of individuals"?[1] One can in fact come to learn a great deal about her, since many of her letters have been preserved and published, while one

---

[1]From Gyllembourg's preface to the reader in *Two Ages*, a novel by the author of "A Story of Everyday Life," ed. Johan Ludvig Heiberg (Copenhagen: Reitzel, 1845) v.

is also, through her daughter-in-law Johanne Luise Heiberg's memoirs[2] and various family histories, given a living impression of her personality and surroundings in the literary cultural life of Copenhagen.

Thomasine Gyllembourg, née Thomasine Christine Buntzen, grew up as the eldest of the five daughters of the well-to-do Copenhagen city broker and inspector of weights and measures, Johan Buntzen (1728–1807). He owned a large property in Nyhavn where he lived with his wife and children and in which mercantile manor several other members of the large Buntzen family also lived for periods. Johan Buntzen was far from being a typical paterfamilias of the time. He took care of his daughters with interest and love, ensuring them a good education with the help of able teachers, especially in music and languages. Among these teachers was the popular political writer, playwright, and translator P. A. Heiberg (1758–1841). Because of his great linguistic talents, Heiberg had acquired a close connection with Johan Buntzen, who often in his work needed help from a language expert. Because of his friendship with the father, P. A. Heiberg agreed to teach his quite young daughters French, German and Italian.[3]

The lessons continued for almost a couple of years, after which, finally one day, to the astonishment of old Johan Buntzen but even more of the young girl, P. A. Heiberg asked her father for her hand in marriage. He was highly flattered by the proposal, just as the little modest girl felt that one could not possibly give such a man a refusal.

---

[2]Johanne Luise Heiberg, *Et Liv Gjenoplevet i Erindringen* (Copenhagen: Gyldendalske Boghandel Nordisk Forlag, 1944).

[3]About Thomasine's first language lesson with Heiberg, Johanne Luise Heiberg many years later tells us that: "The little girl . . . regarded it as a great honor to be taught by him. With a tremendously beating heart . . . she arrived for the first lesson with her books under her arm and with anxiety about displeasing the clever teacher. But everything went better than she had hoped. The lessons continued, and she made her best effort and received continual praise for her industry and carefulness." *Peter Andreas Heiberg og Thomasine Gyllembourg*, an account made on the basis of their letters by Johanne Luise Heiberg, 4th rev. ed. with appendix and information by Aage Friis and Just Rahbek (Copenhagen: Gyldendal, 1947); hereafter PAHTG. PAHTG, 7.

The engagement was thus celebrated between the fourteen-year-old, recently confirmed girl and her far older teacher, and on May 7, 1790, they were married. She was then scarcely seventeen. On December 14, 1791, their son Johan Ludvig was born. Opinion is divided as to how far this marriage was based on mutual sympathy, but their marriage later came, in a tragic manner, to reflect the profound differences that existed between the way two ages understood life. He still belonged to the age of rationalism, when reason and equanimity were prioritized, and when one did not expose one's feelings. "God, Virtue and Immortality" were the truths on which one built one's life.[4] She, by contrast, entirely belonged to the romantic period, characterized by a passion for Rousseau, the German romantic poets, and French novelists. For her, romantic love was the fundamental element in marriage. These contrasts speedily led to fatal misunderstandings between the married couple. He did not speak to her about his work, but sat silent and brooded over his worries, and he found her emotional reactions overexaggerated and sentimental. He often reacted to them with a wounding sarcasm, being sharp and ironic, qualities that also gained him many enemies among the politicians and government officials who were made the objects of his critical but witty pen.[5]

---

[4]See Bruce Kirmmse: *Kierkegaard in Golden Age Denmark*, (Bloomington: Indiana University Press, 1990) 35-36.

[5]One example of Heiberg's lack of understanding towards his wife was supplied by Thomasine herself to her daughter-in-law. Their little boy, who was her great comfort in the loveless marriage, was seriously ill, and in her fear of losing him she sat silent at the meal table, so that Heiberg asked her what was the matter: "Crying, she said: 'Oh I am so distressed about my little boy! I hope Our Lord has mercy on me and watches over this child so I keep him'. Heiberg smiled ironically and said: 'Our Lord! He cares no more about the boy than about the herring lying here on the plate.' " And to her daughter-in-law she added: "You have no idea how I suffered at his words! I was strictly brought up in my Christianity and was by nature of a religious temperament. . . . I speculated day and night as to whether it really could be so, that God did not care at all about this child and my pain" (PAHGT, 16). That Heiberg, however, could himself also seek consolation in a higher justice is shown by the following lines that he wrote down on a scrap of gilt-edged paper in 1794:

Thou God of Truth! thou great all-searching eye!
To whom our thoughts, our spirits open lie,
Grant me they [sic] strength; and in that needful hour,

In 1794 a charge had in fact been brought against him for having expressed himself offensively about the English king in a club song. Together with his friend, Knud Lyhne Rahbek (1760–1830), who had let the song be printed in "Den danske Tilskuer" 43, he was fined three hundred rigsdaler.[6] The economic worries that resulted from such fines were to a great extent the reason for the despondency to which he yielded at home and which pained Thomasine so much. But outwardly he was ever the freedom-loving friend of revolution and affable socialite when he was together with his friends in the club, just as in his home he was an excellent host, the soul of jollity and wit, while his wife felt herself insignificant and superfluous.

In the middle of the 1790s, however, a French delegation came to Copenhagen to promote goodwill for the new republic in a neutral country. With it came representatives who were to establish trade connections, for which reason they were also given a good reception by the upper classes in the world of commerce. These delegates were of course obvious guests in the Heiberg home, where the freedom-loving host had followed the great upheavals in France with interest. Nor was it long before "the French" (as these foreigners were called in Copenhagen) noticed the pretty hostess who was also able to converse with them in their own language with the greatest of ease. At such gatherings Heiberg began to feel almost proud of his wife, and she herself livened up at suddenly seeing herself an object of admiration and "the Frenchmen's" rather unconstrained flirtation.[7] In spite of her

---

Should it e'er come when Law submits to Pow'r,
With firm resolve my steady bosom steel,
Bravely to suffer, tho' I deeply feel!

(From the poem "Independence" by the English satiricist Charles Churchill [1731–1764], PAHTG, 413.)

[6]In comparison with the modest income he could earn as translator and author, 300 rigsdaler must have been a very large amount. It was a disappointment to him that he did not get the vacant state notary appointment, in connection with which great use had been made of his linguistic skills (PAHTG, 21).

[7]Thomasine Gyllembourg gives us a description of such a party many years later in part one of Two Ages. She even mentions one of the participants by his actual name, Honoré Duveyrier, TA, 31.

natural shyness and modesty she discovered that she liked "to please." But at the same time she perceived that one of the more frequent guests, the approximately forty-year-old talented and charming Honoré Duveyrier, began to threaten her tranquillity of heart by his persistent courtship. She saw herself suddenly as object of the passionate love which her romantic soul had always lacked in her husband, who had openly declared to his friends that he had never been in love with his wife.[8] But the new situation disturbed her. She felt herself bound to be faithful to her husband even emotionally. When, however, she one day expressed her concern to her husband, who conceited and proud felt sure of his wife's fidelity, he replied: "Oh, nothing more than that, you have your freedom," words that only wounded her and which she took as a sign that he had never loved her.

Luckily for Thomasine, Duveyrier was suddenly recalled to France, and the danger was over—this time. But the experience had given her a new self-confidence as a woman and had liberated her personality in a manner hitherto unknown to her as merely a useful adjunct to her husband.[9] In the short story *Ægtestand* [Married Life] (1835), of which Kierkegaard speaks with approval (EPW, 66), Thomasine Gyllembourg many years later portrayed a similar situation in a marriage which in many ways seems to be a mirror image of her situation and Heiberg's. But it is characteristic of Thomasine Gyllembourg that the story ends with the wife breaking off the relationship when the lover reveals the true demonic character of his passion, and that the married couple thereafter talk things through and again find and appreciate each other.

---

[8]PAHTG, 17.

[9]This can be concluded from a letter she wrote some years later to her close friend and relative Lene Kellermann (PAHTG, esp. 353-54). One can note that Thomasine has gone through a development like Cordelia's in Kierkegaard's "The Seducer's Diary," and which Carl Henrik Koch in his book, *Kierkegaard og det interessante* (Copenhagen: C. A. Reitzels Forlag, 1992) 28, describes as follows: "The Seducer (here, P. A. Heiberg) first neutralizes 'through prosaic commonsense and mockery' Cordelia's spontaneous femininity, her secure resting in herself, so that she begins to reflect about it and through this to doubt herself as an erotic being, that is, to her self she loses her femininity. Through the agency of the Seducer (here, Duveyrier), she regains it, but on a higher and more conscious level."

This did not happen to Thomasine and Heiberg. When "the French" had gone and the entertaining gradually ceased, Thomasine again lived in relative loneliness in her home where she still, however, had her little loving and talented son to take care of. Her consolation was that on the lonely evenings when her husband was out with his political and literary friends at one of the many clubs of the time, she had rich opportunity to acquaint herself thoroughly with the broad range of foreign literature in Heiberg's library. In her reading in this period she read for the first time the works of Rousseau, with whose thoughts she was already partly familiar. Here she encountered a new ideal of marriage, where marriage for the woman does not only consist of fulfilling a man's social and sexual need, but is a love relationship where man and woman are equal and in which reason and feeling are united. It is this view of marriage that later comes to characterize her "Stories of Everyday Life," in which the heroines are women who with their love are capable of modestly but actively making sure that the daily life of the home functions, not only in practical matters, but also in the atmosphere of security and beauty they create.[10] But this ideal she had little possibility of realizing in a marriage to the chilly and ordinarily reserved Heiberg.

This must be part of the explanation why the young, unhappy, exiled Swedish nobleman, Carl Frederik Gyllembourg (né Ehrensvärd), made such a deep impression on her. After being sentenced to exile for his privy knowledge of the assassination of the Swedish king Gustav III in 1792, he became a permanent resident in Denmark from 1798. During the winter of 1798–1799 he came regularly to the homes of Heiberg and his friends. He was deeply interested in farming, and in 1800 he bought the farm "Ruhedal"

---

[10]This is the same ideal picture of marriage and woman as wife and mother that we encounter in Kierkegaard's pseudonym Judge William (see esp. EO, 2:93-154), but it was also an ideal of womanhood that already from the end of the eighteenth century had gained a footing in middle-class society. K. L. Rahbek in 1801 published as a "New Year Gift" his book *Den Kunst at være lykkelig med Mænd, efter Göthe, Lafontaine, Wieland og J. J. Rousseau* [*The Art of Being Happy with Men, according to Goethe, Lafontaine, Wieland, and Rousseau*], in which woman is hailed as the unifying center of the family. See Klaus P. Mortensen, *Thomasines oprør* (Copenhagen: G. E. C. Gads Forlag, 1986) 60-73.

in Mid-Zealand. Heiberg regarded him, despite his noble ancestry, as a freedom-loving and welcome friend, and with his friendly, cultivated, and discreet behavior, Gyllembourg soon also won Thomasine's heart. She listened attentively to his complaints about being cut off from his fatherland and a glittering military career, and it meant much to her self-esteem to meet one who valued her friendship and loving concern.[11]

Gradually, as Thomasine came to understand the nature of her feelings for Gyllembourg, she felt it her duty to let Heiberg know she was ready to give up seeing Gyllembourg so often, before it perhaps one day became too difficult for her to do so. Heiberg replied that he was well aware that it was only friendship between them, and proud as he was, and perhaps also anxious not to give expression to any form of jealousy, added: "Act in the matter as if I didn't exist."[12]

However in 1799 the catastrophe happened to Heiberg that he was charged with partly seriously attacking, partly ridiculing, unfortunate aspects of the official administration in the quarterly *For Truth*. As a bold member of the opposition he had, as mentioned before, many enemies in government circles who were therefore only too interested in getting rid of him. He thus received the following sentence: "Translator P. A. Heiberg *must be expelled from the realms and lands of the king*." The sentence was made known to him on Christmas Eve. He was put under house arrest until, on February 7, 1800, he had to leave his country, never more to return. He settled in Paris, but a couple of years went by before he

---

[11]They also shared an interest in literature and music. She could accompany his guitar playing on the piano, and they enjoyed singing duets together. Heiberg apparently disliked this form of entertainment and he often postponed his return home or else had to retreat from the warm living room in order to have peace for his work.

[12]The irony that has also surely lain behind his words, namely, the implication that she did that already, Thomasine failed to grasp. She took his answer literally, and it was for her a fresh confirmation of the fact that her husband did not love her. "She then decided privately that he would have a sister and friend in her throughout life but if possible *nothing more*." It never occurred to her to break up her marriage with Heiberg. She would love Gyllembourg as a friend, as a brother. "In her inexperience she did not suspect the battle she was going to encounter because of this decision," writes Johanne Luise Heiberg. PAHTG, 52.

was able to support himself as translator.[13] In this period he was helped by his father-in-law, old Johan Buntzen, in whose home Thomasine and her son now had to live, since the Heiberg home had to be sold when he left, in order to cover his debts.

The majority of people at the time thought that Thomasine ought to have gone with her husband into exile, but from the letters left to us, it does not seem as if this possibility was ever discussed by the couple, probably, among other possible reasons, because Heiberg hoped soon to be able to return to Denmark. Because of people's hard judgement (without knowledge of the couple's personal situation) of Thomasine's relationship with Gyllembourg and her later divorce application, her daughter-in-law a number of years after her mother-in-law's death felt impelled to make public some of the material concerning the divorce that came to her on the death of her own husband Johan Ludvig Heiberg. By so doing she hoped to "make it possible for the observer to make an impartial judgement" of both Thomasine and Heiberg's actions. This became the publication of "all important letters from the two concerned," together with what she herself knew about "the truth of the matter."[14]

However there must have existed a large number of other letters that have since disappeared, since Heiberg told the Danish authorities that he had received over a hundred letters in the period between his departure from Denmark and September 11, 1801 when Thomasine wrote to him asking him for a divorce. Thomasine also tells us that she sent letters to Paris "every post day," probably once a week. It is to her credit that she kept up a regular correspondence with her exiled partner, even though this

---

[13]In 1803, because of his unusual linguistic skills, he received an appointment with the French Minister of Foreign Affairs Talleyrand, whom he later accompanied on journeys all over Europe. See also Kirmmse, *Kierkegaard in Golden Age Denmark*, esp. 21, 266.

[14]PAHTG, xii. The first edition of the book appeared in 1882, soon followed by a second and third edition. In 1947 a fourth edition came out, supplied with full notes made possible by the opening to the public of the Heiberg-Gyllembourg archives in 1940. From these notes one gains an interesting insight into how much people in the top levels of society in Thomasine's time knew each other and often were connected to each other through complicated family relationships. This aspect of social life in Denmark is also illustrated by *The Stories of Everyday Life.*

has surely been a contributing factor to her "Letter of Termination" being such a violent shock to him.

After Heiberg's departure, the relationship between Thomasine and Gyllembourg developed ever more intensely, even though her residence in her father's house, where she was under the eye of sisters and aunts, made it difficult for them to be together, just as it was often difficult for Gyllembourg to be away from his newly acquired property in Mid-Zealand. When the Buntzen family in the summer of 1800 moved to their summer residence "Voxblegen" outside Copenhagen, relationships were freer, and it is possible that their love affair was consummated that summer.[15]

Through all the following winter and summer, in which her longing to share a home with Gyllembourg grew greater, Thomasine lacked peace of mind until she had honestly told her husband about her relationship with Gyllembourg, which, in her view, must result in a divorce without further ado. She was convinced that her husband would not oppose it, since, because of his revolutionary ideas about freedom, he could have nothing against the idea of dissolving a marriage that was only one in name. She did not understand that a marriage for him was still a lifelong institution that indeed rested on practical social principles, but also on a personal promise in which a man "places his honor in the hands of a woman."[16] A marriage was not something one could break up for such incidental emotional reasons as a love affair or a discreet relationship outside the marriage.

After many deliberations Thomasine finally wrote on September 11, 1801, the letter she herself calls "la lettre remarquable," the

---

[15]Thomasine's letters to Gyllembourg became more and more passionate. E.g., she writes, June 1800 from "Voxblegen":

Listen my beloved friend! Our love is hurting no one, it can indeed make us unhappy, but not deserving of punishment as long as we do not sadden anyone through it, deceive anyone because of it, and never will I reproach myself, never will I regret, that I truly and deeply loved you and forgot the rest of the world when I only thought that you were happy in my arms. (PAHTG, 68)

[16]Ægtestand, in Skrifter af Forfatteren til "En Hverdags-Historie," collected and published by Johan Ludvig Heiberg (Copenhagen: C. A. Reitzel, 1849–1851) 3:124, cf. 30: "Quand on le sait, c'est peu de chose; ce n'est rien, quand on l'ignore." (From Lafontaine's story La Coupe Enchanté.)

notable letter, which it also apparently took her several days to compose. In this she unfolds all the diplomatic ingenuity that apparently is, in her view, needed in order to persuade Heiberg. The letter, which must have run to about ten handwritten pages, begins by formally emphasizing what Thomasine calls "the *beautiful* aspect" of his character, his love of freedom and truth, his hate of prejudice, his personal nobility and pride. At the same time she emphasizes self-consciously that she is now taking a step "that not many of *my* sex would be able to venture," and she reminds him that their marriage for many years has not been a marriage but a friendship. That he has a couple of times, with others present, said that he had never been in love with her, she could only understand negatively and as a sign that he had never loved her, for which reason she also had decided from that time that they should be only friends.[17] To maintain a marriage without love was to "overturn the law of nature." She reminds him that she once asked him straight out whether he minded that she "so often and gladly" saw Gyllembourg and she describes her thankfulness to Heiberg for his reply: "Act in the matter as if I didn't exist." She thus feels that she now openly and honestly can admit that the situation is that she and Gyllembourg can no longer live without each other. She again appeals to Heiberg's lack of prejudice and to his nobility, making him the proposal: "give me my freedom back," and receive instead my and Gyllembourg's eternal respect and thankfulness and "the admiration of the entire world." Their son Johan Ludvig she is astonishingly enough prepared to give up and let him be brought up by her sister and brother-in-law.[18]

Heiberg, who, as mentioned, regularly received letters from her telling him about things at home, usually took her letters with him to his club where he shared the news they contained with his Danish friends. He thus also took Thomasine's unusually fat letter of September 11 with him to the club, looking forward to having

---

[17]Heiberg has, however, a different understanding of this decision and in his replies tells her that her memory must have deceived her: "Your coldness, as wife, is of a far older date. Examine yourself, and say whether you with good conscience can deny that this coldness starts the very first day of our marriage" (PAHTG, 122).

[18]PAHTG, 103-11.

a lot of fresh news to report. As he first read the letter through to himself as usual, his friends swiftly perceived that something was wrong. He went pale, did not say a single word, and one of those present, a doctor, went home with him. His reply, which he writes during the next few days, shows the shock Thomasine's request has been. Marriage was for him, as said, first and foremost a commitment one had taken upon oneself and from which one could not run, and this view, he writes, is not a prejudice; freedom does not lie in violating one's duties. He begs her forgiveness for the mistakes he has apparently made, and pleads with her to give up her intention. How shaken he is can be seen especially from the fact that he is ready immediately for her sake to sacrifice his honor and request pardon of the government authorities, and if it is not granted, then to defy the sentence and return illegally to Denmark (something, he would of course on sober reflection never do).

The whole of his long letter bears the stamp of his shaken frame of mind, but between the lines one can read an appreciation of Thomasine that he has never before been able to express. He therefore also chiefly blames Gyllembourg as the one who has seduced his wife from him. His repeated assurances of his love and respect make, however, not the slightest impression on Thomasine. She was passionately taken up with getting her own way. On October 13 she writes: "I will never be *yours*, never! I can't and I won't," and pointedly she comments: "you say you are my lover: 'Well! then you became that a month ago, G. has been it for three years.' " She asks him whether he "as philosopher" can "assert that the rights of marriage are more holy than those of love" and thinks that according to her "premises" she has nothing with which to reproach herself.[19]

After receiving, as Heiberg ironically comments, "a heap" of letters "all telling me that a wife has a right to leave her husband and child, and that consequently, I who assert the opposite am wrong," he writes: "I have done what I can—I believe done what I ought—everything is in vain. So in God's name! You have your freedom back. May God make you happy!" His sole request is that she give up all rights to their son. She must herself apply for a

---

[19]PAHTG, 144-46.

divorce and let him have a draft of what he is to sign. At the same
time he reproaches her with the fact that she has not sent off his
application for pardon as he asked her to, since it is now even
more important to him to return to Denmark out of regard for
Johan Ludvig, whom he cannot look after abroad.[20]

Heiberg's application for pardon and Thomasine's application
for a divorce therefore lay at the same time in the hands of the
government authorities, and it gave Heiberg reason to think that
intrigues must be involved when his application was refused,[21]
while the divorce was allowed. A knowledgeable lawyer, J.M.V.
Nellemann, has however later shown (in *Nordisk Tidsskrift* 1883)
that Heiberg's suspicion was unjustified. It was, "putting it mildly,
naive to think" that Heiberg's sentence to lifelong exile could be
repealed without further ado after such a short passage of time.
But the decision made him very bitter against Gyllembourg and
Thomasine, who were now free to marry. Heiberg retained his
parental rights to his son, however, but was right-minded enough
to let him remain in Denmark until he was mature enough himself
to decide where he wished to continue his education.[22] Thomasine
was not allowed to meet her son or to write to him.

The letters of Thomasine and Heiberg illustrate with all desir-
able clarity how the different ideals of two ages can contribute to
tragic misunderstandings between two people. Each of them, as it
is said of Claudine in *Two Ages*, was "a victim of the current ideas
of the age."[23]

The aforementioned lawyer, J. M. V. Nellemann, expresses a
similar view when he writes: "Both seem to have formed their
opinions according to certain coherent philosophical concepts that
conformed with the tendency of the time, . . . and both seem to

---

[20]PAHTG, 154-57.
[21]among other things, with the explanation that it was not "penitent."
[22]Heiberg's opinion was that "no father in the world has the right to change
his son's nation and thus kill his nationality and give him one other than nature
has decided for him" (PAHTG, 170).
[23]TA, 79. In Kierkegaard's copy (to be found in the McGill Gregor Malantschuk Søren Kierkegaard Collection, Montreal) there is a dogear on this page and
vertical lines made beside this quotation.

have been rather distant from the actual legal situation."[24] This is probably one of the reasons why Thomasine gave up her son. Because of Heiberg's sentence of exile she could have acquired parental rights to him if she had delayed her marriage. But this renunciation also shows how much power her passionate love for Gyllembourg had over her—she had only one single wish: to be married to Gyllembourg. The marriage was thus celebrated on December 17, 1801, a few days after the divorce became absolute (December 11, 1801).

Thomasine moved to "Ruhedal" a few days later, but just before, she writes to Gyllembourg: "[N]o one can understand my happiness except the one who for the first time in her life feels freedom and joy, real joy, and who has bought it dearly as I have, but *not* at the expense of conscience."[25]

Apparently it was a happy marriage, even though they had to battle for a long time with economic worries. "Ruhedal" could not give the return Gyllembourg had expected. However, it burnt down completely in 1806 after being struck by lightning, and the compensation for damages was so large they could install themselves comfortably in the capital where they also soon acquired a large circle of friends and acquaintances.

In 1815 Gyllembourg died after a short illness, and as a widow without means Thomasine soon again became dependent on her family. On top of this came the fulfillment of the agreement that Johan Ludvig, as soon as he had completed his education in Denmark and done his doctorate in philosophy, should go to his father in Paris for a period of study. He remained in Paris for three years. So Thomasine offered to live as a teacher in her cousin Andreas Buntzen's home where there were eight children to take care of. She became especially attached to the little sickly Georg (according to a family tradition really a son of Johan Ludvig Heiberg), and he went with her also when she went to live in Kiel where Johan Ludvig on his return from Paris had got a lectureship in Danish Language and Literature at the university. Residence in Kiel proved no success, and it was a relief when the family in 1824

---

[24]PAHTG, 442-43.
[25]PAHTG, 171.

could move back to Copenhagen, where Johan Ludvig's vaude-villes had now secured him a position at the Royal Theatre. At the same time he began his publication of the paper *Kjøbenhavns flyvende Post* [Copenhagen's Flying Post]. He sometimes found it difficult to get enough material for the three weekly numbers, so he suggested to his mother that she could probably help him. He may have had a suspicion that hidden within her she had ideas for stories that could prove suitable for entertaining reading in serial form for a wide public.

So the fourth number of *Kjøbenhavns flyvende Post* came out in January 1827 with a fictitious letter "From a lieutenant to the edi-tor of *The Flying Post*," which was continued in the following numbers. It was written in the form of an explanation to do with an authentic advertisement in the first number of "Addressea-visen" for 1827. The advertisement went as follows: "*Reply* to *the Lieutenant* who on last December 16 sent a *young lady* a letter is waiting sealed at the post office where he can collect it without payment."[26] This advertisement has apparently fired Thomasine Gyllembourg's imagination, and the letter she wrote as the lieutenant's reaction to the sealed letter provoked great interest from the public, since many took it seriously.[27] This fictitious exchange of letters served first and foremost as the framework for Thomasine's first story "Claras Skriftemaal" [Clara's Confession], but the entire thing came out later as *A Story of Everyday Life* under the title: *Familien Polonius* [*The Polonius Family*]. It became the intro-duction to the long series of "Stories of Everyday Life" that gradually also appeared as independent stories by "the Author of 'A Story of Everyday Life,' " still with Johan Ludvig Heiberg as publisher. The last of these stories was *Two Ages* in 1845.

During these years Thomasine Gyllembourg lived together with her son, whom she found it so difficult to let go that she moved into his new home together with adopted son Georg on the occasion of Johan Ludvig's marriage to the very young actress

---

[26]*Thomasine Gyllembourg Familien Polonius og En Hverdagshistorie samt Fru Gyllembourgs litterære Testamente* (Copenhagen: Gyldendals Trane-Klassikere, 1968) 46; hereafter Trane.
[27]Kierkegaard writes that "we were fooled and could not tell if it were fact or fiction" (TA, 17).

Johanne Luise Pätges in 1831, a match that Thomasine had had a hand in. Johanne Luise paints a sympathetic picture of their family life in *Et Liv Gjenoplevet i Erindringen* [*A Life Relived in Recollection*],[28] but the drawbacks can be guessed at from some sections that were left out of the first edition, also from her article: "Don't Go to Live with your Children" from the end of the 1850s.[29] Under Thomasine Gyllembourg's strong influence on the entire arrangement of the home as well as on the daily running of the house, the Heiberg home during these years became a significant part of the city's cultural life and not because the family's socializing excelled itself by any form of extravagance, although regarding pleasantness and beauty nothing should be lacking. For Thomasine "the sense of beauty in domestic life was so developed in her that it cast its glitter on everything that surrounded her. The simplest meal acquired a certain festive stamp from her sense of order and care, and the friends she gathered to her table always felt themselves enlivened and communicative." This is what her daughter-in-law writes in a postscript to Thomasine Gyllembourg's so-called "Literary Testament."[30]

There are not many of the well-known "Golden Age" personalities who have not from time to time visited the Heibergs. Some few (among these the composer C. E. F. Weyse (1774–1842) and the poet Henrik Hertz (1797–1870)) came nearly every day for a time. Whether Kierkegaard had visited the family more than once is not known. Hertz mentions in his diary for June 6, 1836, Kierkegaard and Poul Martin Møller as guests in the home[31] when there was a farewell to the Heiberg couple before their visit to P. A. Heiberg in Paris. On the other hand, Hans Lassen Martensen, whom the Heibergs came to know in Paris, was a frequent and prized guest from that time onwards, and Thomasine Gyllembourg often discussed ethical and religious questions with him.[32]

---

[28](Copenhagen: Gyldendal, 1891–1892).

[29]Printed in *Omkring Johanne Luise Heiberg* by Just Rahbek (Copenhagen: Gyldendal, 1948) 103-16.

[30]Trane, 16, 19.

[31]*Dansk Litteratur Historie* (Copenhagen: Politikens Forlag, 1976) 3:255.

[32]Cf. KAUC, 21: Kierkegaard is possibly referring to this when he advises Martensen to confine himself to talking only "in the parlor, over a cup of tea with

Thomasine Gyllembourg gained ideas and inspiration for her writing through her large circle of friends and acquaintances and the many other people she also made contact with in such a little capital as Copenhagen. Her sharp perceptive powers of psychological observation brought it about that she, as her daughter-in-law tells us, "easily and speedily searched out the human weaknesses, and not many she came in contact with went away unknown by her" but "she did not have the heart to tell others what she saw and searched out"; she "kept all these observations and experiences for the quiet consideration of her soul until her inner being could no longer contain them. Then out sprang the living figures in stories, figures in whose mouth she placed what had long been worked out in her private thoughts."[33]

That she thus acquired her material from her own daily surroundings was one of the reasons why anonymity was so essential for her that she never let herself be persuaded to give it up. Thomasine Gyllembourg herself explains the anonymity as "the necessity to me of a freedom, a loneliness in an enlarged sense of this word, but it follows just as naturally from this that all my stories are true 'stories of everyday life.' "[34] Another essential reason why she insisted on remaining anonymous was that she was "amazingly shy about this writing activity. . . . It was her view that women must not be involved in such a thing," and if she heard of other women who wrote she could exclaim: "So, she is writing too! Good Lord! I think we women have enough to take care of without getting involved in that sort of thing as well. We must leave that to the men!" exclamations that highly amused her relatives. Yet the family "almost never saw her writing in daily life. In the late evening hours she stole away to that work about which she felt a maidenly embarrassment."[35]

It has not solely been the inspiration from her surroundings, from the fate of friends and members of the family that has formed the background of Thomasine Gyllembourg's novelistic ability. An

---

a woman and some prating friends" (translation revised). Thomasine also valued J. P. Mynster's sermons highly.

[33]Trane, 16-17.

[34]Trane, 36.

[35]Trane, 14, 20.

essential impulse has also come to her through the dramatic tension she had herself experienced between the duty to be faithful to her husband and her passionate love for another, where she without hesitation chose love, sure that she was right—on the basis of her "premises." For it looks as if already while Gyllembourg was still alive she has come to doubt this and atten.pted to search her conscience to find out why she once had been able to do an action that she felt did not accord with her true character. To her best friend and relative she writes in 1809: "Why hasn't my behavior been as pure and simple as my heart, so that I could surrender my soul to God as pure as when I received it from his hands." She has basically always known, she writes, that "there is no other way of resisting temptation other than the one: to *avoid it*, to break with it as soon as the least disagreement between my better and worse self appears."[36]

Therefore we also see that this is how her heroines, the pure and innocent young women, usually behave. They realize the ideal she thought she had betrayed, even though it was her view that she in *her* situation could not have acted otherwise. In her most personal novel *Ægtestand* [Married Life] her own experiences reflect themselves especially in the admonition she gives her lady reader at the conclusion of the story. This addition Kierkegaard emphasizes as an example of the fact that the reading of these stories can be "a truly upbuilding study." "My dear young lady reader! You who perhaps have picked up this book to distract yourself from thoughts that you scarcely dare admit to yourself: to you especially this simple story is dedicated with an unknown friend's warm wishes for your victory!" (EPW, 66n.).

A much-treated theme is the conflict between duty and love, which is often due to the relation of opposition between the generations. The elders demand first and foremost obedience from their children, also when it has to do with choice of partner, while love, despite a possible difference in rank, is decisive for the young. Yet more controversial subjects are also dealt with in the stories: the seduced girl's unhappy situation, the unharmonious

---

[36]PAHTG, 353. Cf. CA, 109: "whoever yields to temptation is himself guilty of the temptation." See also CUP, 1:459-60.

marriage, adultery, children outside marriage, adopted children,
women who, because of bad treatment from their partner, break
out of the marriage, or who, for personal emotional reasons do not
wish to marry. Thomasine Gyllembourg's psychological empathy
shows itself especially in her true-to-life reproduction of the
characters' thoughts, conversations or letters, by which their nature
and deeds are indirectly illuminated and explained. This also holds
for the instances where "complexes" or possible childhood traumas
appear and demand a deeper justification and a special solution.

In short, the stories of everyday life have to do with situations
which most people encounter in their daily existence, but it is
characteristic of Thomasine Gyllembourg that in her presentation
of all these problems she is open and free of prejudice, never
sitting in judgement, but above all sympathetic. Her freedom from
prejudice concerning all kinds of subjects—although they are
treated with a never-failing "delicacy"—occasionally met with criticism in her generation, a criticism which, however, was by no
means shared by Kierkegaard. He emphasizes precisely her
"mastery in exposition and description," her "powers of observation," her "balanced and dignified faithful reproduction of
actuality" by which everything acquires "such authenticity that it
becomes interesting precisely for that reason" (TA, 33). But the
most essential for him is that in all the stories there is "the same
closeness to the actuality of daily life and . . . the same distance in
understanding" (TA, 14).

In his comment on the stories Kierkegaard however also notes
that it is "in the older generation, whose life-view is the premise
for their coming into existence," that they "must seek their truly
sympathetic readers." Though there also in the stories is given
expression to "the joy that has conquered the world," so that also
a younger generation will be able to see that there is a "toast
worth drinking: To genius, beauty, art, and the whole glorious
world! To what we love and what we have loved!" (EPW, 67).[37]

---

[37]This exclamation Kierkegaard has taken from the story *Extremerne* [*Extremes*]
(1835), in which also religious questions are debated. The painter Palmer has, in
contrast to his brother-in-law the count, liberated himself from all empty conventional ties and lives only for his art. Although he usually takes his themes from
the surrounding nature, he has once, preoccupied with religious ideas, set himself

For the reason that behind these short stories there lies a view of life which first and foremost is to be found in the older generation and which was carried by a voluntary "resignation," one coming from "the joy that has conquered the world," they cannot in Kierkegaard's view acquire essential significance for the growth of society and the politicians, because these have an eye for nothing but *realpolitik*. This view of the short stories as an entirety is probably the reason why Kierkegaard, as he admits himself, had to read through Thomasine Gyllembourg's last story *Two Ages* more than once in order to see that it had precisely a social-political dimension, what Kierkegaard calls "the reflection of the age in the work." On the other hand, in his admiration of the "author's ingenuity" (TA, 112), he writes a hundred-page-long appreciative review on the basis of precisely its convincing description of the political and social development that has taken place in the course of a generation, and which has led to the levelling of all values. In his introduction to this review Kierkegaard again pays tribute to "the author of a story of everyday life," but especially because "he" has remained true to himself and his view of life for nearly twenty years. This can be explained only by the fact that "The life-view that sustains *A Story of Everyday Life* . . . must come to maturity in the author before he begins his writing." He possesses a view of life with which he can, as no other author, "reconcile [people] with actuality," and he can do that because the ways found to solve the conflicts are the ways belonging to actuality. Sorrow changes to sadness and bitterness to resignation and forgiveness. But the author does not take up problems that can find only a religious solution—his view of life "lies on the boundary of the aesthetic and in the direction of the religious" (TA, 14, 15, translation revised).

---

the task of painting a picture that will show Christ coming to the disciples "through closed doors." The special light that is to come from the figure of Christ he finds, however, impossible to achieve. It is only several years later that he succeeds in painting a "pale reflection" of what he had seen in his imagination. Strangely enough Kierkegaard also fastens on the expression "closed doors" from a religious almanac several years later in a personal Journal entry (JP 5:5313). Could it be the case that Kierkegaard has here got "one or two of these novels woven into the recollection of his own life"? (TA, 18, translation revised).

Finally Kierkegaard points out that the author of the *Story of Everyday Life* that was to be the last one has posed himself a difficult task. For it is natural to assume that whether it has to do with a younger or an older author, the difficulty will lie in being objective in relation to one's own time and being clearly able to see what it is that particularly characterizes it in relation to a previous or a later time.[38] It has to be said, however, that Thomasine Gyllembourg had very special qualifications for making such observations, her life, as stated, being stamped by all of three ages. In her earliest youth she was married to a man whose view of life was decisively marked by the rationalism of the age of enlightenment, while she herself felt enthusiasm for revolution's and romanticism's liberated and romantic expressions of erotic and romantic love. As a mature woman she was later disappointed by the lack of commitment and spontaneous enthusiasm in the 1830s and 1840s, the time's superficial wish to impress in externals, its "currying of favor" and reflective commonsense.[39] On the basis of her human experiences through the many years and with her ability cleverly to observe and evaluate her fellow human beings, Thomasine Gyllembourg was able through her last story to draw a sure picture of both the previous period's spontaneous passion and enthusiasm and of the pseudoexistence of the present age.

Two Ages became the conclusion of Thomasine Gyllembourg's authorship but she also left behind what later was called her "literary testament," which was first published ten years after her death in the second edition of her "Collected Writings," Copenhagen 1866. In this "testament" she acknowledges her authorship of *The Stories of Everyday Life*, a literary production that she, in 1834, in two fictitious letters had in a skilful indirect manner denied

---

[38]Kierkegaard later sent J. L. Heiberg two copies of his review, one to Heiberg as the publisher, and one to the author. Besides Heiberg's thanks Kierkegaard also received three weeks later a letter from "the author of *A Story of Everyday Life*," in which he especially thanks for being "understood . . . comprehended with as much love" as that with which Kierkegaard has examined her latest story (LD, letters 134, 135, 138).

[39]Cf. Johannes Climacus: one "more and more turns away from a primitive expression of existence. . . . One does not love, does not have faith, does not act, but one knows what erotic love is, what faith is . . . ," which results in an "extinction by which the actual life becomes a shadow existence" (CUP, 1:344).

writing.[40] Since it occurred to her that she here "has lied to that public who has shown my stories so much favor and tolerance," she thinks she owes her readers an explanation concerning the anonymity, that she basically regarded activity as an author as incompatible with "the *feminine calling* in close and distant relationships, a calling whose high importance none can sufficiently acknowledge."[41]

Thomasine Gyllembourg was a person full of contrasts, and she can scarcely be better characterized than she was by her daughter-in-law who, in her postscript to Thomasine Gyllembourg's "literary testament" among other things wrote:

> While she wandered here on earth . . . she was loved by all who had eye and spirit to comprehend this fine, remarkable woman's nature, composed of such noteworthy elements opposed to each other, at the same time so conscious and so unconscious, so soft and so sharp, so early tried and yet so inexperienced, so wise and so naive, so pious and so worldly, a lady of the world and yet all her life through preserving the innocence of childhood, the young girl's virginity. . . .[42]

It belongs to the picture of Thomasine Gyllembourg that over the years she also became reconciled with Heiberg. While Johan Ludvig still lived with him in Paris she wrote a letter in 1821 to her former husband in which she begs him from the bottom of his heart to forgive her what wrong she has done him. And she adds: "The thought that I have saddened you, that I have made bitter

---

[40]In *Kjøbenhavns Flyvepost's Interimsblade*, 29 & 30; see Trane, 23-42.

[41]Trane, 9. Of course people tried to guess at the time who was behind the anonymous authorship, and many thought J.L. Heiberg definitely had a share in it. Johanne Luise Heiberg tells us that one of those who became clear that only Thomasine Gyllembourg could have written the stories was Poul Martin Møller, who belonged to the inner circle of guests at the Heiberg home. Thomasine Gyllembourg also suspected that he gave her away. She "therefore exclaimed to her intimate friends: 'Poul Møller is my undoing! It is he who has circulated the rumor about me' " (Trane, 13). That Kierkegaard through his good friend Poul Møller has got to know the real truth is therefore highly probable, but he respected her anonymity and always referred to the author as "he."

[42]Trane, 12.

many a day of your life has always been extremely painful to me and cost me many a tearful lonely hour."[43]

Happy at seeing his son again, in whom he recognizes many of his mother's "good and lovable characteristics," Heiberg replies: "Of course dear Thomasine all the past ought to be forgotten. The best we could both do is to stop trying to find out which of us can come up with the most and the greatest reproaches against himself."[44] This correspondence was continued in a cordial tone in the following years, but it is characteristic of Thomasine that she never says a single word to her former partner about the *Stories of Everyday Life* in which people (just as she did in her own life) always ended by reaching a reconciliation—the *Stories of Everyday Life* which, as Kierkegaard said, are not only "a consummate story but are stories of consummation" (TA, 16, translation revised).

[43]PAHTG, 292.
[44]PAHTG, 294.

6

"Cosmopolitan Faces":
The Presence of the Wandering Jew
in From the Papers of One Still Living

George Pattison

Introduction

In this essay I shall seek to interpret Kierkegaard's *From the Papers of One Still Living* through the heuristic figure of Ahasverus, the Wandering Jew. The justification for this project does not lie on the surface of Kierkegaard's text, for we will not find in it any explicit reference to Ahasverus. Nonetheless, the motif of the Wandering Jew throws light on a number of important connections between the text and the contexts of Kierkegaard's own developing authorship and of the social and literary situation of the 1830s. Let us briefly anticipate the yield we expect from this interpretative venture.

Firstly, we shall strengthen our understanding of the continuity between *The Papers* and the themes of Kierkegaard's early journals. Secondly, and in close connection with this, we shall gain a valuable insight into Kierkegaard's intellectual association with Poul Martin Møller (sometimes held, in the light of his death shortly before its publication, to be the implied dedicatee of the review's title). Thirdly, we shall be able to forge connections between the literary and political dimensions of the text (and, more generally, of Kierkegaard's development at this point). Fourthly, we shall confirm Kierkegaard's own judgement that the figure of the Wandering Jew has a singular relation to the age of modernity. Fifthly, and focussing in more specifically on our chosen text, we shall see how the theme of the Wandering Jew is to be found in Andersen's novel *Only A Fiddler* and how this relates to Kierkegaard's critique.

This is the yield we expect. To achieve it let us prepare the ground in two stages. The first will consist of an overview of the history of the legend itself, up to and including the 1830s and the second of a brief examination of the theme of the Wandering Jew in Kierkegaard's early journals.

The Legend of the Wandering Jew[1]

The legend of the Wandering Jew seems to have originated in the period of the crusades. A number of thirteenth century sources, notably Roger of Wendover, Matthieu Paris, and Philip of Navarre refer to a Jew, variously named as Malchus (the High Priest's servant whose ear was cut off by Peter), Cartaphilus, and Jean Boutedieu, who, though a contemporary of the Christ, was believed to be still alive. He is variously said to have been baptized by Ananias, to have supernatural knowledge, to be able to cure illnesses and to find hidden treasures; despite his appearance as a poor pilgrim he is really wealthy, he cannot succumb to torture or even execution, but is condemned never to remain more than three days in one place.

The sixteenth century saw a significant development and popularization of the legend (as was also the case with Faust). Matthieu Paris's account, translated into German in 1586–1587, became the basis for the virtually definitive account published in 1602 under the title *Kurtze Beschreibung and Erzehlung von einem Juden mith Namen Ahasverus welcher bey der Creutzigung Christi selber Persönlich gewesen auch das Crucifige Über Christum habe helfen schreyen* (*A Short Description and Narration of a Jew called Ahasverus who was personally present at the Crucifixion of Christ and who also helped to call down the "Crucify Him" on Christ*). This text relates the claim of one Paul de Eitzen, doctor of Theology and bishop of Schleswig, to have met and spoken with the Jew in Hamburg in 1572. Other sightings were common—in Spain, Vienna, Poland, Paris, and Silesia as well as in Northern Germany. From this period texts begin to multi-

---

[1]For the material in this section I am particularly indebted to Edgar Knecht, *Le Mythe du Juif errant. Essai de Mythologie Litteraire et de Sociologie Religieuse* (Grenoble: Presses Universitaires, 1977). See also G. K. Anderson, *The Legend of the Wandering Jew* (Providence RI: Brown University Press, 1965).

ply—in some cases taking on an anti-Semitic flavor (in Spain the spread of the legend can be connected with the expulsion of the Jews).

The main features of the story are that Ahasverus, a cobbler in Jerusalem, having been part of the crowd which called for Christ's crucifixion, is standing by his front door on the road up to Golgotha when Christ arrives carrying his cross. Christ asks if he can sit down and rest, but Ahasverus rebuffs him, and is told that it is he, Ahasverus, who must now keep on walking until the end of the world.

Apart from performing the function (in an age of nascent historicism) of eyewitness to the saving events of the Christian religion, Ahasverus became the focus of many legendary accretions. Some of these, as already indicated, had an anti-Semitic bias, using the legend (in Girard's sense) as a "text of persecution." Thus, Ahasverus is blamed for the perpetual covering of snow on the Alps, whilst his presence is sometimes said to bring sterility. Yet he is also celebrated as having instituted apple growing in one region of France, and protects against serpents as well as bringing good harvests. Some legends have him at work amassing faggots with which to burn the earth on the last day.

He is characteristically an artisan figure, sometimes said to have been a mason who worked on the temple. In this respect, as with regard to his suffering, he is often a sympathetic figure, whose complaint is narrated with compassion, whilst remaining a warning to the impenitent.

In the seventeenth and eighteenth centuries the legend undergoes a number of permutations. In the Age of Enlightenment his travels and historical knowledge make of him a mouthpiece for enlightened values of universal curiosity, tolerance and the critique of religious and social institutions that claim a premature absolutism. In the words of Edgar Knecht the story is transformed from a "history" to "memoirs" and from "myth" to "fable."[2]

With the Romantic movement further dramatic transformations are set in motion.

---

[2]See Knecht, Le mythe du Juif errant, 74 and 81.

A major text is "Der Ewige Jude," a poem by C. F. D. Schubart, whose imprisonment for ten years by the then Duke of Württemberg in the late eighteenth century helped establish the poet's credentials as a romantic "hero" and role model.

The theme of longing for death is recurrent in Schubart's work. It is often treated in the language and in the tone of pietistic devotion, but in "Der Ewige Jude" it is powerfully dramatized in Ahasverus's passionate complaint.[3] Ahasverus is discovered in a cave on Mount Carmel, angrily throwing down the skulls of his father, his wives and his children—all of whom have been able to die, whilst he is denied "Death's sweet comfort, the comfort of the grave's peace. . . . " Having vainly sought death in battle or as the prey of wild beasts he challenges the Almighty: "Fearful wrathful One in Heaven / Have you in your armory / Any more fearful punishment? [than not to be able to die.]" Ahasverus in this way becomes the voice of protest against heavenly (and, by implication, earthly) despotism, though, at the end of the poem, he is promised release by an angel, who says, "Now sleep . . . Ahasverus, / sleep a sweet sleep; God is not angry for ever! / When you awake, he will be there / Whose blood you saw flow at Golgotha; / And he—you too will forgive." (It is an indication of Schubart's sensitivity to the theological implications of a "hard" reading of the legend that the initial doom on Ahasverus is not spoken by Christ but by the angel of death: the poet wishes to draw a clear line between the [Christian] God of love and the ideological image of God as an arbitrary despot.)

The image of the Wandering Jew continued to haunt German Romanticism. Schiller (in *Der Geisterseher*), A. W. Schlegel (in *Die Warnung*), Nicholas Lenau and Achim von Arnim (*Halle und Jerusalem*) were amongst those who took up the theme, using the figure of the Jew to explore the "anguished problem of human impotence in the face of destiny"[4] and to give expression to the *mal du siècle*. Sinclair Lewis in *The Monk* and Charles Maturin in

---

[3]In *Gesammelte Schriften und Schicksale* (Hildesheim and New York: Olms, 1972) 4:65ff. The translation here, and from other foreign language titles cited, is my own.

[4]Knecht, *Le Mythe du Juif errant* 156-57.

Melmoth the Wanderer incorporated the Jew into the genre of the gothic novel.

In Britain, Schubart's poem, in a "dirty and torn" copy was picked up by Shelley from a bookstall in Lincoln's Inn Fields and inspired him to use Ahasverus as a prototypical Promethean figure in "Queen Mab," giving the Jew the task of declaiming a massive and relentless indictment of divine injustice. Here Ahasverus answers the question "Is there a God" with the response

> . . . ay, an almighty God,
> And vengeful as almighty!

Even Christ is implicated in the terrible wrath of God's "tyrannous omnipotence":

> . . . humbly he came,
> Veiling his horrible Godhead in the shape
> Of man, scorned by the world, His name unheard,
> Save by the rabble of His native town,
> Even as a parish demagogue. He led
> The crowd ; he taught them justice, truth, and peace,
> In semblance ; but he lit within their souls
> The quenchless flames of zeal, and blessed the sword
> He brought on earth to satiate with the blood
> Of truth and freedom His malignant soul.
> At length his mortal frame was led to death.
> I stood beside Him : on the torturing cross
> No pain assailed his unterrestrial sense ;
> And yet he groaned. Indignantly I summed
> The massacres and miseries which His name
> Had sanctioned in my country, and I cried,
> "Go! Go!" in mockery.
> A smile of godlike malice reillumined
> His fading lineaments.—"I go," He cried,
> "But thou shalt wander o'er the unquiet earth
> Eternally."—The dampness of the grave
> bathed my imperishable front. I fell,
> And long lay tranced upon the charmèd soil.
> When I awoke Hell burned within my brain . . .
> But my soul
> From sight and sense of the polluting woe
> Of tyranny, had long learned to prefer

Hell's freedom to the servitude of heaven.[5]

This is the quintessential expression of the Romantic Ahasverus: the voice of anguished protest against a human condition which is experienced as both politically and metaphysically unjust, a voice pleading for liberation and for the advent of a new era of freedom.

A Danish Ahasverus appeared from the hand of B. S. Ingemann, whose *Leaves from the Pocket Book of Jerusalem's Shoemaker* appeared in 1833 and was noted by Kierkegaard.[6] Ingemann's work, which consists of a sequence of short poems, has little of Shelley's tone of rebellion. His Ahasverus is more an "Everyman" who is confronted with the riddle of a temporal existence in a finite world that nonetheless has intimations of immortality. In the poem "Thoughts of Death" he laments that: "My eye looks beyond clouds and stars / For the way, by which Enoch ascended above. / I search for Jacob's ladder: / Is there a bridge to heaven from the realm of death?" It concludes: "Immortal, [yet burdened] with the dark thought of death, / My soul hovers between heaven and the abyss." In this situation of questioning doubt, "The veil of eternity is nowhere torn" in such a way that we might catch glimpses of the other side. Yet—and as opposed to other Romantic Wandering Jews—this Ahasverus finds some comfort in the continuity and companionship of nature. In "My Mother's House" Ahasverus proclaims "Abandoned no longer, no more do I go alone: / Here stirs a spirit which understands me. / I talk to the flower of the field, to wood and lake, / And a thousand voices answering bring comfort to my soul." Nor is he without final hope. The concluding poem, "Redemption's Word," looks to the day when Ahasverus, with all of Israel, shall hear God's voice calling him to share the life of the Kingdom.

Ahasverus also journeyed to France in this period, from whence the most remarkable of all the Romantic reworkings of the

---

[5]From Percy Bysshe Shelley, "Queen Mab" in *The Poetical Works of Percy Bysshe Shelley*, vol. 1, *Lyrics and Shorter Poems* Everyman's Library (London, Toronto, and New York: J. M. Dent & Sons; E. P. Dutton & Co., 1907) 98-100.

[6]B. S. Ingemann, *Blade af Jerusalems Skomagers Lommebog* (Copenhagen: Andreas Seidelin, 1833). See JP, 5:5193.

legend was to come: Edgar Quinet's poetic drama written in the form of a mystery play—*Ahasvérus* (1834). Best remembered as a precursor of Flaubert's *The Temptation of Saint Anthony*, in its own time it inaugurated a flood of Wandering Jew literature, plays and even opera in France in the 1830s and 1840s. The genre included Eugène Sue's enormously successful novel of 1844 in which the Jew becomes the spokesman for anticlericalism and socialism. In this novel, as in other contemporary French works (e.g., A.-L. Constant's *Trois Harmonies* of 1845) the Jew champions the values of the common man and of the masses—"the people."[7]

Let us briefly examine Quinet's *chef d'oeuvre* as one of the supreme examples of this literature and as representative of the cultural profile of the Wandering Jew in the period when Kierkegaard began to take an interest in the topic. Although there is no evidence of Kierkegaard having read this work, the life and literature of Paris were discussed in the contemporary Danish press and, in this case as in many others, Paris (even in the "market-town" of Copenhagen) may fairly be taken as "the capital of the nineteenth century," that is, as embodying the "whole newer development" with which Kierkegaard is at this time taking issue.[8] The significance of Paris in this respect is, as we shall see, alluded to by Kierkegaard in the course of *From the Papers of One Still Living* and Quinet's drama may fairly be taken as epitomizing the intellectual and cultural tendencies that Kierkegaard discerns in the Wandering Jew and that *The Papers* sets out to address.

The work is, in effect, nothing less than a mythological retelling of the history of the world, from the dawn of creation to Judgement Day and beyond. It is, God says in the prologue, "A long story by which even I am oppressed."[9] It is divided into four "Days," with prologue and epilogue.

---

[7]The same chord has been struck more recently in Stefan Heym, *The Wandering Jew* (New York: Holt, Rinehart & Winston, 1984; German: *Ahasver*, 1983).

[8]Many of the authors, such as Scribe, St.-Georges, and Sue who dealt with this theme were certainly familiar to Kierkegaard in other connections. For Kierkegaard's relation to contemporary French culture see G. Pattison, *Poor Paris! Kierkegaard's Critique of the Spectacular City* (Berlin: Walter de Gruyter, 1999).

[9]Edgar Quinet, *Ahasvérus* in *Oeuvres Complètes* (Paris, 1858) 7:64. Further references are to act and scene numbers.

Day 1, Creation, begins in the Orient, and narrates the rise and fall of the ancient Empires of the East: India, Iran and Egypt. The cities of the ancient world are shown discoursing among themselves until Jerusalem announces the advent of a new God. By means of the three Kings the Eastern cities pay their tribute to this new arrival. They present a chalice filled with tears from which each of them have drunk and a crown with studs of gold, which Mary sees as drops of blood and spines of Judaean wood. The gifts are, as yet, too heavy for the infant to bear. Returning, the Kings find their former realms devalued and worthless.

Day 2 deals with the Passion and depicts the decisive encounter between Christ and Ahasverus. This is considerably embroidered and lengthened. Thus, Christ asks for water and Ahasverus replies that the well is dry; Christ asks for help in carrying the cross, Ahasverus refuses; Christ asks to sit down on the bench by Ahasverus's door but is told "No room"; Christ asks if he might sit on the threshold—"No"; again, Christ asks if he might have a stool—"No."

> A: Be on your way.
> Christ: I wished to save you.
> A: Prophet, get out of my shadow. Your way lies in front of you. Walk, walk.
> Christ: Why did you say that, Ahasverus? It is you who will go on walking until Judgement Day . . . in my place you will carry the burden which I will lay down on the cross. To quench your thirst you will drink what I have left in the bottom of my chalice. . . . You will inherit my eternal sorrow. . . . You will be the man who never dies.

Via the Sack of Rome, Ahasverus arrives for Day 3, "Death," in a medieval Rhineland Town. Here we are introduced to Rachel, an erstwhile angel who, because she shed a tear for Ahasverus has been sent down to earth to assist Mob, the witch-like figure of Death. Although not initially recognizing each other Rachel and Ahasverus fall in love and he begins to wonder whether his long torment will soon be over. Mob, however, ridicules the power of love—"Nature is made up of atoms, and that's all there is," she says (Day 3:10). "The sphere of the worlds is a great zero which traces its emptiness in empty space" (3:12). In a later scene, showing herself in her true skeletal form, she lists her own names :

"Void, abyss, desert, ruination, nothingness,[10] dust, / And, finally, in every case, I am NOTHING"[11] (3:17). With only their love, rejected by the Church, by society, by everything, Rachel and Ahasverus set out to wander the earth, until the Last Day, until Christ's cup of sorrows will have been finally drained.

Day 4 takes us many centuries further to that Last Day. The world is desert-like. "God is dead," says the mythological voice of ocean, "let us perform his funeral rites." "The last night, the immense night, will come," sighs Ahasverus. Yet even when the world is ended, he fears, sorrow will still remain, "Sorrow without name, sorrow without voice, sorrow without form. . . . There still remains in his glass a taste of bitterness . . . a word called despair." Yet, following scenes of cataclysmic judgement that offer a recapitulation of world history, there is a final reconciliation between Ahasverus and Christ.

> Christ: Have you drunk all that remains of the world's sorrow?
> A: Rachel has drunk it with me.
> Christ: Do you want to return to your home in the Orient?
> A: No. I ask for life, not rest. Instead of the steps of my house on Calvary, I would like without pausing to mount the steps of the universe. Without taking breath, I would like to whiten my soles on the dust of the stars, to climb, always to climb, from world to world, from heaven to heaven, without ever redescending, in order to see the source from which you have made to issue the centuries and the years. . . . Bless me, and I will leave this evening towards these future worlds which you already inhabit.
> Christ: Who will follow you?
> The Universe: No—we don't want to go forward.
> Rachel: I will.
> The Universe: A woman caused my loss, a woman has saved me.
> Christ: Yes, this voice has saved you, Ahasverus. I bless you, the pilgrim of the worlds to come and the second Adam. (4:13)

Mob (Death) cannot now follow Ahasverus and Rachel, for Ahasverus is, as The Father Eternal confides to Christ, "the ever-

---

[10]French: *néant*.
[11]French: *le RIEN*.

lasting man." Yet this is not the last word. The epilogue finds
Christ alone. Since Ahasverus has returned the chalice, his wounds
have reopened and his tears fall into the abyss. Why, he asks
himself, has the Universe collapsed about him?

> Ah! How the sky is empty; how I am alone in the firmament.
> One after the other the angels have folded their wings. . . . Mary
> my mother is dead; And my Father, Jehovah, said to me on his
> deathbed: Christ, my time has come. . . . Go! Your father is dead.
> The Universe has shaken its God from off its branch like a fig
> tree [shakes off] its leaves.

Christ doubts himself.

> Who have I been ? Who am I ? Who will I be tomorrow? Word
> without life? or Life without Word? World without God? or God
> without World? Equally nothing. (Epilogue)

Eternity calls on him to accept a new death, a new sepulchre,
from the dust of which a new heaven and a new Adam might be
created. Christ thereupon dying, Eternity buries both Father and
Son in a frozen star without fellow or light. Eternity and Nothingness are left.

> Nothingness: At least, me, you will keep me. I take up little
> room.
> Eternity: But you make too much noise. Neither Being nor
> Nothingness; I want nothing but myself.
> Nothingness: Who then will keep you in your desert.
> Eternity: I!
> Nothingness: And, if not I, who will put in place your crown.
> Eternity: I! (Epilogue)

Finis! The love of Ahasverus and Rachel, it seems, may in some
sense transcend the power of death and the material extension of
the visible universe—but there is a final absolute, eternal but without quality, thought or feeling in the face of which even love and
even the personal divinity of Christian theology come to an end.

If Quinet's excessive and often heavy-handed symbolism—of
which we have glimpsed only the merest tip of the iceberg—seems
far removed from the simplicity of the original medieval legend,
it is clear that he uses that legend to explore fundamental issues in
the understanding of religion and modernity. The new universe
uncovered by science, the historical relativity of the world's vari-

ous religions, empires and philosophies, the problem of time and issues of cosmic justice are all explored in the light of radical humanism and nihilism. Half a century before Nietzsche the death of God is placed firmly on the religious agenda. That the story of Ahasverus could thus be used to bring so many of the decisive themes of the contemporary critique of religion into focus is highly significant for what we shall now see of Kierkegaard's exploration of the Jew and for his reading of Andersen's novel. We turn first to the understanding of the Wandering Jew found in Kierkegaard's early journals.

The Wandering Jew in Kierkegaard's Early Journals

In the early Journals the figure of the Wandering Jew occurs chiefly in association with the complementary figures of Don Juan and of Faust, defined by Kierkegaard as "three great ideas" "representing life in its three tendencies, as it were, outside of religion" (JP, 1:795). These are discussed chiefly in the light of their role as subjects for artistic representation or as they are represented in works of art by Mozart, Goethe and Lenau.[12] At the same time they are seen to be connected by a historical dialectic, by which they represent, respectively, more and more intensely conscious manifestations of the separation of the subject from the religious substance of a homogenous social and cosmic order (JP, 2:1184; JP, 1:737).[13]

Of the three figures the Jew is dealt with least extensively (and, we may add, is less obviously present in Kierkegaard's published authorship—a situation which this essay is particularly concerned to address). Although there are a total of fourteen entries in which he is mentioned[14], most of these are somewhat cursory. Yet it is

---

[12]See, e.g., JP, 2:1177, 1178, 1179, 1180, 1183, 1184; JP, 4:4397; JP, 5:5092.

[13]For a fuller justification of this reading see my *Kierkegaard, the Aesthetic and the Religious: From the Magic Theatre to the Crucifixion of the Image* (Houndmills, Basingstoke, Hampshire UK: Macmillan, 1992) 48-49; or, more extensively, my Ph.D. thesis (of which *Kierkegaard* is a revision), "Kierkegaard's Theory and Critique of Art: Its Theological Significance" (University of Durham, 1983) 152-57.

[14]JP, 1:737; JP, 2:1179, 2206; JP, 5:5087, 5109, 5110, 5111, 5112, 5193, 5194, 5195, 5196 and 5197. Also, in the Danish edition, I C 63 (a quotation from E. T. A. Hoffmann which describes the Jew as wandering "durch das bunteste Gewühl der

clear that Kierkegaard took pains to inform himself both about primary sources for the legend as well as reading what he could of its more recent literary reworkings. His own understanding of the Jew's significance is well illustrated by some critical remarks made in one of the lengthiest entries dealing with the subject that deals with a late eighteenth century German treatment of the legend. This plainly concentrates on what might be called the curiosity value of the Jew, who is depicted in conversation with representatives from four different nations at the Leipzig Easter Fair. Kierkegaard comments:

> [H]e is here conceived, as in most adaptations, more as the *temporal* Jew than as the *eternal* Jew [in Danish, as in German, the "Wandering" Jew is known as the "Eternal Jew"], that is, completely atomized time is presented in its multiple, variegated forms, but on the whole, instead of the more inwardly turned eye, signifying the deepest, most silent despair, there is the perception of external objects in and for themselves, and he is endowed with a good bit of garrulousness (ἀλαζονεία), characteristic of an adventurer. (JP, 5:5196)

Alongside this definition of the Jew as the representative (when properly understood) of "the more inwardly turned eye, signifying the deepest, most silent despair" we should set this summary statement: "The present age is the age of despair, the age of the wandering Jew (many reforming Jews)" (JP, 1:737). From the juxtaposition of these texts (dating from 1837 and 1836 respectively) we may establish a definitive correlation between the figure of the Jew and the concept of despair, a correlation borne out by other entries. Moreover, we see this correlation extended to a definition of the present age and, in particular, of what might be called the political (and by implication the literary) "left," the reformist tendency, represented in Denmark by those with whom Kierkegaard crossed swords in his polemical articles attacking the liberal newspaper *Fædrelandet* and in his 1835 address to the Student Association. It is this political manifestation of modernity ('the whole newer development' EPW, 60) that Kierkegaard targets in *From the Papers*

Welt, ohne freude, ohne Hoffnung, ohne Schmerz, in dumpfer Gleichgültigkeit, die das caput mortuum der verzweifelung ist, wie durch eine unwirthbare trostlose Einöde. . . . "

of One Still Living with particular ferocity, describing its progeny as "a whole brood of select abstract *Cosmopolit-Gesichter* [cosmopolitan faces]" (EPW, 64). In addition to his Danish opponents we must also (and importantly) count the left wing literary movement known as "Young Germany" amongst these "cosmopolitan faces" (see EPW, 94n.).

To summarize: the Wandering Jew symbolizes for Kierkegaard the despair of the present age, a despair rooted in its separation from the substantial ground of religion and manifesting itself in both political reform movements and philosophical nihilism. Also, as we shall see, this despair is central to the problematic of contemporary literature, a problematic that might be defined in the form of a question: How can good literature be written in a cultural situation of fragmentation and the decay of tradition? That is to say: How can good literature be produced "outside of religion"?

To explore these questions further we turn now to the figure of Poul Martin Møller with a view to examining his significance both for Kierkegaard's understanding of the Wandering Jew (as reflected in the early journals) and for the question of literature and the life-view as that is raised in *The Papers*.

Poul Martin Møller and Nihilism

Central to Møller's philosophy was the concept of "the life-view" (or "worldview"), a concept which is also central to Kierkegaard's critique of Andersen. For Møller, as later for Kierkegaard, this concept performed a synthesizing role in bringing together a whole range of concerns: philosophical, moral, cultural and aesthetic.[15]

Although idealistically grounded, Møller's thought was characterized by a degree of empiricism and a strong sense of the in-

---

[15]For the relationship between Kierkegaard and Møller, see W. Glyn Jones, "Søren Kierkegaard and Poul Martin Møller" in *Modern Language Review* 60 (1965) 73-82; Gregor Malantschuk, "Søren Kierkegaard og Poul M. Møller" in *Kierkegaardiana* 3 (1959) 7-20; G. Pattison, "Nihilism and the Novel: Kierkegaard's Literary Reviews" in *The British Journal of Aesthetics* 26/2 (1986): 161-71; idem., *Kierkegaard, the Aesthetic and the Religious*, 28-34. Traces of Kierkegaard's admiration for Møller can be found in JP, 5:5302, 5305; CUP, 1:34 and, most famously, in the dedication to *The Concept of Anxiety*.

violable integrity of the personality that made him an early Danish critic of Hegel. (For him, as for Ingemann—and somewhat differently for Kierkegaard also—this issue crystallized around the question of immortality.) For Møller there can be no absolute or presuppositionless beginning, because the human subject is always already immersed in and shaped by a given social and empirical reality.

> Purely on his own, as a single individual, no one would come to consciousness of religious concepts: he who believes that he has put aside external authority and solely by free self-activity of thought has gained a new result, which is his purely personal possession, has nevertheless . . . always received a significant impetus from the tradition, without which his thought would have lost itself in subjective, fruitless fancy.[16]

The empirical and social bases of an authentic worldview are firmly indicated in the following passage:

> The Christian tradition, empirical experience, as well as the higher experience in which the supersensuous encounters us in a real form at particular times and places give the discrete points which must have their place in a proper worldview, and the systematic, philosophic exposition only expresses with formal perfection that knowledge which is first present in an immediate way and in an inarticulate form.[17]

Uffe Andreasen has shown that Møller was preoccupied over many years with the phenomenon of nihilism, as manifested in aspects of Romanticism and, philosophically, in Schopenhauer[18], and he was dubious as to the extent to which a "proper" worldview could be attained by those living in the present age. The repudiation of tradition by the left specifically removes one of the main buttresses of the worldview. Anticipating Kierkegaard's critique of the Romantic appropriation of Fichtean irony Møller wrote, "[I]rony is a consequent development of the fruitless struggle to construct a self-enclosed ethical system from the stand-

---

[16]Poul Martin Møller, "Om Udødeligheden" in *Efterladte Skrifter* 3rd ed. (Copenhagen: Reitzel, 1856) 5:67.

[17]"Om Udødeligheden" 5:69-70.

[18]See Uffe Andreasen, *Poul Møller og Romantismen* (Copenhagen: Gyldendal, 1973).

point of the individual. This method must necessarily end with the loss of all content, with moral nihilism."[19]

Once such irony has been unleashed on the world it is hard to see where it will stop:

> I nurture a doubt as to whether the basic view, for whose defence these pages give a provisional contribution, can, by any amount of effort be vindicated in the present time. It is very possible that [the spirit of] negation has still not reached the point which must be reached, so that it can be made apparent that the desolation it brings with it is not the sphere in which the human spirit is at home.[20]

This nihilism has, for Møller, clear political implications. In one of his poems he says of the child of "nineteenth-century rational man" that he "is an old man who never jokes, / His music the ringing chimes of rebellion; / He is pale with wrath, / And murder is his game."[21]

The life-view, or lack of it, is, moreover, crucial to the situation of the artist. Møller's view is most succinctly summarized on this point by his statement that "he, who feels himself in discord with himself and with existence, cannot possibly be a genuine poet."[22]

In all these dimensions of the philosophy of the life-view, Møller provided the philosophical framework which Kierkegaard was to put to use in the Andersen review. Kierkegaard's definition of the life-view as 'the transubstantiation of experience . . . an unshakable certainty in oneself won from all experience' (EPW, 76) and his subsequent lambasting of Andersen for lack of such a starting point are thoroughly within the sphere of Møller's personalistic philosophy.

Yet there is far more to the Kierkegaard-Møller axis than that. It is not the case that Kierkegaard simply "lifted" a positive response to nihilism from Møller's thought. It is more accurate to see both Kierkegaard and Møller recognizing the political, intellectual and cultural power of contemporary nihilism and spelling out the problematic that arises out of this for those who

---

[19]Møller, "Om Begrebet Ironie" in *Efterladte Skrifter* 3:152.
[20]"Om Udødeligheden" 5:41.
[21]Idem., "Kunstneren mellem Oprørerne" in *Efterladte Skrifter* 1:134.
[22]Idem., "Recension af Extremerne" in *Efterladte Skrifter* 6:67-68.

would be advocates of a more "sound" view. If *The Papers* criticizes the disintegration of the elements of the life-view as that is
manifested in Andersen's novel, it is clear that this is not merely
an individual failing on Andersen's part. It is rather that Andersen
represents one point at which the general destiny of the age becomes manifest. This destiny—we might say doom—lay upon the
age as a whole. Kierkegaard's own early journals are replete with
aphorisms that can be read as expressive of the nihilistic mood, as
can the aesthetic stance described in *Either/Or* Part 1. To what
extent this represents the confessional self-purgation of a penitent
and to what extent Kierkegaard simply observed the phenomenon
from the outside are not questions which need to detain us here.
In either case it is clear that the phenomenon was one which he
regarded as important and compelling, requiring the engagement
and activation of his best intellectual and literary energies.

Kierkegaard was not alone in identifying the Wandering Jew
as a symbolic representative of the despair of the present age.
Møller too wrote a series of fragments, dated between 1836 and
1837 (a time when Kierkegaard was closely associated with the
older philosopher), entitled *Ahasverus*, which use the Jew as a representative of moral nihilism. Frithiof Brandt suggested that these
aphorisms constitute an intellectual portrait of Kierkegaard himself
during his own "nihilistic" phase, but whatever truth there may be
in such a speculation, the intellectual proximity of these aphorisms
to, for example, the "Diapsalmata" of *Either/Or* is striking.[23]

> "Your ignorant half-philosophers believe that every philosophical
> system which comes out is new; but I have experienced in many
> circles that philosophy has run through its natural stages many
> times and I have heard the same squabbles about the same
> problems. To me the whole thing is only a cycle of pieces in a
> barrel organ."
>
> "Your ignorant priests believe that there is an absolute difference
> between good and evil, but they do not observe that I stand
> precisely at the zero point on life's thermometer."
>
> "Amongst a shower of merry bachelors I began by playing the
> part of a good-humored old fellow who was young with the

[23]See Walter Lowrie, *Kierkegaard* (London and New York: Oxford University Press, 1938) 143.

young; but as I saw the mood of the gathering pass through every gradation from smarminess through to self-satisfied uprightness and from loving embraces through to disharmony—then my face took on an expression of utter weariness with the whole of existence, and I let out, with an unspeakable grimace: Bah! Everyone dropped their glasses, and it became as still as the grave. It was a Medusa's head I had showed them. . . . "

Ahasverus wills nothing. He regards himself as infinitely higher than those who will anything.

Ahasverus has such complete consciousness of all his movements and of what is characteristic of his utterances, that there is no longer anything spontaneous about him; but it follows from that that he is essentially always playing a role, for he must plan out what should occur spontaneously.[24]

The whole collection is, to be sure, sketchy at best. But we can see important anticipations of Kierkegaard's depiction of contemporary nihilism: the drawing of cynical conclusions affecting both morals and knowledge from a relativistic philosophy, the problem of boredom as symptomatic of a rootless society, the displacement of natural immediacy by contrivance and deception. If Møller's *Ahasverus* lacks the political dimension touched on in some of his other writings (and strongly hinted at by Kierkegaard in the Andersen review as well as in his polemical articles) it nonetheless sets out the basic premisses which underlie what both men regarded as the political and cultural malaise of their time. Ahasverus is the doom hanging over an age which is no longer capable of the healthy and health-giving "life-view."

The Fiddler and the Jew

If it is accepted that the figure of Ahasverus belongs somewhere in the intellectual background of the Kierkegaard of *The Papers*, there may still be some question as to how directly relevant he is to the specific case of "Andersen as novelist," more particularly, Andersen as author of *Only a Fiddler*. Andersen himself appears in the review as a very different figure from the Jew. For if Ahasverus is identified in texts from Shelley to Quinet and Møller (not to mention Kierkegaard's own early journals) as

---

[24]Møller, "Ahasverus" in *Efterladte Skrifter* 3:159-62.

representing the dynamic forces of contemporary relativism and nihilism, Andersen is represented by Kierkegaard as victim rather than as agent of this tendency. To be sure, by producing literature devoid of a properly synthesized life-view, Andersen also participates in the further propagation of the age's essential sickness—but, even so, he is a manifestation rather than a source of the problem. Ahasverus, on the other hand, is in himself representative of the essence of nihilism. What, then, is the specific justification for relating Ahasverus to this review in particular, other than in the light thrown by the theme on Kierkegaard's general concerns at this point in his authorship? To answer this question we must turn to Andersen's novel itself.

The novel opens in the little Fyn town of Svendborg, home to Christian, the novel's "hero" and the fiddler of the title. Christian's father (Christian is only a little child at this point) and an old soldier friend are observing the storks nesting on a neighboring roof. Their reflections on the birds' migrations lead them to speak of their own travels and a strong contrast is drawn between the world of "little Denmark," a cosy world of familial intimacy, and the magical, mysterious world beyond, a world promising novelty and adventure.

But the stork is not the only symbol in the novel of this wider world. It is no accident that the neighbor on whose roof the storks are seen nesting is an old and wealthy Jewish moneylender, who lives with his granddaughter, Naomi. One day Christian, whose father is only a poor tailor, breaks through the dividing wall into Naomi's garden. Everything about her and about the garden has an overwhelming effect on him. It is as if a new and exotic world has opened up. "He stood in a land of dreams, losing himself in the sight."[25] Naomi's "gazelle eyes" evoke her "Asiatic race." The flowers, the scents, the garden house and the game invented by Naomi (money lending!) transport Christian into a new "hesperidean world, which seemed far removed from his usual home. . . . Never had he played so happily before."

---

[25]Hans Christian Andersen, *Kun En Spillemand* (Borgen: Det danske Sprog- og Litteraturselskab, 1988) 18.

The next day, however, the hole in the wall has been blocked up and the magical world is closed to him. But he is soon to be brought together with Naomi again, for her grandfather's house catches fire and is burnt to the ground. The old man himself dies and Christian's parents take Naomi in. The old man's remains are taken away by boat to be buried in a Jewish cemetery in Fredericia. In Christian's imagination the journey is one to "a far, far-off land of fantasy, perhaps not far distant from Jerusalem, the Jews' royal city."[26] Maria, Christian's mother, comments, "The poor people. They don't even find rest in death. They must travel to be put in the earth." Shortly afterwards a grandly appointed coach arrives and an elderly, noble lady descends to take Naomi off to a new life. This, however, is only the first of many wanderings for her, wanderings which include Vienna, Italy and Paris (seen as the city or atheism *par excellence*: EPW, 94n.) and an escapade with a band of gypsy circus riders.

From the very beginning Naomi, the Jewess, stands for the exotic, for all that lies beyond the frontiers—intellectual, moral and geographical—of "little Denmark." The novel ends with Christian's humble funeral procession, comprising a handful of local peasant folk, having to step off the road to make way for a coach and four occupied by Naomi and her husband, a French marquis (although we know that despite its external splendor, the marriage is unhappy, Naomi being blackmailed by her husband into putting up with his adultery). As we can learn from Kierkegaard's review (EPW, 94n.), Naomi is also—and importantly for our argument— linked to the intellectual movement known as "Young Germany," that is, the literary and intellectual movement most closely identified with what Kierkegaard and Møller regarded as nihilism. The fact that Young Germany itself was shortly to be outstripped in political radicalism by the "Vormärz" movement of the 1840s would scarcely have surprised these Danish critics, who (as the opening pages of *The Papers* make clear) regarded them as only the vanguard, only harbingers, of worse to come. The relationship is very much like that between the older and the younger Verkhovensky in Dostoevsky's novel *The Possessed* in which the idealistic

---

[26]*Spillemand*, 25.

liberalism of one generation literally fathers the materialistic and revolutionary radicalism of the next.

Andersen's novel, then, puts into play a sequence of clearly structured dualities, between the safe world of homely Danish traditions and peasant life on the one hand, and the wider and newer worlds represented in Naomi on the other. It is in the context of this sequence that the significance of Christian's failure to achieve a life-view is best appreciated.

As we reflect on this, we can see that many of the themes thrown up by *The Papers* are not as arbitrary or as unconnected as they might at first seem. The philosophical and political polemics of the opening pages, the celebration of the philosophy of the life-view as exemplified by Madame Gyllembourg and the critique of Andersen's understanding of selfhood all reflect the situation of a society suddenly caught up into a process of rapid transition and modernization, a situation reflected equally in other early polemical writings dealing with issues of feminism and censorship. Over this whole situation hangs the doom of absolute nihilism—and that, for Kierkegaard, is the doom of Ahasverus, the doom of the uprooted, stateless, relativistic wanderer across the face of the earth and through time, the living exponent of the bad infinity, of experience and of history without goal, purpose or end. If, as has been suggested, Andersen is a reactive rather than an active figure in this process, he matters to Kierkegaard precisely in this respect: that in his novel we begin to see the consequences of nihilism, of the doom of Ahasverus working itself out on contemporary Danish culture. The argument is in this way not merely about "what it is to be a person." It is an argument about Danish society and about Danish values in a world in which a new, levelling universalism is poised to sweep away the institutions that had given that society and those values their distinctive cast. Ahasverus is the supreme symbol, the avant-garde, as it were, of that new world of "cosmopolitan faces."

So far this study has been preeminently exegetical. We cannot, however, avoid facing a difficult question raised for the contemporary interpretation of Kierkegaard by what we have read. For, as is all too well known, the figure the "Eternal Jew," precisely understood as a symbol of left-wing politics and cosmopolitanism, was to be a characteristic feature of anti-Semitic propaganda later in the nineteenth and on into the twentieth century, becoming especially prominent in the Third Reich. The "Eternal Jew" was indeed the title of the most notorious of all Nazi propaganda films.

It is at the very least embarrassing that Kierkegaard seems to have espoused a complex of political and cultural perceptions that were to play such a large role in the ideological preparation for what was arguably the most horrific of all the twentieth century's horrific crimes against humanity. When, in his epochal *Kierkegaard*, Walter Lowrie remarks that "In [Kierkegaard's] day the Jews (men without political attachments) were prominent as instigators of liberal reform in Denmark, as they were also in other lands, and as they are today [1938!],"[27] we cannot but feel uncomfortable. The comment was, minimally, untimely. But although we should not be blind to the fact that later reactionary ideology in Europe was both to appropriate aspects of Kierkegaard's thought and also to put to sinister use the kind of image of the Wandering Jew developed by, but not unique to, Kierkegaard, it is essential for us to have a sense of historical perspective and to take into account the differences between Denmark in the 1830s and 1840s and the age of European totalitarianism. There is no element of intentional racism in what Kierkegaard says about the Wandering Jew, and, if he had been significantly anti-Semitic, the fact that his most bitterly disliked literary enemy, Meïr Goldschmidt, editor of *The Corsair*, was Jewish, would have provided him with ample occasion for showing it, if only in the pages of the journal (where he could be extremely inventive in abusing the targets of his wrath). In fact, prior to "the Corsair Affair," Kierkegaard seems to have been essentially well-disposed towards Goldschmidt, regarding him as one of the more promising young Danish writers (particularly in connection with Goldschmidt's novel *A Jew*).[28]

The central point can be put like this: Kierkegaard's concern with the Wandering Jew is not directed towards delineating the Other, the One-who-we-are-not, but as articulating a condition that belongs to the inner destiny of all who have drunk from the bitter

---

[27]Lowrie, *Kierkegaard*, 91.
[28]See COR, vii-xxxi, for the relationship between Kierkegaard and Goldschmidt.

waters of modernity. Indeed, Kierkegaard's critique of Andersen implies that it is precisely by depicting the Jew (Naomi) as the Other and projecting onto this Other the responsibility for Christian's decline and fall, that Andersen obscures the issue as to where responsibility for contemporary nihilism really lies. If Christian is a victim of nihilism, he is, according to Kierkegaard, ultimately responsible for being so. In the last resort, corruption cannot come from without, but only from within. As an ideal type the Wandering Jew is an existential possibility for Jews and non-Jews alike—just as a modern Don Juan or a modern Faust need not be Spanish or German[29]—and the fate of the Wandering Jew, condemned to a life without end or purpose, has to be seen as the fate of all who bear within themselves the condition of modernity. The responsible acceptance of this fate—a recognition that each of us is, in a sense, Ahasverus—(understood in the spirit of Kierkegaard's own later formulation that the single most efficacious because most radical remedy for despair is—despair) may even be a necessary first step in the rebirth of religious faith beyond the wasteland.

---

[29]For a fuller discussion of the question of anti-Semitism in relation to Kierkegaard's portrayal of the Wandering Jew, see Håkon Harket, "Kierkegaards evige jøde" in Joakim Garff, Hakon Harket, Poul Erik Tøjner and Eivind Tjønneland, Innøvelse i Kierkegaard. Fire Essays (Oslo: Cappelen Akademisk Forlag, 1996). Harket also concludes that the charge of anti-Semitism is misplaced.

7

Kierkegaard's Anticipation of Authorship: "Where Shall I Find a Foothold?"

David Cain

Julia Watkin observes, "Although the authorship proper did not begin before *Either/Or*, some of its themes appeared in both published and unpublished material prior to 1843" (EPW, vii). This is strikingly the case. The more one looks, the more one finds. Anticipation of authorship in Kierkegaard's early writings abounds and attests to the "holistic," unified, consistent, and persistent character of Kierkegaard's reflection. On his own terms, Kierkegaard is an "essential author" and not a "premise-author."[1] The major concern here is to identify some of this anticipation in *The Battle between the Old and the New Soap-Cellars* (*Striden mellem den gamle og den nye Sæbekielder*) and perhaps to shed some light on this curious text. *Soap-Cellars*, unfinished and unpublished (by Kierkegaard), is Kierkegaard's one attempt to write a play. The attempt suggests that he could not do it.

Foothold

"But where shall I find a foothold [*Fodfæste*] . . . ?" asks Mr. von Jumping Jack, a "philosopher" in *Soap-Cellars* (EPW, 115). This is also the question of young Søren Kierkegaard. From the middle of a decade of intellectual wanderings, twenty-two-year-old Kierkegaard describes his discomfort in lacking a sense of direction. He

---

[1] "The premise-author is easily recognized and easily described, if only one will remember that he is the exact opposite to the essential author, that while the former is outwardly directed, the latter is inwardly directed" (OAR, 6; see OAR, 3-18).

is concerned with finding a foothold when he writes on 1 June 1835:

> Here I stand before a big question mark. Here I stand like Hercules, but not at the crossroads—no, here there are a good many more roads to take and thus it is much more difficult to choose the right one.[2] It is perhaps my misfortune that I am interested in far too much and not decisively in any one thing; my interests are not subordinated to one but instead all stand coordinate.[3] (JP, 5:5092)

A search for a place to stand is a large part of Kierkegaard's decade at the University of Copenhagen during the 1830s. The declaration attributed to Archimedes—"Give me a place to stand and I will move the world"—becomes a touchstone to which Kierkegaard returns again and again.[4] Here are telling "Diapsal-

---

[2]But must there be a right *one*? What becomes one of Kierkegaard's favorite places, Otteveiskrogen (the Nook of Eight Paths) in Gribskov, a forest in northern Sjælland, affords an appropriate image of many different paths and coordinate lures. In "In Vino Veritas: A Recollection," part of *Stages on Life's Way*, the pseudonym William Afham writes: "In Gribs-Skov there is a place called the Nook of Eight Paths. . . . Indeed, the name itself seems to contain a contradiction, for how can the meeting of eight paths create a nook, how can the beaten and frequented be reconciled with the out-of-the-way and the hidden? . . . The eight paths—heavy traffic is only a possibility, a possibility for thought, because no one travels this path except . . . that fugitive that only the fatal bullet overtakes, which indeed explains why the deer now became so still but does not explain why it was so restless" (SLW, 16-17). The deer's restlessness is Kierkegaard's.

[3]This passage may be part of a "literary" letter from a series of "Faustian letters" (see JP, 5:n.245); but even if this is the case, these words surely reflect back upon young Kierkegaard and his sense of his situation.

[4]See, e.g., SLW, 261 and n. 162. In the courtyard of the venerable student residence at the University of Copenhagen, Regensen (1618–1628), is a celebrated *lindetræ* (lime tree). On a bench at the base of the tree is a small plaque engraved with Archimedes' words: *Giv mig et fast punkt, hvor jeg kan stå, så skal jeg dreje jorden*. Is there a special relationship between Regensen and a place to stand? Is Regensen the *fast punkt* from which one can whirl the world? Did Kierkegaard first become aware of or take to himself Archimedes' words, having encountered them at Regensen (the first reference to "Archimedean point" in the journals is 11 September 1834 [JP, 1:117] during Kierkegaard's university years of which Regensen was a part)? Apparently not. Iben Thranholm of Regensen has kindly investigated, and she writes me: "In Regensen, we have these 'circles' [societies] . . . one of the circles is named after the tree. It is called *Tilia*, the Latin name for

mata" from *Either/Or*, I: "My foot slips. My life nevertheless remains a poet-existence. Can anything worse be imagined?" (EO, 1:36). A slipping foot means no foothold. And even though no foothold is mentioned, the problem of standing is implicit here: "My observation of life makes no sense at all. I suppose that an evil spirit has put a pair of glasses on my nose, one lens of which magnifies on an immense scale and the other reduces on the same scale" (EO, 1:24). If there is a place to stand, the speaker cannot get it in focus. "The disproportion of my body is that my forelegs are too short. Like the hare from New Holland, I have very short forelegs but extremely long hind legs. Ordinarily, I sit very still; if I make a move, it is a tremendous leap . . . " (EO, 1:38). Is there not a relationship among close-up and wide-angle views, kange-roos and leaps, and the footing problem of no place to stand?

Finding an Archimedean point is central to the Kierkegaardian quest. Finding a foothold is more than an anticipation of Kierke-gaard's authorship. It is motivation and substance as well.

Occasion

An occasion of *The Battle between the Old and the New Soap-Cellars* was student experience and involvement. A major student voice during Kierkegaard's university years was that of Peter Martin Orla Lehmann (1810–1870). In 1839, "liberal" Lehmann led the way in requesting of King Christian VIII a representative constitution.[5] He provided Kierkegaard with a target (see EPW,

---

Lindetræ; and in 1985 when the institution of the tree was two hundred years old [the plaque bears the dates: 1785–1985], this circle gave the inscription as a birthday gift to the tree. . . . So the inscription is only twelve years old. Nobody seems to know why that inscription was chosen." Must we settle for coincidence? Among many references to Archimedean point in the journals are these: "that Archimedean point from which he can lift the whole world, that point which precisely for that reason must lie outside the world, outside the restrictions of time and space" (JP, 5:5099). "Pastor Grundtvig is alive, a man who is far superior to Archimedes and does not even need or dream of needing a fixed point in order to move heaven and earth—no, he does it without a foothold [*Fodfæste*]" (JP, 5:5740). "Fixed point" and "foothold" are here closely related.

[5]See Bruce H. Kirmmse, *Kierkegaard in Golden Age Denmark* (Bloomington: Indiana University Press, 1990) 49-51.

xix-xxiii)—Kierkegaard thrived on targets—and with the idea for the character "Hr. Holla [Orla] Hastværksen"[6] in *Soap-Cellars*.

Another occasion of *Soap-Cellars* was Kierkegaard's stepping out into Gråbrødretorv (Grey Brothers [Franciscans] Square-Market-Place). Probably on 1 September 1837, Kierkegaard, now twenty-four, moved from the Kierkegaard family home at Nytorv 2 into an apartment at Løvstræde 7, on the east corner of Løvstræde and Niels Hemmingsens Gade, looking out over Gråbrødretorv to the west.[7] Daily encounter with rival soap-cellar signs on Gråbrødretorv (see EPW, 260) may well have set young Kierkegaard musing.[8] This musing issued forth in ink and fragmentary form, perhaps during the summer of 1838.[9]

---

[6]See Niels Thulstrup, *Kierkegaard's Relation to Hegel*, trans. George L. Stengren (Princeton NJ: Princeton University Press, 1980) 194, and EPW, xxxii, 262n.10. Stengren translates the name "Harry Rushjob"; Julia Watkin translates "Holla Hurrison."

[7]The actual building was demolished in 1938.

[8]But Kierkegaard had come upon the soap-cellar rivalry earlier. See JP, 5:5156, dated 10 August 1836, where the soap-cellars are treated as signifying, not two rival student organizations as is possibly intended in Kierkegaard's play (see EPW, 260), but "the orthodox and the rationalists" in religious conflict, and JP, 5:n.202: "The reference is to the competition between three soap stores located in the half-flight basements of buildings on Graabrødretorvet near the University of Copenhagen." Apparently, there were not two but three such soap-cellars: "One had a sign, The Old Soap-Cellar, another, The Original Old Soap-Cellar, the third, Here Is the Original Old Soap-Cellar where the Old Soap-Cellar People Live."

[9]However, see Thulstrup, *Kierkegaard's Relation to Hegel*, 192-96. Bringing other considerations to bear such as an identification of the "Prytaneum" in *Soap-Cellars* with *Den akademiske Læseforening* (the Academic Lecture Association or the "Academy"), founded in April 1839, Thulstrup suggests a later date, "after July 1839" (196). (The Academy is not to be confused with *Studenterforeningen* [the Student Association], founded in 1820.) Nonetheless, Thulstrup also notes that, at the beginning of the play, Willibald "escapes" from a tea party and "hurries home to his room" (EPW, 107). Thulstrup proposes, "This gives us an indication of the date of this text, when we note that the young man did not have an apartment but only a single room, and compare that with the fact that Kierkegaard himself had moved out of home in his father's house (Nytorv 2) in September 1837, to rent a room at Løvstræde 7 in Copenhagen" (181). This "indication" does not necessarily argue for an earlier date, but it permits the consideration.

Henning Fenger thinks that *Soap-Cellars* and *From the Papers of One Still Living* "form a chronological entity." He concludes, regarding the date of *Soap-Cellars*, "Nothing indicates 1839, everything indicates the spring and summer of 1838"

The date of the draft is uncertain and debated. Julia Watkin identifies several significant considerations (see EPW, xxiv, esp. n. 66). One alternative title for the piece is "From the Papers of One Still Living / against his will published / by S. Kierkegaard" (EPW, 105). This links *Soap-Cellars* to *From the Papers of One Still Living: Published Against His Will* [7 September 1838] *by S. Kjerkegaard*, without ruling on the date.

Kierkegaard seems to have been back on Nytorv by 10 July 1838.[10] If moving did not disrupt writing, certain events might have done so. This spring-summer of 1838 is a critical time for Kierkegaard (see EPW, xiv, xxiv): March grief, May joy, and, in August, grief again. Poul Martin Møller, Kierkegaard's teacher and friend, died on 13 March 1838.[11] Two months later, Kierkegaard records a contrasting event: "an indescribable joy. . . . Not a joy over this or that, but the soul's full outcry . . . " in an exclamation of a journal entry dated 10:30 a.m., 19 May 1838 (JP, 5:5324). Then comes another journal entry dated 11 August 1838 and marked with a cross: "My father died . . . " (JP, 5:5335).[12]

These events are dialectical in relation to dating *Soap-Cellars*. Did they suspend writing or impel it—or both? A factor, too, is Kierkegaard's teaching. In 1837–1838, Kierkegaard taught Latin at

---

(Henning Fenger, *Kierkegaard, the Myths and Their Origins: Studies in the Kierkegaardian Papers and Letters*, trans. George C. Schoolfield (New Haven CT: Yale University Press, 1980) 142.

For further consideration of the date of *Soap-Cellars*, see EPW, xxxii, 259, under "Title Page," and Thulstrup, 198.

[10]See JP, 5:5330 and A. Egelund Møller, *Søren Kierkegaard om sin kjære Hoved- og Residensstad, Kjøbenhavn* (København: Attika, 1983) 10-11. Kierkegaard may not have moved directly back to Nytorv after his time at Løvstræde 7. He may have taken advantage of Copenhagen's *april flyttedag* (April moving day, see EPW, xxivn.65) to move to another apartment of unknown address before returning to his father on Nytorv in late spring or early summer 1838. See A. Egelund Møller, *Søren Kierkegaard om sin kjære Hoved- og Residensstad, Kjøbenhavn* (København: Attika, 1983) 10.

[11]Kierkegaard expresses his appreciation of Poul Møller in Vigilius Haufniensis's commemorative dedication to Møller of *The Concept of Anxiety* (see CA, 5).

[12]Kierkegaard goes on to write that his father "died on Wednesday (the 8th) at 2:00 A.M." (JP, 5:5335). His father, Michael Pedersen Kierkegaard, died on 9 August; 8 August must have been fixed in Kierkegaard's experience as the day of dying. Crossing midnight does not matter.

Borgerdydskolen (the School of Civic Virtue), where he himself had been a student in the 1820s.[13] These considerations yield no firm date for the actual writing of *Soap-Cellars*; but late spring or early summer 1838 remain possibilities, in spite of later datings. The daily impress of Gråbrødretorv's soap-cellar signs would have remained relatively fresh with Kierkegaard in this time before the momentum of writing *From the Papers of One Still Living* took hold. Perhaps he hurried through *Soap-Cellars*, leaving it rough and unfinished[14] because *From the Papers* upstaged it.[15]

Anticipation

What follows is a selective "commentary" on *Soap-Cellars*, which seeks to identify anticipation of authorship. A reading of the play in light of the authorship shows how what were to become central concepts and concerns in Kierkegaard's authorship were already finding their way into young Kierkegaard's thinking and pen.

The first words[16] Kierkegaard writes in his sketch are "A heroic-patriotic-cosmopolitan-philanthropic-fatalistic drama" (EPW,

---

[13]Borgerdydskolen is located on Klareboderne just across Købmagergade from Løvstræde, where Kierkegaard conveniently resided during part of this time.

[14]Kierkegaard begins act I "After a brief monologue . . . " (EPW, 107), which he does not write. Three times the words *nonnulla desunt* (something lacking) occur as a heading (EPW, 110, 116, 118). Is this the author's reminder to himself or somehow a part of the play—or both? Kierkegaard does employ *nonnulla desunt*, almost like a refrain, elsewhere (see JP, 5:5092). But possibly this is an editorial addition (see JP, 5:n.104). There is this note: "N.B. In this book [*I denne Bog*: book—and not "drama" or "play"] only the train of thought will be indicated for what follows; the rest will have to be gradually worked out on pieces of paper" (EPW, 112). And this: "(This speech should naturally be worked out in far greater detail, but I will now merely give a suggestion of it)" (EPW, 121). Indication and suggestion await gradual working out and greater detail, but they wait in vain.

[15]Though the possibility remains that *From the Papers* was written first (see EPW, 260n.5) or even that *Soap-Cellars* was written alongside *From the Papers*, which "was composed in the period between late April or early May and mid-August 1838 and was published on September 7, 1838" (EPW, xxivn.66).

[16]The first two pages are chaotic (see the manuscript reproductions, EPW, 208-209), so sometimes one cannot be sure what was written first. See "A Note on the Manuscript," 156-57, below.

105). Mockery fills every adjective but the last. "Fatalistic" is jarringly different—not at all what one might expect to bring up the rear of this "heroic-patriotic-cosmopolitan-philanthropic" parade. The parade is playful and satirical. Is it also "genre-defiant," a way of excusing oneself—already—from becoming a paragraph in "the system,"[17] of saying, with Johannes Climacus, "Let no one invite me, for I do not dance" (PF, 8)? Climacus' *Concluding Unscientific Postscript* is characterized as "A Mimical-Pathetical-Dialectical Compilation" (CUP, 1:1). These terms have a different and genuinely descriptive significance, but the formal resemblance to *Soap-Cellars* is clear.

Now we are promised a drama "in several episodes" (EPW, 105), as if the author does not know and does not care just how many acts and scenes there are to be. The tone is somehow hurried, impatient, as if the author were beyond the piece even as he is writing it.[18] Some characters listed at the outset do not appear in the play—"A Ditto, nephew of the above-mentioned, a Hegelian" (the "above-mentioned" is "A Fly, who has wisely wintered for many years with the late Hegel and who has been so fortunate as to have sat on his immortal nose . . . "); "A Ventriloquist"; "A Pedestrian"; "A Fighter for Orthography"; and "Wholesalers" (EPW, 106). "Wholesalers" may signal the economic imagery Kierkegaard commonly employs—buying, selling, lowering prices, raising prices, bargain prices (see, e.g., FT, 5, 121). But "in the world of the spirit" (FT, 27), there are no bargain prices, no wholesalers, no cheating.[19] Other characters appear in the play without being

---

[17]"The system is hospitable! Just as a bourgeois-philistine, without regard to compatibility, takes along every Tom, Dick, and Harry when he goes on an excursion to the woods, inasmuch as there is room enough in the four-seated Holstein carriage, so also is the system hospitable—there is indeed plenty of room. . . . Poor Hamann, you have been reduced to a subsection. . . . Poor Jacobi! . . . the subsection plow plows under all your eloquence, all your inwardness, while a few paltry words are being registered about your importance in the system" (CUP, 1:250-51).

[18]See n. 14 above.

[19]Wholesalers and lower prices fit with "making things easier." On the other hand, "Once when the price of spices in Holland fell, the merchants had a few cargoes sunk in the sea in order to jack up the price. . . . Do we need something similar in the world of the spirit?" (FT, 121). Raising prices fits with "making

named in the cast (*Personer*). Theoretically, these include the "entire
company" as well as the "hostess" at the tea party, which party is
not dramatized (EPW, 107); "the physician" (EPW, 111); three men
identified as "revivalists" (EPW, 112);[20] "a police agent" and "the
police" (EPW, 113). The most prominent of "uncast" characters is
"The President" of the prytaneum, who appears abruptly in act II,
scene 3 (EPW, 118).[21] Then there are "the other members of the
prytaneum" (EPW, 116), perhaps including some cast members;
"beadles" (*Pedellerne*), in this case prytaneum attendants (EPW,
110); "Philologists etc." (is this what becomes of "A Fighter for
Orthography"?—EPW, 120); and "Several speaking at once"—
"A.", "B.", "C.", and "D." (EPW, 122). But these latter are surely
among "the other members of the prytaneum."

Depending upon the number of students, wholesalers, police,
prytaneum members, etc., the cast extends to twenty or more.
Willibald, "a young man," and Echo, "his friend," are paired
(EPW, 106). Echo echoes Willibald, while "friend" (*Ven*) is not
innocent. Mr. von Jumping-Jack (Springgaasen) is "a philosopher."
Mr. Holla Hurrison (Hastværksen) is described as "a provisional
[*foreløbigt*, temporary, interim] genius" (EPW, 106). But a determination of the concept of "genius" is precisely the provisional. That
is, genius, however great, is quantitative and vanishing. Kierkegaard writes in 1846–1847: "The genius may well have something
new to contribute, but this newness vanishes again in its gradual
assimilation by the race, just as the distinction 'genius' vanishes
when one thinks of eternity" (OAR, 105). Mr. Phrase is "an
adventurer, member of several learned societies and contributor to

---

things more difficult." See below, 142-43.

[20]Watkin writes, "It has been suggested that the three revivalists represent
Kierkegaard's brother Peter Christian (1805–1888), Jacob Christian Lindberg (1797–
1857), and Andreas Gottlob Rudelbach (1792–1862). All three at that time were
staunch Grundtvigians" (EPW, 264n.39). The suggestion has been made that
Nikolai Frederick Severin Grundtvig (1783–1872) himself is represented by "A
Horn" (EPW, 262n.14).

[21]Carl Ploug (1813–1894) may stand behind "The President," especially if the
identification of the prytaneum with *Den akademiske Læseforening* is credited (see
EPW, 262n.14 and Thulstrup, 192). Ploug was the first president of the Academy.
See Svend Aage Nielsen, *Kierkegaard og Regensen* (København: Graabrødre Torv's
Forlag, 1965) 76-92, and Kirmmse, *Golden Age*, 61-62.

numerous journals"; and Mr. Ole Wadt, "formerly writing-master," is "acting military adviser" (EPW, 106). We are told that the four "misters" (*Herrer*) are "maintained at public expense in the prytaneum" (EPW, 106). Some seventeen years later, in the so-called "attack on Christendom," the philosophical-professorial misters are joined by priests in being "maintained at public expense": "this silly business of having royal functionaries, which does not so much as require one to have a religion for oneself, but merely to lecture *qua* royal functionary, paid by the State, protected by the State . . . " (KAUC, 134).[22]

"This piece begins very merrily [we should be suspicious], progresses very dismally, yet ends very joyfully" (EPW, 105). Is a drama which is finally "fatalistic" capable of ending *meget glædeligt*?

Kierkegaard refers to "a frontispiece [*et Titelkobber*, a title-copper] showing Luther sitting in a hazel tree cutting switches for people who ask useless questions. Some of them [switches] are to be seen lying on the ground; others will be found scattered around in the book. The inexperienced will perhaps mistake them for dashes" (EPW, 105). How does one stage a frontispiece—or show switches which can be mistaken for dashes "scattered around *in the book*" (italics added; *rundt om i Bogen*)? What *book*? Is this not intended as a *drama*? Or is this anticipation of "theater of the absurd" as well as of Kierkegaard's authorship? Or is this "not

---

[22]See 155, below. Evidence is clear that Kierkegaard had certain associates in mind as models and that a large part of the point of this "drama" was to address (not necessarily to be) the topical: Willibald (Kierkegaard or no?), Echo (Henrik Hertz?), von Jumping-Jack (Johan Ludvig Heiberg? Hans Lassen Martensen?), Holla Hurrison (Orla Lehmann), Phrase (Hans Lassen Martensen?), Ole Wadt (Jens Finsteen Giødwad). See EPW, 260-62, and Thulstrup, 183, 188-92. The tea party, which is mentioned but is not actually in the play, may indeed recall aspects of the famous Heiberg gathering of 4 June 1836. Kierkegaard draws, here as later, upon autobiography; but this does not mean that the party "is" the Heiberg party, that Willibald "is" Kierkegaard, or that autobiography is the "key" to understanding. Watkin assesses the situation: "although, like many an author, Kierkegaard identified himself closely with his literary models, some ideas were already in the literary atmosphere. . . . Thus one probably should not view Willibald as more than a parody of a young Faustian doubter flying into the arms of Hegelianism" (EPW, 261n.7).

quite theater" in a sense similar to that in which Kierkegaard is "not quite" so many other things? Paul Holmer says well that Kierkegaard "shall be to the historians . . . not quite a philosopher, not quite a theologian, not quite a poet."[23] So Kierkegaard is not quite a dramatist (genre-defiance and role-defiance reign) who cannot quite write a play. This is a highly literary work, with quotations, descriptions of "impossible" happenings, and promises of monologue and dialogue threatening to eclipse characters' lines. Stage directions become scene stealers. There is some truth in Henning Fenger's assertion that Soap-Cellars is "proof . . . that Kierkegaard the playwright lacked the talent to write dialogue and to create figures for the stage."[24] Kierkegaard lacked not the talent. This is clear from the authorship which contains much drama and cannot resist first-person speeches, enlivening diverse perspectives.[25] Kierkegaard lacked the interest or, better, pursued his own interests in his own ways. He insisted on being director as well as playwright, and his direction is in the text of his play.

Two references to dedicating the work have in common "mad" (gal)—"Dedicated to the four mad brothers in Claudius" and "Dedicated to the seven madmen of Europe . . . " (EPW, 105). Another considered title is "The Crazier [galere] the Better" (EPW, 105), which may belong together with the From the Papers title. Madness and Soap-Cellars have an affinity for one another.[26] Yet

---

[23]Paul L. Holmer, "Kierkegaard and the Truth: An Analysis of the Presuppositions Integral to His Definition of the Truth," diss. (Yale University, 1946) xi.

[24]Fenger, Kierkegaard, the Myths and Their Origins, 141.

[25]Stephen Crites sees this: "[Kierkegaard] . . . himself had such a deep kinship to the craft of the actor or director or playwright. There is the same keenness of psychological observation, the sense of dramatic development and appropriate dramatic form, the ability to adapt his style to widely divergent personae. He does not simply define in general the various ways of life which are set forth as alternatives to the Christian, but exhibits them concretely from within, projecting himself dramatically into their roles" (C, 43). Anti-Climacus presents one vivid example of Kierkegaard's "first-person proclivity," of the tendency to dramatize in the first person, with his roll call of imagined contemporaries reacting variously to Jesus (see PC, 42-52). Kierkegaard writes, "it became my task to create author-personalities and let them enter in the actuality of life in order to get men a bit accustomed to hearing discourse in the first person" (JP, 6:6440).

[26]Kierkegaard writes, in what is surely a pseudonymous voice, "No. I will not leave the world—I will go into an insane asylum, and I will see if the profundity

one more title option is "The All-embracing Debate on Everything against Everything" (EPW, 105). "Everything" connotes "the system," which pretends to be all inclusive (see, e.g., CUP, 1:133-34). Kierkegaard notes of the title, *The Battle between the Old and the New Soap-Cellars*, that it "seems to imply a misplaced coquetry [*Coquetterie*] . . . " (EPW, 105). A flirtation with the "New"? Willibald's concluding more-than-flirtation with "you absolute spirit who are no longer a secret to me but whose hidden depths I can now plumb" (EPW, 123)? (Here is warrant for "fatalistic drama.") Where is coquetry rightly placed?

"A concluding vignette [*Slutnings-Vignet*] should show Zacchaeus in the sycamore tree" (EPW, 105): this could be staged as a tableau. The reference is to Luke 19:1-10. Zacchaeus "sought to see who Jesus was" and climbed a tree in order to see over the crowd. Luther and Zacchaeus—and both are up a tree. Where shall they find a foothold? Zacchaeus, who sought to see who Jesus was, is looking for a foothold beyond the bounds of *Soap-Cellars*. The proposed "vignette" thus offers an anticipation of the kind of "break away" which is important in the authorship. Writing of Kierkegaard's "pseudonymous theater," Stephen Crites observes that "in every case the point of view from which the work is written is itself transcended within the work, *aufgehoben* or at least rendered problematical, its limitations revealed."[27] So a sermon from a pastor "on the heath in Jylland" breaks away from *Either/Or*, II (EO, 2:337-54). Abraham breaks away from Johannes de Silentio (FT, e.g., 37). "Repetition" breaks away from *Repetition* (FT, 220-22). "Sin" breaks away from *The Concept of Anxiety* (CA, e.g, 21). Christian faith breaks away from *Concluding Unscientific Postscript* (CUP, 561-616). Etcetera. And Zacchaeus breaks away from *Soap-Cellars*—to see what he can see, not within but outside of the play. This is, after all, "a concluding vignette"; and Kierkegaard loves "conclusions" which do not conclude, conclusions which open up and surprise, which confuse and disorient.

---

of insanity will unravel the riddle of life" (JP, 5:5186; see JP, 5:n.245, and JP, 5:n.278).

[27]Stephen Crites, "Pseudonymous Authorship as Art and as Act," *Kierkegaard: A Collection of Critical Essays*, ed. Josiah Thompson (Garden City NY: Doubleday, 1972) 217. Crites's discussion is perceptive and helpful: see esp. 217-19.

How does one present dramatically a quotation in Latin from Sallust's *Jugurtha*? "They will surely be convinced that it is rather from justifiable motives than from indolence that I have changed my opinion, and that greater profit will accrue to our country from my inactivity than from other's activity" (EPW, 106). The inactivity / activity contrast pervades the authorship (thought / existence, possibility / actuality). One implication of this contrast is that changing an opinion is inactivity rather than activity. Activity is not changing an opinion but acting upon it.

More prose (directorial comment) follows: "However, in order that this piece will be useful for something . . . " (EPW, 106). The word "useful" warns that Kierkegaard is up to something; he and his pseudonyms often confess to being—or pride themselves upon being—useless. And lo!—

> Postscript. Since I see, however, that a writer of verbiage at the office of *Kjøbenhavnsposten* always steals a march on me, I must admit with pain that my book [*min Bog*: book again; is this a slip?] is entirely useless, indeed, not even suitable for hammering a nail in a wall. So I am compelled to omit this part in order to avoid being useless. (EPW, 107)

Later, the pseudonyms steal many a march on (*Forkjøbet*, anticipate, preempt) Johannes Climacus: "What happens? . . . *Either/Or* is published. What I aimed to do had been done right here" (CUP, 1:251). "What happens? A book comes out: *Fear and Trembling*" (CUP, 1:261).

One way of being useless is failing to make things easier. In a famous passage in which he smokes a cigar or two at Restaurant Josty in Frederiksberg and determines to become an author (CUP, 1:185-88), Climacus meditates:

> [W]herever you look in literature or in life, you see the names and figures of celebrities, the prized and highly acclaimed people, prominent or much discussed, the many benefactors of the age who know how to benefit humankind by making life easier and easier, some by railroads, others by omnibuses and steamships, others by telegraph, others by easily understood surveys and brief publications about everything worth knowing, and finally the true benefactors of the age who by virtue of thought systematically make spiritual existence easier and easier and yet more and more meaningful—and what are you doing? (CUP, 1:186)

In the world of spirit, where there is no cheating, "easier and easier" amounts not to more meaningful but to less. Climacus reflects:

> [W]hen all join together to make everything easier in every way, there remains only one possible danger, namely, the danger that the easiness would become so great that it would become all too easy. So only one lack remains, even though not yet felt, the lack of difficulty. Out of love of humankind, out of despair over my awkward predicament of having achieved nothing and of being unable to make anything easier than it had already been made, out of genuine interest in those who make everything easy, I comprehended that it was my task: to make difficulties everywhere. (CUP, 1:186-87)

The ironic relation of easy-useful, difficult-useless is present as well as the earnest relation of easy-useless, difficult-useful: "if I were objectively sure (which I as a *subjective* author naturally am not) of the usefulness of my medicine and that this did not depend simply and solely on the way it is used, so that the manner of use is actually the medicine, I would be the first to promise every one of my readers a *raisonnable douceur* (reasonable sweetness) . . . " (CUP, 1:187-88).

Not so suddenly, after struggling through the dense clutter of cryptic introductory notes, we arrive at act I, where as much is described as is dramatized. A "map" will mark the description and help us find our way through this fragmentary, fragmented play.

Act I
Willibald monologue (N.D.)[28]
Tea party—Willibald meets Echo, who echoes Willibald's brilliance and wit (N.D.);
Willibald escapes home to his room (N.D.)
A possibility: Willibald singing and Echo singing[29]—but Echo's echo is inadequate (N.D.)
Scene (not numbered)

---

[28]"(N.D.)" stands for "not dramatized," meaning that Kierkegaard has announced, described, or promised but not written the requisite lines. We are not shown but told.

[29]Echo's song refers to madness: "must one really not go mad [*blive gal*]?" (EPW, 107). See 140 and n. 26.

> Willibald monologue with pipe and books; Echo condenses from a cloud of pipe smoke; dialogue between Willibald and Echo

nonnulla desunt (EPW, 110)

> Echo exits to fetch a physician at the direction of Willibald, who is spitting blood (see EPW, 263n.34) after swallowing a bit of quill pen; now Kierkegaard has Willibald running out of the house and away in a rage
>
> Enter Echo and physician (no articulation of scenes); dialogue with Echo and physician
>
> Return to Willibald (no new scene), who encounters three revivalists (N.D.); Willibald leaves the revivalists, hurries on, is nearly arrested by a police agent out to arrest the revivalists, eludes arrest and "is no longer to be found on earth" (N.D., EPW, 113)

Act II—"A fantastic region. The prytaneum . . . " (EPW, 113)

    Scene 1

> "Ole Wadt   Holla Hurrison" (EPW, 113)
>
> Dialogue between Wadt and Hurrison: soft and steel pens; Hurrison departs in anger

    Scene 2

> "The same[30] Phrase von Jumping-Jack" (EPW, 114) Hurrison, still departing, is halted by Phrase; dialogue among Phrase, von Jumping-Jack, Wadt, and Hurrison: the people, doubt and philosophy, style, life, and finding a foothold

nonnulla desunt (EPW, 116)

    Scene 3

> Willibald discovers himself in the prytaneum with von Jumping-Jack, Phrase, The President, and "the other members of the prytaneum" (EPW, 116); dialogue and von Jumping-Jack's "short account of modern philosophy" (EPW, 116) from beginning (Descartes) to end (Hegel)

nonnulla desunt (EPW, 118)

> Expulsion of von Jumping-Jack; adjournment of prytaneum meeting; Willibald's referral to "the *World-Historical College*" (N.D., EPW, 119), his acceptance of prytaneum views, and his question about

---

[30]Apparently, part of "The same" is the presence of Wadt and Hurrison. But if the scene is "The same," why not have Phrase and von Jumping-Jack enter "*Scene 1*," especially since such an entrance would manifest the uneven legs of von Jumping-Jack? See 148-51, below.

unchanging sunlight in the prytaneum—which occa-
sions a "General Meeting" (N.D., EPW, 120)
General Meeting[31]
"President   v. J. Phrase   Ole Wadt   Holla Hurrison
Polytechnic Students   Philologist etc." (EPW, 120);
The President presents the question of the static light
(N.D.); dialogue between Hurrison and von Jump-
ing-Jack: "out-views," "in-sights," and a "leap"
(EPW, 121-22); more general dialogue, leading to
requests for a vote and a committee; Willibald enters
to explain that his question meant to suggest an
eternal aspect of the prytaneum (N.D.); adjournment
(N.D.)

Act III—"(He is walking in a fantastic region near the prytan-
eum.)" (EPW, 123)
Willibald exults in "wisdom's native land" and "my immor-
tal teacher von Jumping-Jack" (EPW, 123); enter an
Hegelian fly, a political horn, and a "soft" Wadt; Willi-
bald and Wadt exit "arm-in-arm" (EPW, 123)
Suddenly (no indication of entrance or scene change),
Willibald and Wadt are present again: "Willibald, von
Jumping-Jack, Holla Hurrison, Ole Wadt, Phrase, etc."
(EPW, 123); discussion of a new-old name for the
prytaneum
Erecting of a monument and general celebration (N.D.)
The End

(One can almost hear Kierkegaard breathe a sigh of relief.)

Consider, map in hand, further anticipation of authorship. In
act I, *Scene,* a troubled Willibald is in search of self and determined
to break free of "an erudite and very learned professor's . . .
decimal and algebraic calculations" and to "be freed from all
condolences . . . " (EPW, 108). Calculations smother individuality,
and condolences are one of the evils of friendship.[32] A cloud of
smoke from Willibald's pipe prompts reference to "these fog
masses" (*disse Taagemasser*). Kierkegaard wrote in 1835–1836 of "the

---

[31]This "General Meeting" might have been a fourth scene—or a fifth, if one
allows a scene for the Willibald interlude.

[32]After sending Echo off for a physician, Willibald exclaims, "Finally I got rid
of him. Oh, why have I become a social animal, a human being, why not an owl
or a bittern, then I would be free from the worst torment—from friends" (EPW,
110; see EO, 1:33).

way every Christian concept has become so volatilized, so completely dissolved in a mass of fog [*saa aldeles opløst i en Taagemasse*], that it is beyond all recognition" (JP, 5:5181). What can happen to concepts can happen to potential individuals. Frater Taciturnus thinks that "the statistical joy they have in Paris over so and so many superlative people . . . [can] . . . intrude disturbingly and churn the individual [*den Enkelte*] into a froth so that life has no meaning . . . " (SLW, 487). Like fog, like froth: both obscure clarity of concepts and clarity in regard to illusory individuals. Willibald reflects on "these fog masses": "so that is the kingdom where I belong. Oh, look how they condense and *seem to become figures*. . . . Well, now, if I am going to be a shadow myself, I will at least compose a new one, I will create one.[33] . . . (with great feeling) Let there be a person [*et Msk: menneske*, person, human being]. . . . (at that very moment the cloud assumes the form of Echo) What do I see? Is it not my tormentor—my other self . . . " (EPW, 108, italics added; see JP, 5:5186). Something Faustian and demonic is insinuated.

Echo somehow emerges from a cloud of Willibald's tobacco smoke. Willibald strikes at Echo, who is but one of "the whole flock of parrots" (EPW, 108), with a sword; but Echo disappears. Willibald proceeds to direct the sword at himself "but just then happens to cough violently"[34] (EPW, 108) because of accidentally

---

[33]The shift from "compose" [*digte*] to "create" [*skabe*] could suggest a shift from human to divine—to playing God.

[34]Walker Percy has caught this Kierkegaardian irony brilliantly—not with a cough but with toothache and nausea. Will Barrett descends into Lost Cove cave with great deliberation "to settle the question of God once and for all"—that is, to await a sign from God or to die: "Unfortunately for the poor man awaiting the Last Days and raving away at God and man in the bowels of Sourwood Mountain directly below thousands of normal folk ["fog masses"] playing golf and antiquing and barbecuing and simply enjoying the fall colors . . . unfortunately things can go wrong with an experiment most carefully designed by a sane scientist. . . . In the case of Will Barrett, what went wrong could hardly be traced to God or man . . . but rather to a cause at once humiliating and comical: a toothache. So in the end not only did he not get a clear answer to his peculiar question, not a yes or a no or even a maybe—he could not even ask the question. How does one ask a question, either a profound question or a lunatic question, with such a pain in an upper canine that every heart beat feels like a hot ice pick shoved straight up into the brain? The toothache was so bad it made him sick. He

getting part of a quill pen caught in his throat. Now Echo "is heard clearing his throat" (EPW, 108). He knocks on the door and enters. After allusive exchanges, Echo says, "I don't understand you." Willibald comments, "Well said" (EPW, 109). Honesty, understanding, misunderstanding—all are in motion and embedded in the authorship. One example among so many: Climacus instructs, "it is exactly right not to be understood, for one is thereby protected against misunderstanding" (CUP, 83).

In the dialogue which follows, Echo enacts his name:

E. . . . You are bored by parties, so am I.
W. Oh, no, I think they are amusing.
E. Of course, many of them . . . . . you seek solitude.
W. You do, too.
E. Oh, how sad it is to be misunderstood, not to dare to open one's whole heart, yes, misunderstanding, yes, misunderstanding. [The understanding-misunderstanding theme continues.]
W. (with an ironic smile) Yes, but there are cases in which the person concerned can be well served by it.
E. I do not deny that . . . up to a point.
W. All novels lie.
E. I, too, have noticed that. (EPW, 109)

Echo . . . echoes.

Echo's "up to a point" [*til en vis Grad*, to a certain degree] taps another fundamental theme—and irony—in Kierkegaard's authorship: the way in which the quantitative assaults the qualitative and tries, futilely, to attain it. "To a certain degree" is closely associated with "little by little" [*lidt efter lidt*] as a way of trying to trick the qualitative out of its . . . quality (see, e.g., PC, 27-28). Later, Phrase voices his opinion that "one should write for the educated middle class, for wholesalers,[35] polytechnic students, for capitalists, and if one modified the style a little more [*lidt mere*] . . . " (EPW, 115). Wadt wants to "round off the forms [of "modern philosophy"] a little more [*lidt mere*] . . . " (EPW, 115). Von

---

vomited.

"There is one sure cure for cosmic explorations, grandiose ideas about God, man, death, suicide, and such—and that is nausea" (Walker Percy, *The Second Coming* [New York: Farrar, Straus, Giroux, 1980] 186, 213).

[35]See 137 and n. 19 above.

Jumping-Jack maintains that "Kant carried through this skepticism only to a certain extent [*til en vis Grad*] . . . " (EPW, 118). Willibald is "gradually [*efterhaanden*, gradually, by degrees] won over to the views current and recognized in the prytaneum . . . " (EPW, 120). All of this awaits the qualitative concept of "leap," which is introduced in *Soap-Cellars*, but playfully. Von Jumping-Jack:

> I move in the true speculative zigzag. Just as we see that the common fish, the common bird, the common animal, in their mode of travel always move in a simple straight line following the nose, whereas the noble bird of prey, the dignified predator fish, the proud beast of prey, are seen to seize their quarry with a leap [*Spring*], so it goes with the genuine speculative movement. . . . (EPW, 121)

Hurrison, who wants to get on with "life," addresses the general meeting of the prytaneum and refers to von Jumping-Jack (*Spring gaasen*, whose every step is a kind of leap—or "jump"): "Indeed, we are surely right to leap over all his leaps [*ja vi springe vistnok med Rette over alle hans Spring*]" (EPW, 122). This leap anticipates the leap which becomes a central image in the authorship.[36]

After running into the first of the three revivalists and apologizing for so doing, Willibald is to be told (because this "scene" is not dramatized but described) that: "he need not make any apology, for the man well knew he was a great sinner, and it would only please him if he might meet with the good fortune of suffering something for the sake of Christ" (EPW, 112). These words anticipate the important—and problematic—issue of suffering and specifically Christian suffering in the authorship (see, e.g., PC, 108-109). The note, "Great contest between three revivalists . . . as to who is the greatest sinner" (EPW, 112) raises the issue of spiritual pride, which is profoundly developed by Anti-Climacus in *The Sickness unto Death*:

> [D]espair over sin is not averse to giving itself the appearance of being something good. Then it is supposed to be the mark of a deep nature, which therefore is so sensitive about its sin. . . . " I will never forgive myself." This is supposed to show how much good there is in him, what a deep nature he has. It is a subterfuge. . . . He will never forgive himself—but now if God would

---

[36]See JP, 3:2338-59 and JP, 3, p. 794.

forgive him this, well, he certainly could have the goodness to forgive himself. . . . When the sinner despairs of the forgiveness of sins, it is almost as if he walked right up to God and said, "No, there is no forgiveness of sins, it is impossible," and it looks like close combat. (SUD, 111, 114)

At the beginning of act II, we are reminded once again that the "previously mentioned" members of the prytaneum "are maintained at public expense" (EPW, 113). "Everything is arranged triangularly" (EPW, 113): "triangularly" means that Hegel is at hand. In *Scene 1*, Ole Wadt tells Holla Hurrison that his pen is not soft enough ("regarding style") and plays on the meaning of "steel pens" as descriptive of pen and of what is written—and of how. Hurrison: "It has certainly a profound practical meaning, a symbolic significance, that steel has been transferred in this way from lances and spears to pens" (EPW, 113). Is Kierkegaard thinking of the words from Isaiah, "[A]nd they shall beat their swords into plowshares, and their spears into pruning hooks; nation shall not lift up sword against nation, neither shall they learn war any more" (Isaiah 2:4, RSV)? Is the "pen mightier than the sword" because it can function either as a plowshare or as a pruning hook? Wadt identifies "time's sword" with the present and "the soft, flexible, elastic loveliness" with the past (EPW, 113). Hurrison is not interested in the past, "an idyllic state of innocence," but with responsible action in the present, with being "men" (*Mænd*), with "earnestness" (*Alvor*, EPW, 113-14). "Earnestness" becomes a weighty concept in the authorship.[37]

In act II, scene 2, rather cruel sport is made of von Jumping-Jack, "whose one leg is a good six inches shorter than the other . . . " (EPW, 114). In 1846, Kierkegaard paid for such sport—ironically, coincidentally, and painfully, in "*The Corsair* affair" (see COR), when "all of Copenhagen" was obsessed with the length of Kierkegaard's trouser legs: were they indeed uneven?

Phrase expresses concern to "make the great results of scholarship accessible to the people; our time's development ought to gain

---

[37]See David Cain, "Treasure in Earthen Vessels: Johannes Climacus on Humor and Faith," in *Irony and Humor in Søren Kierkegaard*, ed. Niels Thulstrup and Marie Mikulová Thulstrup, Liber Academiae Kierkegaardiensis VII (København: C. A. Reitzels Forlag A/S, 1988) 86-90.

in extensity what it loses in intensity" (EPW, 114). The paramount theme of equality is engaged along with the "'extensity'-easy-superficial / 'intensity'-difficult-meaningful" contrast. In the words of Johannes de Silentio, which are at the heart of Kierkegaard's authorship: "Faith is a marvel, and yet no human being is excluded from it; for that which unites all human life is passion, and faith is a passion" (FT, 67). This formulation guards fundamental ethical-religious equality. To gain in extensity what is lost in intensity is nonsense; for if "extensity" is not the enemy (and equality says there is a basic sense in which it is not), then "extensity" is won through "intensity" and not at the expense of "intensity."[38]

Kierkegaard has fun with von Jumping-Jack's claim to "infinite doubt." "Yes," says von Jumping-Jack, "sometimes I have been troubled by a truly scholarly doubt as to whether I have indeed doubted enough . . . " (EPW, 114). Von Jumping-Jack identifies doubt with "modern philosophy" (see EPW, 264nn.47-48). Wadt joins Phrase in concern about "the style of writing": "Remove some of the sharpness, the angularity, the excessive spikiness, from the many-sidedness of modern philosophy, round off the forms a little more . . . " (EPW, 115). Wadt ever wishes to round and soften the sharp and the hard (steel pens). Von Jumping-Jack declares:

> v. J. . . . Also at stake here is the newer philosophy's profound requirement δός μοι ποῦ στῶ [give me a place on which to stand].[39] But where shall I find a foothold [hvor skal jeg faae Fodfæste] in the vulgar sphere of reasoning? δός μοι ποῦ στῶ.
>
> H. Yes, you must certainly always find it difficult to find a foothold, and that is the case with almost all philosophers who are as poor on foot as you are, Mr. Jumping-Jack.
>
> v. J. That's a low attack.
>
> Wadt. Yes, he lacks form. The offensive shows up so very strongly in his every utterance. (EPW, 115)

Wadt wants to soften the offensiveness and says that Hurrison lacks form [Formen]. (Wadt forgets, perhaps, that he has just called for rounding off the forms [Formerne] of "modern philosophy.") As is characteristic of Soap-Cellars and of Kierkegaard, passion and

---

[38]See 142-43 above.
[39]See 131-33 and n. 4 above and EPW, 265n.53.

earnestness underlie playfulness and jest. Hurrison's "low attack" suggests the "down" moment in von Jumping-Jack's walk. Kierkegaard gives "down" another turn in describing von Jumping-Jack at the beginning of this scene:

> (Mr. von Jumping-Jack is a little unimpressive man, whose one leg is a good six inches shorter than the other, and, in order to illustrate his philosophical ideas, after first having raised himself on the longer leg, he used to desert this illusory standpoint [*Standpunkt*], as he usually expressed it, to win the deeper reality.) (EPW, 114)

(How does one put this meaning on the stage?) Hurrison's "low attack" also underscores the ironic appropriateness of von Jumping-Jack's quest for a place to stand. Von Jumping-Jack's exaggerated condition calls attention to a solemn need for a nonillusory place to stand which, in the name of fundamental human ethical and religious equality, Kierkegaard attributes to us all, and which, as his university years are drawing to a close, he keenly recognizes in himself.

Kierkegaard seems to forget that he is writing a play when he adds: "When von Jumping-Jack was really expounding his skepticism, he used to lay his finger significantly on his nose in order, as Hurrison observed, to have at least one fixed point amid the infinite doubt" (EPW, 115). This is no Archimedean point: one cannot stand on one's nose. In juxtaposition to this concern for a place to stand, Willibald sees the prytaneum and "in joy casts himself on the ground and kisses it" (EPW, 116).

What become rich concepts in the authorship—"appropriation" (*Tilegnelse*) and "repetition" (*Gjentagelse*)—are dropped in passing (EPW, 116). In passing, von Jumping-Jack speaks of a "speculative spiritual adviser" (*speculativ Sjælesørger*), which for Kierkegaard is a contradiction. The following exchanges are a harbinger of Kierkegaard's consideration for communication, direct and indirect:

> *The President.* Since holding such long monologues violates our rules . . . I must, by virtue of my office, interrupt you.
> *v. J.* I would be sorry if I should in any way have been so transported by my eloquence as to transgress the accepted conventions of our society. . . . the reason must be found . . .

with regard to our catechumen [Willibald],[40] whom I wished
to initiate into the correct standpoint [*det rette Standpunkt*: so
von Jumping-Jack has finally found a place to stand] . . . I
venture to call several of the gentlemen present to witness
that the short discourse I otherwise usually hold on modern
philosophy since Descartes, or more correctly, on modern
philosophy, would in no way be too long even in the best
constructed drama [such as this one]. Indeed, Mr. President,
I will wager that it does not last more than one-and-a-half
minutes, because I have prepared it precisely with regard to
our society's requirements.

President. I am obliged once again to call you to order and call
for silence.

v. J. It was Descartes who said. . . .

President. Silentium. . . .

v. J. Spinoza now carried through this standpoint [*dette Standpunkt*]. . . .

President. Beadles, step forward!

v. J. . . . and whereas Kant carried through this skepticism only
to a certain extent [*til en vis Grad*]. . . .

President. Arrest him and take him away.

v. J. Since I see that force will be used, I cannot do the piece on
Schleiermacher, but it was Hegel who. . . .

      (The beadles make as if to seize him.)

Now I have finished, and with Hegel world history is over.

   . . .

Phrase. This is a totally one-sided standpoint [*Standpunkt*] (clears
his throat). Gentlemen, I have gone beyond Hegel; where to,
I cannot yet say very precisely, but I have gone beyond him.

v. J. What do I hear—serpent! Judas! Release me; or must then
the eternal idea always succumb to the mass?

President. Take him away to prison.

      (They lead him away.)

Phrase. I repeat [*gjentager*], gentleman, I have gone beyond Hegel.
      (EPW, 118-19)

(But to repeat is not to go beyond. . . .)

Compare this scene, one of the most amusing in the play, with
the following:

---

[40]This implied confusion of the philosophical and the religious occurs
elsewhere, as when von Jumping-Jack proposes Descartes' words for "confirmation instruction" (EPW, 117).

The object of the communication is consequently not a knowledge but a realization. . . .

An example of the misunderstanding through conceiving instruction aimed at capability as instruction in knowledge. A sergeant in the National Guard says to a recruit, "You, there, stand up straight." Recruit: "Sure enough," Sergeant: "Yes, and don't talk during drill." Recruit: "All right, I won't if you'll just tell me." Sergeant: "What the devil! You are not supposed to talk during drill!" Recruit: "Well, don't get so mad. If I know I'm not supposed to, I'll quit talking during drill." (JP, 1:650, 13-14)

And the recruit grew up to become von Jumping-Jack—or the other way around. The example of the sergeant and the recruit is from a sketch Kierkegaard made in 1847 for a series of lectures on "The Dialectic of Ethical and Ethical-Religious Communication" (JP 1:648-57). Kierkegaard contends, "The ethical does not begin with ignorance which is to be changed to knowledge but begins with a knowledge and demands a realization [or "appropriation"]" (JP, 1:650, 10). Von Jumping-Jack and the recruit fail to turn knowledge into realization. Much of Kierkegaard's authorship explicates, enacts, and contends: "All communication of capability is indirect communication" (JP, 1:651).

Prominent in the authorship as well is the ironic use of "going further."[41] One who claims "to have gone further than" is often one who has not begun to approach that which one claims to have gone farther than. . . . Finally, "going further" betrays confusion or ignorance about that which one claims to have surpassed. So Phrase has gone beyond Hegel but "where to, I cannot yet say very precisely. . . . " *Fear and Trembling* lives with and ends on the irony of going further:

> "One must go further, one must go further." This urge to go further is an old story in the world. . . . Heraclitus the obscure said: One cannot walk through the same river twice. Heraclitus the obscure had a disciple who did not remain standing there but went further—and added: One cannot do it even once. (FT, 123)

---

[41]See David Cain, "Notes on a Coach Horn: 'Going Further,' 'Revocation,' and *Repetition*," in *Fear and Trembling and Repetition*, International Kierkegaard Commentary 6, ed. Robert L. Perkins (Macon GA: Mercer University Press, 1993) 339-45.

The prytaneum suggests that Willibald attend "the *World-Historical College*. This, however, was not yet completed, and only the atrium could be used, but this was so large that four professors lectured there simultaneously without disturbing one another. Indeed, it was so large that the audience could not even hear what the lecturers were expounding . . . " (EPW, 119-20). As writer but not as playwright, Kierkegaard continues in this way, sporting with "professors." The *World-Historical College* is no more complete than is "the system"; and an incomplete system is no system, no matter the size of the "atrium." Does Willibald accept the views expressed—because he "could not even hear what the lecturers were expounding . . . "?

In different ways, both Hurrison and von Jumping-Jack want to go further and to go beyond (EPW, 121-22); and Phrase insists again on his phrase:[42] "I have gone beyond Hegel" (EPW, 122). Hurrison demands a vote. On what? On whether Phrase has gone beyond Hegel? Probably not. Probably the vote is aimed at the problem of light in the prytaneum: is it the "break of day" (Hurrison, EPW, 120) or the "light of evening" (von Jumping-Jack, EPW, 122)? President: "Is it to be by ballot or by show of hands?" (EPW, 122). Hurrison: "I demand that there be a vote on whether there is to be a vote. I am fighting for freedom" (EPW, 122). Wadt hopes for harmony. A Philologist: "I request that a committee of people expert in the study of the past be appointed in order to find out through sound criticism the meaning of the rules" (EPW, 122). (All of this sounds very much like a typical late twentieth-century college or university faculty meeting.) The vote and the committee, too, are Kierkegaard's mockery of numerical advances on truth.

Act III is brief. Willibald has been "won over to the Society's ideas" (EPW, 123) which means: he is lost. He has penetrated the depths of "absolute spirit." The fly and the horn make apocalyptic appearances: "world history is now over . . . " (EPW, 123). Wadt hopes for harmony. Willibald declares: "I think that we should begin a new era and, also to that end, give our Society a new name under which it will nevertheless remain the same. I therefore propose that for the future we call it the New-and-the-Old-

---

[42]"Phrase" = *frase*, but why Kierkegaard's non-Danish spelling?

Prytaneum, written, please note, with hyphens" (EPW, 124). If hyphens may be identified with dashes, we have come full circle and have returned to Luther's switches. Hurrison and von Jumping-Jack respond to Willibald's proposal in what by now has become characteristic fashion. Von Jumping-Jack points out that "the entire incident sheds a remarkable light on a myth that is surely known to everyone present, namely, the battle between the old and the new soap-cellars, and hence the speculative significance of myth is also absolutely evident, that it contains an anticipation of history, a preliminary run, so to speak, to becoming history" (EPW, 124). The soap-cellars' battle has become history in the prytaneum, and history is now completed. Wadt suggests erecting a memorial monument to this great day—with prizes attached: "That reward, both money prizes and official praise, are very beneficial, I have experienced in my time as writing master at Efterslægten"[43] (EPW, 124). Kierkegaard views such external "reward" as destructive of genuine inwardness, as a form of being "maintained at public expense."[44] In the third issue of *The Instant*, dated 27 June 1855, Kierkegaard writes:

> If the State had a mind to put a stop to all true poetry, it would need merely (and remember that poetry is not so heterogenous to this world as Christianity is), it would need merely to introduce 1,000 livings for royal poetic functionaries. In this way the aim will soon be attained, the land will be overfilled continually with badly spoiled poetry, to such a degree that all true poetry becomes as good as impossible. The few who really had a call to become poets will precisely at the critical moment spring [*springe*] away from the effort required to venture out at one's own risk—and into the comfort of a royal office. (KAUC, 136)

Kierkegaard ends his "play" with words written by not quite a dramatist: "Thereupon a monument is erected, on which occasion several enthusiastic toasts are proposed, especially by Willibald" (EPW, 124). Kierkegaard treats toasting, clinking glasses, as an image of superficial alliance, promise, and resolve, as when Climacus contrasts the inwardness of "the pledge for the day

---

[43]"Efterslægten" ("Posterity") is the name of a respected secondary school in Kierkegaard's day (see EPW, 267n.74).
[44]See 139, above.

today" with "that estheticizing hobnobbing [*Klinken*] with our Lord" (CUP 1:488, n.).[45]

Foothold Again

"Where shall I find a foothold . . . ?" *Soap-Cellars* finds Kierkegaard identifying and exploring places, concepts, and themes which will inform his response to this question. At the same time, *Soap-Cellars* has helped Kierkegaard clarify to himself certain directions in which a foothold is not to be found, paths which lead to no existential Archimedean point. Where there are soap-cellars there are soap bubbles which float away, far, far away from a foothold in existence.

A Note on the Manuscript

Niels Thulstrup concludes, "It is, then, hardly possible to arrive at complete assurance on the question of dating. Kierkegaard used the same kind of paper for the whole manuscript and his handwriting is the same, quite neat throughout, so we can not utilize external criteria" (Thulstrup, *Kierkegaard's Relation to Hegel*, 198).

The manuscript is printed as II B 1-21 in *Søren Kierkegaards Papirer*, ed. P. A. Heiberg, V. Kuhr, and E. Torsting, 2nd ed. in 22 vols. supervised by Niels Thulstrup (Copenhagen: Gyldendal, 1968–1970; 1st ed. 1909–1948), 285-306, twenty-one printed pages with five lines on a twenty-second page. Kierkegaard's manuscript is twenty-five and a half pages; but this is misleading because of space equal to half of each page left for marginal notations, additions, etc. The pages are seven and one-half inches wide and nine and three-eights inches high. Kierkegaard wrote the text in what was once a notebook: cardboard covers, brown with blue swirls, stitched together with pages. Regarding the notebook, one page appears to have been torn neatly or cut from the front, whereas nine pages have been ripped from the back. Of what

---

[45]The Swenson-Lowrie translation keeps the image: "this aestheticizing clinking the glasses with Providence" (Johannes Climacus [Søren Kierkegaard], *Concluding Unscientific Postscript*, trans. David F. Swenson and Walter Lowrie (Princeton NJ: Princeton University Press, 1941) 436n.

remains—and this is the text of *Soap-Cellars*—the first four sheets are loose; the other eleven sheets are still part of the notebook. The ink is mainly light brown (sepia) but sometimes dark brown and black. A reddish ink appears to have been used in editing the first two pages, which are a scramble such that what was written first or added later is often unclear. Kierkegaard liked to work in one narrow column down the inside of a page, writing lines about three and a half inches long and leaving an equally or almost equally wide column as outside margin. On the "title page," the cast of characters is written in the inside column, and changes and additions have filled up what was originally the margin column on the outside. On the third page, Kierkegaard underlines "W." and "E." in red to highlight characters' lines. Once launched, Kierkegaard leaves the busyness of the initial pages behind, and the text settles into the writing-column / margin-column pattern with precision and clarity. The written columns are remarkably straight. There are few changes, and the margin columns remain mainly blank. The size of the handwriting varies some but not greatly. The handwriting is small, and there is nothing in the hand which indicates haste (in spite of my suspicion).

8

The Literary Sources of Kierkegaard's
The Battle between the Old
and the New Soap-Cellars

David R. Law

The Battle between the Old and the New Soap-Cellars is the draft of a play Kierkegaard wrote as a twenty-five or twenty-six-year-old student. Despite being the only play that Kierkegaard ever wrote, the *Soap-Cellars* has tended to be neglected by Kierkegaard scholarship.[1] Brandt describes it as "undergraduate nonsense" and writes that "it is easy to understand why Kierkegaard research has given it a wide berth."[2] Similarly, Thulstrup comments, "Earlier researchers passed over it in silence, embarrassed that the great thinker had descended to such things at all."[3] Fenger regards the *Soap-Cellars* as "a further proof—after 'The Master Thief'—that Kierkegaard the playwright lacked the talent to write dialogue and to create figures for the stage."[4] *The Battle between the Old and the New*

---

[1]There has been only a small number of scholars who have devoted their attention to the *Soap-Cellars*, namely, Frithiof Brandt, *Den unge Søren Kierkegaard* (Copenhagen: Levin & Munksgaard, 1929) 419-46; Emanuel Hirsch, *Kierkegaard-Studien* (Gütersloh: C. Bertelsmann, 1933) 432, 556-59; Knud Jensenius, *Nogle Kierkegaard-Studier* (Copenhagen: Nyt Nordisk Forlag—Arnold Busck, 1932) 70-78; Carl Roos, *Kierkegaard og Goethe* (Copenhagen: G. E. Gad, 1955) 130-47; and Niels Thulstrup, *Kierkegaard's Relation to Hegel*, trans. George L. Stengren (Princeton NJ: Princeton University Press, 1980) 180-200; Henning Fenger, *Kierkegaard, the Myths and their Origins*, trans. George C. Schoolfield (New Haven and London: Yale University Press, 1980) 141-42. Walter Lowrie also devotes some attention to the piece in his *Kierkegaard* and in his *Short Life of Kierkegaard*, but simply follows Brandt's analysis. Walter Lowrie, *Kierkegaard* (London: Oxford University Press, 1938) 92, 147; *A Short Life of Kierkegaard* (Princeton NJ: Princeton University Press, 1942) 106.

[2]Brandt, *Den unge Søren Kierkegaard*, 429.

[3]Thulstrup, *Kierkegaard's Relation to Hegel*, 181.

[4]Fenger, *Kierkegaard, the Myths and their Origins*, 141.

Soap-Cellars, then, can hardly be said to be a significant piece in the Kierkegaardian corpus.

Despite the piece's foolishness and apparently trivial nature, however, we must not forget that it was *Kierkegaard* who wrote the *Soap-Cellars*. Consequently, even if the piece is of little value in itself, it may nevertheless provide us with insights into the young Kierkegaard's thinking. The play may, for example, be a practice piece for Kierkegaard's irony and humor and, consequently, be able to shed light on the development of these important characteristics of Kierkegaard's personality and thought. Alternatively, the play may be a transmuted biography and thus provide us with insights into Kierkegaard's early life and his relationship with his contemporaries.

To address such questions and to arrive at a satisfactory assessment of the play and its place in Kierkegaard's intellectual development would require a major study impossible in an essay of this kind. Such a study would demand a thorough investigation of the political, literary, philosophical, and theological developments of 1830's Denmark, as well as a detailed knowledge of the personalities and actions of the students and lecturers at the University of Copenhagen. As Fenger points out, "'The Soap Cellar' is a puzzle the pieces of which can be put in their proper place only after a careful study of the primary sources, in particular the dailies and weeklies of the time."[5]

One of the few things we can be certain of in our interpretation of the *Soap-Cellars* is that it is a parody of Hegelianism. Acts II and III take place in the prytaneum, where Hegelianism reigns and the inhabitants of this exalted realm are constantly engaged in debates concerning Hegelian philosophy and its alleged supersession of all previous philosophies. The philosophical background of the play is thus relatively straightforward. A certain degree of consensus has also been reached with regard to the identity of the *dramatis personae* of the play, at least as far as the major figures are concerned.[6] Less clear, however, is the *literary* background of the play.

---

[5]Fenger, *Kierkegaard, the Myths and their Origins*, 141.

[6]There is a large degree of agreement that Willibald represents Kierkegaard himself. Brandt (*Den unge Søren Kierkegaard*, 421, 430), Hirsch (*Kierkegaard-Studien*, 557), Roos (*Kierkegaard og Goethe*, 145-46), and Thulstrup (*Kierkegaard's Relation to*

It is this question of the literary background of *The Battle between the Old and the New Soap-Cellars* that I wish to consider in this essay. It is hoped that this study of the literary sources of the *Soap-Cellars* may give us some idea of the impulses and influences that led to the formation of Kierkegaard's later thought and to the production of those works that make him such a significant thinker.

Literary Allusions in
The Battle between the Old and the New Soap-Cellars

References to literary issues permeate the *Soap-Cellars*. Kierkegaard has Willibald and Echo discuss Willibald's claim that "All novels lie" (EPW, 109), a discussion which quickly develops into

---

Hegel, 190-91) all argue that Willibald is Kierkegaard. Roos, however, argues that Willibald is a caricature not only of Kierkegaard but also of Martensen and Kierkegaard's generation (*Kierkegaard og Goethe*, 145-46), an argument which is convincingly refuted by Thulstrup (*Kierkegaard's Relation to Hegel*, 189-92). Brandt (*Den unge Søren Kierkegaard*, 421, 430), Roos (*Kierkegaard og Goethe*, 131), and Thulstrup (*Kierkegaard's Relation to Hegel*, 188) all agree that Henrik Hertz is the model for Echo. Hirsch, however, believes that Kierkegaard himself is the model for Echo (*Kierkegaard-Studien*, 557). Both Hirsch (*Kierkegaard-Studien*, 557) and Thulstrup (*Kierkegaard's Relation to Hegel*, 188) are convinced that Ole Wadt is modeled on Giødwad, the editor of the *Fatherland*. According to Brandt, Orla Lehmann is the model for Holla Hurrison (*Den unge Søren Kierkegaard*, 424). Hirsch (*Kierkegaard-Studien*, 557) and Thulstrup (*Kierkegaard's Relation to Hegel*, 188) follow Brandt. There is less consensus over the identity of von Jumping Jack. Roos writes: "The editors of the Papers point to Blicher's *Fjorten Dage i Jylland* (*Fourteen Days in Jutland*) (1836), in which a dancing master, in the chapter entitled 'Gravhøjen' (burial mound), is called Professor Jumping-Jack, and this may well have given an impulse, since Kierkegaard was an admirer of Blicher" (*Kierkegaard og Goethe*, 142). Thulstrup, however, believes that Heiberg is the model for von Jumping Jack, but points out that, exercising the right of poetic license, "Kierkegaard has somewhat changed [Heiberg] in particular and made him say things that historically would more properly belong to Martensen" (Niels Thulstrup, *Kierkegaard and Hegel*, 188). Hirsch, however, believes Heiberg to be caricatured as the president of the prytaneum (Hirsch, *Kierkegaard-Studien*, 557). Both Hirsch (*Kierkegaard-Studien*, 557) and Roos (*Kierkegaard og Goethe*, 143-44) claim that Phrase represents Martensen. Thulstrup too believes that "Mr. Phrase is probably Martensen" (Thulstrup, *Kierkegaard's Relation to Hegel*, 188) and bases his argument on the fact that Phrase's claim to have gone beyond Hegel yet without knowing precisely where, resembles Kierkegaard's comment concerning Martensen in a journal entry made in 1837: "After leapfrogging over all his predecessors he has progressed out into an indeterminate infinity" (JP, 5:5200; n.d., 1837).

a debate on the literary devices employed by novelists (EPW, 109-10). A little later, when Echo has returned with the doctor to minister to the ailing Willibald, only to find that Willibald is no longer in the room, Echo begins to discuss his literary output with the doctor, who beats as hasty a retreat as possible (EPW, 111-12). A further reference to literary matters can be found at the beginning of act II, which opens with Ole Wadt criticizing the style and expression of Holla Hurrison's writings, an inadequacy he attributes to the latter's use of steel pens (EPW, 113; cf. 115).

Alongside these general literary discussions, there are numerous allusions to specific works in the *Soap-Cellars*.[7] Many of these are merely brief quotations. The problem facing the interpreter is that of establishing the significance of these quotations. Does the young Kierkegaard include them in order to impress his audience with how well read he is or are they chosen for more serious reasons? Are they included, for example, because they sum up a particular character's mood or view, or perhaps because they conjure up particular associations in the minds of the audience? If the latter is the case, then such literary allusions play a significant role in carrying the meaning of the play.

The problems of attempting to assess the significance of the literary allusions in the *Soap-Cellar* are well illustrated by Kierkegaard's quotation from Gottfried August Bürger's poem "Lenore."[8] When Echo enters Willibald's apartment (EPW, 108), Willibald

---

[7]There are also occasional references to libretti. In a marginal note to his description of Willibald's return to his room after the unsuccessful tea party, Kierkegaard suggests that "One could also have Willibald sing: Rarely money, but many blows, etc." (EPW, 107), an aria from Mozart's *Don Giovanni*. (This is taken up by J. L. Heiberg in his vaudeville *De Uadskillelige* (*The Inseparable Ones*), first performed at the Royal Theater in June 1827, Hummer's song.) Kierkegaard intended to have Echo sing in reply to this a piece from Scribe's *Bruden* (*The Bride*): "Oh, how bad, Oh, how sad, must one really not go mad?" (Augustin Eugène Scribe, *Bruden*, I,2, trans. J. L. Heiberg, Det Kongelige Theaters Repertoire [Repertoire of the Royal Theater] 35 [1831], pp. 1-2). In this marginal note Kierkegaard also makes a reference to Daniel Auber, the French composer.

[8]Gottfried August Bürger, "Lenore." Kierkegaard presumably used *Bürgers Gedichte* (*Bürger's Poems*) (Gotha and New York, 1828), although this work does not appear in the auction catalogue of his library. A modern edition of the poem can be found in Gottfried August Bürger, *Sämtliche Werke*, ed. Günter and Hiltrud Häntzschel (Munich: Carl Hanser, 1987) 178-88.

addresses him with Lenore's question to her lover Wilhelm: "Wo kommst du hergeritten?" (Whence have you ridden?).[9] Echo replies to Willibald's question by quoting Wilhelm's reply to Lenore: "Wir satteln nur um Mitternacht" (We don't saddle up until midnight").[10] The question that arises here is whether this is merely a passing literary allusion, or whether Kierkegaard wishes to evoke the story of "Lenore" in the minds of his audience. If the latter is the case, then what is Kierkegaard's purpose in doing so and what is the relation of "Lenore" to the plot of the *Soap-Cellars*?

My own view is that Kierkegaard quotes Bürger in order to create some mildly amusing banter between Willibald and Echo. In Bürger's poem the passages quoted by Willibald and Echo form part of a conversation between Lenore and Wilhelm on the latter's return from war. Earlier in the day Wilhelm's army had returned from its campaign in Bohemia and the soldiers had been welcomed with joy by their loved ones. Wilhelm, however, had not been among them, to the great distress of Lenore. In her anguish she doubts the good governance of God and wishes for death. Late that night, however, Wilhelm does appear and persuades Lenore to ride with him into the night to the marriage bed he has prepared for her. They set off at midnight and ride through the night. As dawn approaches, however, Wilhelm becomes visible in his true form: a skeleton with a scythe. It is Death himself that has carried Lenore off. She has received her just punishment for refusing to accept God's will.

Bürger's poem was extremely popular in late eighteenth century and early nineteenth century Europe.[11] It is thus likely that Kierkegaard's intended audience would have been well acquainted with it. By quoting these passages from Bürger, Kierkegaard may have been wishing to conjure up the dark and gothic atmosphere

---

[9]Bürger, "Lenore," l. 112. Kierkegaard's Danish has interfered with Bürger's German, for he misquotes "kommst" as "komst." Kierkegaard has also separated "her" from "geritten," which are written together in Bürger's original.

[10]Bürger, "Lenore," l. 113.

[11]See Peter Boerner, " 'Les morts vont vite' or the European Success of Bürger's Ballad *Lenore*," in *Studies on Voltaire and the Eighteenth Century* 216 (1983): 448-44; Evelyn B. Jolles, *G. A. Bürgers Ballade Lenore in England* (Regensburg: Hans Carl, 1974).

of Bürger's poem. The joke seems to be that instead of following through with the conversation between Lenore and Wilhelm and "saddling up" with Echo, Willibald points out that if Echo intends to saddle up at midnight, then he had better be off, for it is almost one! It is probably the contrast between the gothic atmosphere of Bürger's poem and Willibald's timekeeping that constitutes the "punch line" of this part of the play.

The commentator faces similar problems in assessing the significance of Kierkegaard's literary allusions when attempting to interpret the numerous literary references and quotations with which Kierkegaard opens the *Soap-Cellars*. The first instruction Kierkegaard gives in the preface to the play is that it should be provided with "a frontispiece showing Luther sitting in a hazel tree cutting switches for people who ask useless questions" (EPW, 105). This is then followed by the dedication of the piece "to the four mad brothers in Claudius" (EPW, 105), which is a reference to the four insane brothers of Matthias Claudius' work *Der Besuch im St. Hiob zu*** (The Visit to St. Job's at**).[12] Kierkegaard apparently intended the following verse from this work to be printed in the foreword:

Ach Herr! laß dein lieb Engelein
Am letzten End' die Seele mein,
  In Abrahams Schoß tragen,
Den Leib in sein'm Schlafkämmerlein,
Gar sanft ohn ein'ge Qual und Pein,
  Ruhn bis am Jüngsten Tage. etc.[13]

---

[12]Kierkegaard possessed the 5th ed. of Matthias Claudius, *ASMUS omnia sua SECUM portans, oder Sämmtliche Werke des Wandbecker Bothen*, Werke I-IV (Hamburg: 1838) II:112-15 (ASKB 1631-32). A modern edition of the work can be found in Matthias Claudius, *Sämtliche Werke* (Munich: Winkler, n.d.) 257-59. Kierkegaard seems to have had a moderate interest in Claudius at this time. We find other near contemporary references to Claudius in JP, 4:4406 (dated 26 October 1838), Pap. II A 785 (n.d., 1838), Pap. II B 5 (n.d., 1838), and, eighteen months earlier, JP, 1:770 (dated March 1836).

[13]Claudius, *ASMUS omnia sua SECUM portans, oder Sämmtliche Werke des Wandbecker Bothen* II.(4):115. *Sämtliche Werke*, 259. "O Lord, let your dear little angels / at my end bear my soul / to Abraham's bosom. / Let my body rest in its little bedchamber / peacefully without anguish or pain / until the Day of Judgement."

However, the verse itself does not appear in the text. The instruction to include this verse is then followed by Kierkegaard's request that "a concluding vignette should show Zacchaeus in the sycamore tree,"[14] which is in turn followed by the suggestion of another title for the play, namely "The All-Embracing Debate on Everything against Everything or The Crazier the Better" (EPW, 105). The phrase "the crazier the better" is, Julia Watkin tells us,[15] the refrain from the final song in Johann Herman Wessel's play *Kierlighed uden Strømper* (Love without Stockings).[16] Finally, the preface ends with a second dedication, this time to "the seven madmen of Europe, whom no city has wanted to acknowledge" (EPW, 105). The literary source of this dedication, should there indeed be one, has yet to be identified. It is possible, of course, that it is not a literary reference. Perhaps Kierkegaard is making a joking reference to his circle of acquaintances.

It is very difficult to establish with any degree of certainty what Kierkegaard's purposes are in making these various allusions. What, for example, is the meaning of Kierkegaard's reference to "Luther sitting in a hazel tree cutting switches for people who ask useless questions"? Is Kierkegaard implying by this that Hegelianism is useless and that Luther would be contemptuous of the type of questions debated by the bizarre Hegelian figures that make up the bulk of the play? If so, this statement may indicate a nascent religious critique of Hegelianism in the young Kierkegaard. On the other hand, it is possible that this remark concerning Luther may have been prompted by a conversation—a joke perhaps—among the student friends of Kierkegaard's who would have been the intended audience of the play. If this is the case, then it is highly unlikely that we shall ever discover the meaning of the play's reference to Luther.

It is also difficult to see the significance of the reference to Zacchaeus sitting in the sycamore tree. Is Kierkegaard wishing to

---

[14]Luke 19:1-10.
[15]EPW, 260n.4.
[16]*Johann Herman Wessels samtlige Skrivter* I-II (Copenhagen: 1787) I:119-20. Kierkegaard does not seem to have owned Wessel's works. There is no reference to Wessel in the auctioneer's sales record of Kierkegaard's library.

create a parallel between Luther and Zacchaeus and, if so, what is it? The other three references or allusions in the foreword, however, do seem to have a certain logic about them. They are all linked by the fact that they deal with madness in some way. But why does Kierkegaard make three references to madness on the opening page of his play? Again, it is impossible to arrive at an explanation with any degree of certainty. I would tentatively suggest, however, that the clue to interpreting these references to madness is the linking of Kierkegaard's alternative title for his play "The All-Embracing Debate on Everything against Everything" with the refrain from Wessel's play "The Crazier the Better." The phrase "The All-Embracing Debate on Everything against Everything" has a strong Hegelian ring about it. The Hegelian nature of the title would seem to be confirmed by the contents of the play, which, as we have already mentioned, is primarily a satire on Hegelianism. If the title does indeed refer to Hegelianism, then Kierkegaard's linking of the title with the phrase "the crazier the better" together with the fact that the play is twice dedicated to madmen, would seem to imply that Hegelianism is madness.[17] If we link this with the reference to Luther cutting switches for people who ask useless questions, then Kierkegaard may be implying that Christianity condemns Hegelianism as madness and as guilty of asking useless questions.

After providing a list of the *dramatis personae* of his play, Kierkegaard quotes a passage from Sallust's *Jugurtha*: "They will surely be convinced that it is rather from justifiable motives than from indolence that I have changed my opinion, and the greater profit will accrue to our country from my inactivity than from others' activity" (EPW, 106).[18] Again, the purposes of Kierkegaard in

---

[17]This interpretation would seem to be supported by Kierkegaard's frequent descriptions of speculative philosophy as madness. In a journal entry made in 1839 he writes that philosophers would be well served if they were to adopt "the category of the higher lunacy" he has developed (JP, 2:1581). Other references to Hegelianism as lunacy can be found in EO, 2:158 and CUP, 1:196.

[18]Kierkegaard owned *C. Sallustii Crispi Opera quae supersunt* (*The Surviving Works of Gaius Sallustius Crispus*), ed. F. Kritzius, 2 vols. (Leipzig, 1828; ASKB 1269-70). According to Watkin, the quotation is taken from II:22-23. Kierkegaard also owned *C. Sallustii Crispi Opera* (*The Works of Gaius Sallustius Crispus*), ed. Guil. Lange (Halle, 1833; ASKB, 1271) and *Sallusts Catilinariske Krig* (*Sallust's Conspiracy*

including this quotation are far from clear. Is he making a cryptic reference to a change of opinion on his part? In view of the predominantly Hegelian content of the play, is he confessing that he has revised an originally positive view of Hegelianism to one of hostility? Again, it is impossible to be sure.

Most of the remaining literary allusions and references in the *Soap-Cellars* are merely brief citations that sum up a character's mood or view. This is particularly the case with Willibald's soliloquy in his study, where Willibald makes frequent references to various literary works in order to describe the mental state in which he finds himself. This would seem to be the case with the introduction of Adelbert von Chamisso's *Peter Schlemihls wundersame Geschichte*,[19] which provides the occasion for Willibald's speculation whether he too is a shadow like one of Chamisso's fantasies (EPW, 107). Willibald's reference to "my last fire-breathing gigantic sigh" (EPW, 108) in his soliloquy may be an allusion to Heiberg's *Erasmus Montanus*, while in expressing his dislike of his friend Echo and "the whole flock of parrots" he draws on Suetonius' report in *The Lives of the Caesars*[20] of Caligula's wish that the Roman people had but one neck.

Another indication of Kierkegaard's employment of literary references as a means of characterizing—or perhaps caricaturing—the characters of the play can be detected in the scene in which Willibald flees from his room with the intention of escaping from all human company. As he races away from Echo and from any other form of human company, he hears an out-of-tune clarinet playing a theme from Scribe and Delavigne's *Muurmesteren*: "No, never give up, never give up; friends are always close to

---

of Catiline), trans. from the Latin by R. Møller (Copenhagen, 1811; ASKB, 1273).

[19]Adelbert von Chamisso, *Peter Schlemihls wundersame Geschichte* (*Peter Schlemihl's Wondrous Story*), 3rd ed. (Nuremberg, 1835; ASKB 1630). A modern edition is Adelbert von Chamisso, *Peter Schlemihls wundersame Geschichte* (Stuttgart: Reclam, 1980). Rohde informs us that Kierkegaard bought his copy of this work from Reitzel on 5 January 1836.

[20]Kierkegaard owned C. Suetonii Tranquilli, *Tolv første romerske Keiseres Levnetsbeskrivelse* (*Lives of the Twelve Caesars*), trans. Jacob Baden (Copenhagen, 1802; ASKB 1281).

us,"[21] sentiments which plunge Willibald still further into despair. When, after the interlude of Echo's conversation with the doctor, Kierkegaard again picks up the story of Willibald's flight, we find Willibald reciting aloud to himself a line from Oehlenschläger's *Palnatoke*: "Before, my honor was like a mirror-bright shield of polished steel, . . . now there is a stain of bloody rust on it" (EPW, 112-13).[22] This talk of "bloody rust" attracts the attention of the police, who, however, despite their efforts, are unable to arrest Willibald, for he has now left the earth for the fantastic sphere of the prytaneum.

Goethe

Of more significance than the question of passing literary allusions is the question of what literary models Kierkegaard may have employed in the construction of the *Soap-Cellars*. It is my contention that Goethe's *Faust* plays a significant role in the formation of the *Soap-Cellars*, a view which has also been advocated by Carl Roos, who believes the play to be a parody of *Faust*.[23]

That the *Soap-Cellars* is a parody of *Faust* is indicated by a number of factors. Firstly, as Roos rightly points out, "The basic situa-

---

[21]Augustin Eugène Scribe and Casimir Delavigne, *Muurmesteren*, trans. Thomas Overskou, I.1, *Repertoire* 17 (1829): 1; cf. III.13:18. According to Watkin, Kierkegaard's version deviates slightly from the original text (EPW, 264n.36). Kierkegaard does not seem to have owned this work. He did, however, own *Den første Kjærlighed* (*First Love*), trans. J. L. Heiberg (Copenhagen, 1832; ASKB U 98); *Statsmand og Borger* (*Statesman and Citizen*), trans. Carl Borgaard (Copenhagen, 1844; ASKB U 99); *Verden vil bedrages* (*The World Wants to Be Deceived*) (Copenhagen, 1849; ASKB U 101); (with Mélesville) *Oscar*, trans. A. V. Güntelberg (Copenhagen, 1844; ASKB U 100); and (with E. Legouvé), *Dronning Marguerites Noveller* (*Queen Marguerite's Short Stories*), trans. F. L. Høedt (Copenhagen, 1851; ASKB U 102).

[22]Adam Gottlob Oehlenschläger, *Palnatoke*, V.2 (Copenhagen: 1809) 175-76. According to Watkin, "Palnatoke's lines are somewhat freely recalled" (EPW, 264n.41). Kierkegaard owned *A. Oehlenschlägers Poetiske Skrifter* (*A. Oehlenschläger's Poetical Works*), 2 vols. (Copenhagen, 1805; ASKB 1597-98); A. Oehlenschläger, *Nordiske Digte* (*Nordic Poems*) (Copenhagen, 1807; ASKB 1599); A. Oehlenschläger, *Nordens Guder, et episk Digt* (*Gods of the North: an Epic Poem*) (Copenhagen, 1837; ASKB 1600); *Oehlenschlägers Tragødier* (*Oehlenschläger's Tragedies*), 9 vols. (Copenhagen, 1841-1844; ASKB 1601-1605).

[23]Roos, *Kierkegaard og Goethe*, 141.

tion is the same: a young man who wants to live his life for an idea, a Kaspar Hauser, a dreamer, a madman, is contrasted with those around him, who do not understand him and who, if they humor him, are described as Wagners, Echo, and as windbags."[24]

In addition to this parallel in the situations of the leading characters of the two plays, there are numerous details that indicate that *Faust* provides the basic structure of the *Soap-Cellars*. The clearest indication is Willibald's monologue in his room in act I. The setting and dramatic structure of this monologue resemble two episodes in Goethe's *Faust*. In the first episode Faust is sitting in his study lamenting the fact that all his learning has failed to bring him the knowledge and joy for which he had hoped. To console himself he opens "this mysterious book, written by Nostradamus's own hand."[25] Surely this should be sufficient guide for him, he asks himself. Opening the book, he catches sight of the sign of the macrocosm, that is, a diagram of the magical relations that bind together the elements within the universe and hold the world together. Gazing at the diagram of the macrocosm Faust feels the fire of youthful, sacred *joie de vivre* rushing anew through his body. This, however, is only a fleeting feeling, for he quickly realizes that this diagram is merely a magnificent spectacle[26] that cannot bring him any nearer to his true goal, namely that of grasping infinite nature, of understanding life itself.[27] Disappointed, he turns over the pages of the book and comes across the sign of the Earth Spirit. Gazing at this symbol, he feels closer to the Earth Spirit than he did to the sign of the macrocosm. As he gazes at the sign he feels his powers increase and is imbued with new courage to venture out into the world and to bear the pain, joy, storms, and shipwrecks of life.[28] At this point clouds gather around him, the moon hides her light, the lamp in his study grows dim, mists rise all about him, red shafts of light play about his head, and a shudder descends from the vault of his study and seizes him.[29] Faust senses

---

[24]Roos, *Kierkegaard og Goethe*, 139.
[25]Goethe, *Faust*, ll. 419-20.
[26]Goethe, *Faust*, l. 454.
[27]Goethe, *Faust*, ll. 455-59.
[28]Goethe, *Faust*, ll. 460-67.
[29]Goethe, *Faust*, ll. 468-74.

that the Earth Spirit is hovering about him. He seizes the book and utters the sign of the Earth Spirit in a mysterious fashion. A red flame flares up, in which there appears the Earth Spirit's dreadful countenance. Unable to bear the sight, Faust averts his gaze from the Earth Spirit, who then mocks Faust for resembling more a cringing worm than the "superman" he imagines himself to be.[30]

The second episode in Goethe's *Faust* that possibly underlies the setting and dramatic structure of Willibald's monologue is the entrance of Mephistopheles. While taking a walk on Easter Sunday with his amanuensis Wagner, Faust is followed home by a black poodle. He takes the dog into his study and allows it to sit behind the stove on his best cushion. Faust then embarks upon the task of translating the Gospel of John into German, beginning with the prologue. Faust's efforts to find an appropriate rendering of ἐν ἀρχῇ ἦν ὁ Λόγος disturb the poodle, which begins to howl and bark. Suspecting that the poodle's aversion to hearing the Gospel may indicate that the animal is not all that it seems, Faust attempts by means of various spells to force the creature to reveal its true identity. When these fail to work Faust holds up the cross. This has the desired effect. To Faust's astonishment the animal expands to elephantine proportions before dissolving into mist, out of which there emerges Mephistopheles.[31]

It is my contention that Kierkegaard has modeled act I of the *Soap-Cellars* on these two scenes from Goethe's *Faust*. Evidence to support this claim is provided by the parallels that exist between Willibald and Faust. Both are described by their authors as sitting in a study, surrounded by books and papers; both are absorbed in a book. Faust is reading Nostradamus; Willibald is engrossed in Adelbert von Chamisso's *Peter Schlemihls wundersame Geschichte*. The parallel continues in the fact that both Faust and Willibald evoke a spirit out of flame, smoke, or mist. Faust invokes the Earth Spirit by means of magical incantations and later Mephistopheles emerges from clouds of mist in his study. Willibald creates the character Echo out of cigar smoke.[32] It is this deliberate evocation

---

[30]Goethe, *Faust*, ll. 482-98.

[31]Goethe, *Faust*, ll. 1178-1321.

[32]Roos points to a possible parallel between act I of the *Soap-Cellars* and the dedication with which *Faust* opens: "Like Goethe himself in the dedication to

of Goethe's *Faust* in the minds of his audience that constitutes the joke of act I of the *Soap-Cellars*. Whereas Faust consults the mysterious, magical work of Nostradamus, Willibald chooses von Chamisso's bizarre and humorous novella. Similarly, whereas Faust calls up spirits from the underworld and wrestles with the titanic forces of evil, Willibald creates a counterpart to his own self out of cigar smoke.

In addition to these parallels there may be other allusions in act I of the *Soap-Cellars* to Goethe. Roos[33] links Willibald's comment that he "can soon entertain the hope of adorning a naturalist's study like a freak of nature under a glass bell" (EPW, 107) with the homunculus created by Wagner in a phial in act II of *Faust* II.[34]

Acts II and III of the *Soap-Cellars* also contain allusions to *Faust*, although not to the same degree as act I. Act I of the *Soap-Cellars* ends with Willibald fleeing from the company of his fellow human beings. The police seek to apprehend him after the suspicion of a police agent sent to arrest the revivalists is aroused by Willibald's singing a verse from Oehlenschläger's *Palnatoke*. The failure of the police to arrest Willibald indicates, Kierkegaard writes, that Willibald is no longer to be found on earth. Act II then opens with a description of "a fantastic region" (EPW, 113). It is to this fantastic region that Willibald has been transported (EPW, 116), an event that fills him with joy: "He cries out joyfully at being freed from the whole of that life in which he hitherto toiled like a slave and at finding himself transported to a region where wisdom must necessarily dwell" (EPW, 116). This sudden transition from one realm to another bears some degree of resemblance to the end of *Faust* I and the opening of *Faust* II. At the end of *Faust* I Faust too makes an abrupt departure. Mephistopheles whisks him away from the cell in which Gretchen is imprisoned and where Faust is in danger of himself being arrested. Then, with no explanation of how Faust got there, *Faust* II opens with a description of Faust

---

Faust, [Willibald] sees himself surrounded by clouds of fog which condense into shadows (Ihr naht euch wieder schwankende Gestalten . . . Versuch ich es, euch diesmal festzuhalten), and like Goethe he gives one of the shadows existence, not Faust, but his Wagner, Echo" (*Kierkegaard og Goethe*, 141).

[33]Roos, *Kierkegaard og Goethe*, 141.

[34]Goethe, *Faust*, ll. 6819-7004.

attempting to sleep on a lawn covered with flowers in a "graceful" or "elegant region" (*anmutige Gegend*). The angel Ariel, accompanied by small, graceful spirits, sings to the accompaniment of aeolian harps and lulls Faust into a sleep of forgetfulness, in which he is able to forget the pain and guilt of his relationship with Gretchen and recover the strength to experience the next adventure Mephistopheles has in store for him. Both main protagonists of *Faust* and the *Soap-Cellars*, then, are whisked away from their previous existence and transported to a sphere in which peace reigns. However, whereas this experience equips Faust with the strength to return to reality in order to enjoy the next experience arranged for him by Mephistopheles, Willibald remains in the fantastic region to which he has been transported.[35]

Further evidence for our claim that Goethe's *Faust* underlies the structure of the *Soap-Cellars* is provided by Willibald's first conversation with von Jumping-Jack after having arrived at the prytaneum. Willibald exclaims: "Without actually knowing where I have arrived, it is nevertheless always a comfort to me that we, that I, have left the home of all my afflictions. The external environment, the total impression, has awakened in me a joyful notion, a happy presentiment, that wisdom must be found here, that here I can be healed of all the abominable relativity under which I hitherto have suffered" (EPW, 116). To this von Jumping-Jack replies: "My dear fellow! I fully perceive what ails you. It is the Faustian problem" (EPW, 116). Kierkegaard himself, then, draws attention to the parallel between Willibald and Faust. The connection between them is that both are racked with doubt, dissatisfied with their lives, and are seeking for something to overcome this plight. Whereas Faust turns to Mephistopheles to provide a solution, Willibald's salvation is to come through Hegelianism.

The remainder of act II consists primarily of Hegelian banter and contains, as far as I can ascertain, no further references or allusions to Goethe. Act III, however, opens with what may well be an

---

[35]If this interpretation is correct, it undermines Brandt's claim (*Den unge Kierkegaard*, 421) that there is no connection between act I on the one hand, and acts II and III on the other hand in the *Soap-Cellars*. The connection is the structure provided by *Faust* and, in particular, the transition from *Faust* I to *Faust* II.

allusion to *Faust*. In the scene "Forest and Cave",[36] Faust, all alone, prays to "the exalted Spirit [who] gave me, gave me everything that I asked for."[37] Act III of the *Soap-Cellars* opens with a similar scene, in which Willibald prays to the Absolute Spirit. The similarity between *Faust* and the *Soap-Cellars* continues in that both Faust and Willibald give thanks to the exalted/Absolute Spirit for providing them with knowledge. The nature of this knowledge differs, however. Faust thanks the Spirit for giving him "magnificent nature as his kingdom and the power to feel it and enjoy it"[38] and that it has been granted to him to "gaze into nature's deep breast as if into the bosom of a friend."[39] Willibald, on the other hand, prays to "you absolute spirit who are no longer a secret to me but whose hidden depths I can now plumb" (EPW, 123). Faust, then, gains insight into the essence of nature and receives the power to enjoy it; Willibald, through the good offices of Hegelianism, gains knowledge of the Absolute Spirit itself.

It seems clear, then, that Goethe's *Faust* was a major influence on the *Soap-Cellars*. Much of the dramatic structure of the play seems to be deliberate parody of *Faust*. Willibald's monologue in act I reflects Faust's musings in the early part of *Faust* I. Both Willibald and Faust are dissatisfied with their lives and are searching for something that will give their lives meaning and content. Thus Faust fails to find peace in the works of the ancients or in his various experiments. He craves direct and immediate knowledge of the foundation of all Being. Failing to find this in scholarly activity he turns to magic, the ultimate result of which is the appearance of Mephistopheles, who persuades him to abandon the scholarly life for real life. Willibald, on the other hand, fails to find peace with himself and in the company of other human beings. He makes the reverse movement to that of Faust. He abandons real life for the ideal sphere of Hegelianism. Thus although the dramatic structure is to a large extent due to Goethe, the conceptual content is provided by Hegel. Goethe's *Faust* provides the framework within which Kierkegaard's parody of Hegel can take place. The troubles

---

[36]Goethe, *Faust*, ll. 3217-3373.
[37]Goethe, *Faust*, l. 3217.
[38]Goethe, *Faust*, ll. 3220-21.
[39]Goethe, *Faust*, ll. 3223-24.

of the Faustian doubter Willibald are overcome when he turns not to the pleasures of earthly experience promised by Mephistopheles, but when he makes a different sort of diabolical pact, namely one with Hegelianism.

Eichendorff

The claim that Eichendorff has influenced the *Soap-Cellars* is based first and foremost on the name of the main figure of the play, "Willibald." The name "Willibald" is a German name that is virtually unknown in Denmark. This raises the question of why Kierkegaard should have given this name to the main protagonist of his play.

There are a number of possible sources for this name. Hirsch mentions the opinion voiced by some of his Danish acquaintances that the name may be derived from Willibald Alexis, the nom de plume of Georg Wilhelm Häring, who in 1828 published his *Herbstreise durch Skandinavien* (Autumn Journey through Scandinavia). Hirsch, however, rejects this view on the grounds that Kierkegaard had no knowledge of Alexis.[40] Certainly, a survey of Alastair McKinnon's indexes[41] and Niels Cappelørn's index to Kierkegaard's *Papirer*[42] reveals not a single reference either to Alexis or to his real name. Roos, too, rejects the theory that the name "Willibald" is dependent upon Willibald Alexis, claiming that "nothing in [Alexis'] historical novels with its subject matter from Prussian history could have been thought to have awakened Kierkegaard's interest."[43]

Another possible source of the name "Willibald" is E. T. A. Hoffmann's short story *Die Räuber* (The Robbers).[44] This novella

---

[40]Hirsch, *Kierkegaard-Studien*, 432.

[41]Alastair McKinnon, *The Kierkegaard Indices*, vol. 2, *Konkordans til Kierkegaards Samlede Værker* (Leiden: E. J. Brill, 1971); vol. 3, *Index Verborum til Kierkegaards Samlede Værker* (Leiden: E. J. Brill, 1973).

[42]N. J. Cappelørn, *Søren Kierkegaards Papirer*, vols. 14-16, *Index* (Copenhagen: Gyldendal, 1975–1978).

[43]Roos, *Kierkegaard og Faust*, 144.

[44]See E. T. A. Hoffmann, *Sämtliche poetischen Werke* (*Collected Poetical Works*) (Berlin: Tempel, 1963) III:684-720. Kierkegaard owned E. T. A. Hoffmann, *Ausgewählte Schriften* (*Selected Writings*), 10 vols. (Berlin, 1827–1828; ASKB 1712-16),

describes how two friends, Hartmann and Willibald, take a holiday from their business affairs in Berlin and set out for the south. In Bohemia they are attacked by a band of robbers and Hartmann is wounded. They are taken in by a friendly count, who puts them up in his castle. Strangely, all the people living in the castle have the same names as those in Schiller's tragedy *Die Räuber*. The tragedy described by Schiller then unfolds before Hartmann and Willibald and reaches the same terrible conclusion. Kierkegaard must certainly have known of Hoffmann's *Die Räuber*, for it is mentioned in Eichendorff's *Viel Lärmen um Nichts* (Much Ado about Nothing), with which, as we shall see in due course, he was well acquainted. We also know from Kierkegaard's works and diaries that he was well read in Hoffmann's works. Indeed, references to Hoffmann's works far outnumber those to Eichendorff's writings.[45] Is it then not possible that Kierkegaard derived the name "Willibald" from Hoffmann rather than from Eichendorff? This seems unlikely, because although Kierkegaard frequently cites and quotes Hoffmann in his writings and journals, he nowhere makes any mention of *Die Räuber*.[46]

This does not rule out that Hoffmann may nevertheless have exerted some influence on the *Soap-Cellars*, however. In his critique of Brandt's claim that the relationship between Willibald and Echo and the plagiarism of the former's words by the latter is a parody of Kierkegaard's relationship with Hertz, Hirsch points out that, "the literary form . . . , namely, that one person at a banquet has the ideas, while another person utters them and gains the credit for them, comes from E. T. A. Hoffmann's *Klein Zaches genannt Zinnober* (Little Zach, called Vermilion), a fairy tale that is known to

---

Erzählungen aus seinen letzten Lebensjahren (Stories from the Last Years of His Life), 5 vols. (Stuttgart, 1839; ASKB 1717-21), *Klein Zaches genannt Zinnober* (Little Zach, Called Vermilion) 2nd ed. (Berlin, 1824; ASKB A II 268).

[45]Near-contemporary references to Hoffmann can be found in EPW, 63; LD, letter 8, p. 53; JP, 2: 1688; 2:1699; 5:5109, 5148, 5162, 5223, 5241; Pap. I C 86, p. 239; I C 92; I C 93; I C 94.

[46]The only possible exception to this is if the reference in EO, 2:225 to "a robber chief" is an allusion not to Schiller's *Die Räuber*, as Hong and Hong suggest (EO, 2:489n.68), but to Hoffmann's work of the same name.

have had a very profound impact on Kierkegaard (cf., e.g., XIII 55)."[47]

In her notes on the *Soap-Cellars* Julia Watkin points out that, "A main character is also named Willibald in Christoph Martin Wieland, *Euthanasia*" (EPW, 261, n. 7). We know from a reference to "Wieland's 'irony' " in a journal entry dated 2 June 1837 that Kierkegaard had some knowledge of Wieland's work around the time of his composition of the *Soap-Cellars* (JP, 2:1688). Is it not then possible that it is Wieland rather than Eichendorff who provides Kierkegaard with the name of the main character of the *Soap-Cellars* and who has possibly influenced other features of the play? This seems unlikely for a number of reasons. One reason for doubting Wieland's influence on Kierkegaard is the fact that Kierkegaard adopts Eichendorff's spelling "Willibald" rather than that of Wieland, who prefers "Wilibald." A further and more significant reason is that it is apparent from the auction catalogue of Kierkegaard's library that of Wieland's works Kierkegaard possessed only *Die Dialogen des Diogenes von Sinope* (The Dialogues of Diogenes of Sinope)[48] and Wieland's translation of Horace's letters.[49] It is, of course, theoretically possible that Kierkegaard read

---

[47]Hirsch, *Kierkegaard-Studien*, 557. A modern edition of Hoffmann's novella can be found in E. T. A. Hoffmann, *Sämtliche poetischen Werke*, 3 vols. (Berlin and Darmstadt: Tempel, 1963) 1:979-1072. Klein Zaches is a deformed dwarf with a growth on his back and legs as "thin as hazel switches" (*Werke* 1:982). Despite these disadvantages he is able to work his way up to Minister of State by means of three magic hairs placed on his head by the fairy Rosabelverde. By means of these magic hairs, Hoffmann writes, "everything excellent that somebody else thinks, says, or does in [Klein Zaches's] presence is credited to *him*, so that in the company of well educated, sensible, and intelligent persons, he too is regarded as well educated, sensible, and intelligent. Indeed, he is considered to be the most perfect of the genus with which he is in conflict" (*Werke* 1:1047).

[48]C. M. Wieland, *Die Dialogen des Diogenes von Sinope* (Leipzig, 1770; ASKB, H 474). This work can be found in the republication in 14 vols. by the Hamburger Stiftung zur Förderung von Wissenschaft und Kultur (The Hamburg Foundation for the Promotion of Science and Culture) of the 39 vols. edition of Wieland's *Sämmtliche Werke* published 1794–1805: C. M. Wieland, *Sämmtliche Werke*, 14 vols. (Hamburg: Hamburger Stiftung zur Förderung von Wissenschaft und Kultur, 1984) vol. 12.

[49]*Horatzius Briefe* (*The Letters of Horace*), trans. C. M. Wieland (Leipzig, 1816; ASKB, AI 164-65).

Wieland extensively without actually owning his works. However, the sparsity of references to Wieland in Kierkegaard's works and journals would seem to make this unlikely. Furthermore, with one single exception all references to Wieland occur in entries written after 1847, almost a decade after the composition of the *Soap-Cellars*. The one exception to this is the journal entry of 2 June 1837, which, as mentioned above, makes a reference to "Wieland's 'irony.' " This, however, fails to provide sufficient evidence to support the claim that Wieland has influenced Kierkegaard's writing of the *Soap-Cellars*, for, as Howard and Edna Hong point out, the reference to Wieland's irony is "possibly a reference to the ironic sayings of Diogenes of Sinope," with which Kierkegaard had become acquainted through Wieland's translation of Diogenes' dialogues and perhaps through Wieland's *Nachlaß des Diogenes von Sinope* (Unpublished Works of Diogenes of Sinope). Of Kierkegaard's later references to Wieland we find two references to *Agathon* (JP, 6: 6813 (date: 1852); 3: 3530 (date: 1853)) and to *Aristipp und seine Zeit* (Aristippus and his Age) (JP, 5: 6036 (date: 1847); 3: 3328 (date: 1850)). The picture that emerges from our discussion so far, then, is that Kierkegaard used Wieland as a source of information concerning the ancient Greeks but for little else.

The only direct reference to Wieland's *Euthanasia* occurs in a journal entry made in 1847 and, significantly, it indicates that, almost a decade after the composition of the *Soap-Cellars*, Kierkegaard had *not* read *Euthanasia*: "Sometime I should read a book by Wieland: *Aristipp und seine Zeit*, also one of his latest treatises, *Euthanasia: "wie hat es der Mensch anzufangen um heiter und schmerzlos zu sterben"* (Euthanasia: 'what must the human being do in order to die cheerfully and painlessly')" (JP, 5:6036).

This should provide sufficient evidence that Wieland's *Euthanasia* is not a literary source for the *Soap-Cellars*. This conclusion is further supported by the contents of Wieland's book. *Euthanasia* consists of three conversations between Wilibald, his sister Blandine, and a friend Selmar concerning the possibility of life after death. In these conversations the character of the Willibald of the *Soap-Cellars* bears little resemblance to that of the Wilibald in *Euthanasia*. The former is a restless figure, troubled by self-doubt and in search of a greater meaning in life. The latter is a somewhat cold individual, who seems to live by logic alone. The conclusion to which we are inevitably drawn, then, is that Wieland's *Euthanasia* must be excluded as a possible literary source for the Soap-Cellars.

The most likely source for the name "Willibald" is, as Hirsch points out,[50] Eichendorff's *Viel Lärmen um Nichts*.[51] We can point to both external and internal evidence for Eichendorff's influence on the *Soap-Cellars*. The external evidence consists of references and allusions to Eichendorff's works written around the time of the composition of the *Soap-Cellars*. While this external evidence does not actually prove Eichendorffian influence on the *Soap-Cellars*, it does at least show that Eichendorff's writings were occupying Kierkegaard's attention at this point in his authorship.

We know from Kierkegaard's writings and diary entries that he had some interest in Eichendorff around the period in which he was writing the *Soap-Cellars*.[52] He seems to have been drawn in

---

[50]Hirsch, *Kierkegaard-Studien*, 432.

[51]Although dependence on Eichendorff is probably the best explanation of the inclusion of the name "Willibald," there may be a much more mundane explanation. The name Willibald is a composite of the German words "Wille," meaning "will," and "bald," which is an archaic German word meaning "bold." The German *Stammbuch der Familie* (a book for the recording of family events), issued by the Registrar of Marriages to all newly wed couples and which contains a list of first names permitted to children by German law, translates it as "der Willenskühne," the bold of will. Kierkegaard had, even prior to his visit to Berlin in 1841–1842, a good reading knowledge of German, and it may be that the idea of an individual who was "bold of will" particularly appealed to him. If Kierkegaard was aware of the meaning of the name, it may tie in with the comment on the title page of the play that the play is published against *his will* "from the papers of one still living." This thesis does not, of course, in itself undermine the contention that Eichendorff's *Viel Lärmen um Nichts* constitutes a significant literary source of the *Soap-Cellars*. Indeed, it may indicate one of the reasons why Eichendorff's novella has influenced the play.

[52]We also know from the auctioneer's catalogue of Kierkegaard's library that he owned Joseph von Eichendorff, *Dichter und ihre Gesellen* (Poets and their Companions) (Berlin, 1834; ASKB 1633), *Gedichte* (Poems) (Berlin, 1837; ASKB 1634), and *Viel Lärmen um Nichts* (in a volume together with Clemens Brentano, *Die mehreren Wehmüller und ungarishen Nationalgesichter* [The Several Melancholy Millers and Hungarian National Faces]) (Berlin, 1833; ASKB 1850).

particular to a verse from *Dichter und ihre Gesellen* (Poets and their Companions):[53]

> Zwei Musikanten ziehn daher
> Vom Wald aus weiter Ferne,
> Der eine ist erliebt gar sehr,
> Der andre wär es gerne.
>
> Die stehn allhier im kalten Wind
> Und singen schön und geigen:
> Ob nicht ein süßverträumtes Kind
> Am Fenster sich wollt zeigen?[54]

In a letter to Regine Olsen (LD, Letter 21, pp. 67-68; JP 5:5480, n.d., 1840) Kierkegaard quotes both stanzas, writing of the first: "What is here separated in two, love unites; he is in love, and yet at the same time he is constantly wishing to be so: a restiveness, a yearning, a longing make him wish at every moment to be what he already is at that very moment" (LD, Letter 21, p. 67). Kierkegaard applies the second stanza to Regine herself. In particular he applies to her the phrase "süßverträumtes Kind" and comments, "I hope this phrase may be applied to you and that you have not become too anxious at the thought that I might suddenly measure one foot between the eyes" (LD, Letter 21, p. 68). We also find the first two lines of Eichendorff's verse in the "Seducer's Diary", where it is adapted to apply to women rather than men in love (EO 1:356).

A further possible reference to Eichendorff may appear in the *Concept of Irony*, when Kierkegaard writes: "In the poetry of the romantic school . . . a *Taugenichts* (good-for-nothing) is always the most poetic character . . . " (CI, 281). This reference to *Taugenichts* may well be an allusion to Eichendorff's *Aus dem Leben eines Taugenichts* (From the Life of a Good-for-nothing), the novel which established his reputation.

---

[53]Since Kierkegaard quotes this with reference to *Dichter und Gesellen*, it is probable that he knew it from this source and not from the poem "Vor der Stadt" ("Before the Town"). See Eichendorff, *Werke* 1:58-59.

[54]Eichendorff, *Werke* 2:303. "Two musicians journeyed thence / from the forest far away / One of them is much in love / the other would like to be. / They stand here in the chilly wind / and sing beautifully and play their fiddles / hoping that a sweet dreamy child / might appear at the window.

By far the most important external evidence for Eichendorff's influence on the *Soap-Cellars*, however, is Kierkegaard's review of *Viel Lärmen um Nichts*, written sometime in 1836 (*Pap.* I C 86, pp. 238-40).[55] A number of factors emerge from this passage that are significant for our discussion of the literary sources of the *Soap-Cellars*. Firstly, it is clear from the review that Kierkegaard is very much taken by the novella, for he praises it highly. It is also interesting to note that he recognizes the novella to be a satire on the romantic movement, a movement which he regards as being guilty of abandoning the real world for a dream world. He understands Eichendorff to be making the point that such abandonment of the real world is impossible and that reality before long breaks into the dream-reality created by romanticism: "As this movement aimed at abandoning real life in order to dream itself into a vanished age, this situation became still more withdrawn and anxious (instead of just giving life freshness and strength, as it should) by the fact that there is a reaction in time against it, so that its attempt to tear itself out of the world became still greater, principally by means of a movement which aimed at forgetting the present; time, however, continued to exert its pressure upon them." (*Pap.* I C 86, p. 239).[56] Kierkegaard is also impressed by the irony and humor of the novella, writing that, "It is also quite remarkable that the irony [of the piece] is carried through completely. This irony expresses itself as the ridicule of single individ-

---

[55]Hirsch claims that Eichendorff's *Krieg den Philistern* (*War on the Philistines*) may also have influenced the *Soap-Cellars*. He writes: "[T]he literary form [of the *Soap-Cellars*] is that of the romantic satirical comedy with secret, tragic background. Of the romantic productions of this kind that are known to me, Eichendorff's *Krieg den Philistern* is the most closely related" (*Kierkegaard-Studien*, 557). Unfortunately, Hirsch does not provide any arguments to support this suggestion. It is true that we have a rivalry between two opposing groups in *Krieg den Philistern*, namely, between the poets and the petty bourgeois, and that this may be reflected in the rivalry between the two Hegelian groupings in prytaneum, but there is sufficient material of this kind in *Viel Lärmen um Nichts* to make recourse to *Krieg den Philistern* unnecessary. In addition to this, Hirsch's claim is further undermined by the fact that, as far as I have been able to ascertain, Kierkegaard nowhere mentions or alludes to *Krieg den Philistern* in either his works or journals.
[56]All translations of Pap. I C 86 are my own. A translation of Pap. I C 86 does not appear in JP.

uals or larger crowds of people; simply the contrast between the sentimentality of such individuals and the real external circumstances in all their true, prosaic nakedness causes the comical" (*Pap.* I C 86, p. 239). Perhaps most significant of all is Kierkegaard's comment that "One of the features which otherwise gives the novella its characteristic stamp is the simultaneous abandonment of real life and the ideal conflict with real life. This seems to me to be a great work, in which the surrounding life breaks in on those living in fantasy and with their gaze fixed on the past as suddenly as the chorus in Shakespeare" (*Pap.* I C 86, p. 240). Kierkegaard, then, is attracted by the irony and humor of the work and in the clash between reality and ideality that it portrays.

What is the significance of all this for our claim that Eichendorff's *Viel Lärmen um Nichts* is one of the literary sources of the *Soap-Cellars*? Firstly, it is clear that Kierkegaard was attracted by the piece and regards it as a fine piece of satire. It is customary for human beings to imitate that which they admire, so it may well be the case that at this period of his authorship Kierkegaard regarded *Viel Lärmen um Nichts* as a good model for the prosecution of his own satirical interests. Secondly, many of the features Kierkegaard comments upon in Eichendorff's piece are features that are present in the *Soap-Cellars*. It lies near at hand to suggest that the satirical elements of the *Soap-Cellars* may thus have been prompted or at least colored by Eichendorff's irony and humor. To justify this claim, however, we must turn from our consideration of the external evidence of Eichendorffian influence to a comparison of the *Soap-Cellars* with *Viel Lärmen um Nichts*.

The title of *Viel Lärmen um Nichts* is derived from the Tieck-Schlegel translation of Shakespeare's *Much Ado About Nothing*, namely, *Viel Lärm um Nichts*. The basic plot of *Viel Lärmen um Nichts* concerns a beautiful lady called Aurora. A certain Herr Publikum (Mr. Public) has invited her to his residence. Arriving at the same time at Publikum's residence, Prince Romano, a poet and romantic probably modeled after Pückler-Muskau, makes Aurora's acquaintance in comical circumstances and resolves to woo her. The rest of the novella centers around Romano's attempt to win Aurora's hand, although this basic plot is frequently interrupted by amusing anecdotes and digressions. The reader is led to believe that Romano has achieved his goal, for emerging out of the forest after various adventures, Romano finds that a wedding with Aurora has been prepared for him. Far from being pleased at this unexpected sight, however, Romano beats a hasty retreat, disappearing into the forest never to be seen again, leaving Herr Publikum to marry Aurora. The sting in the "tale" and the reason for Romano's sudden departure is that Aurora is not in fact Aurora but Aurora's maid. The true Aurora had disguised herself as Florentin, a young hunter. Her heart belongs to Willibald. The novella concludes with the two lovers setting off for Italy, watched by the anonymous author, who knew Willibald from their student days together in Halle.

The novella is concerned first and foremost with the relation and misrelation of appearance and reality. According to Cornelia Nolte,[57] this contrast between reality and appearance (*Sein und Schein*) functions on two levels and is expressed in two different treatments of "appearance" that occur in the piece. Firstly, there are those individuals who strive to appear to be *more* than they really are. Secondly, there are those who appear to be something *other* than what they really are. The chief representatives of the first form of appearance are Romano and (false) Aurora.

The misrelation between Romano's appearance and reality emerges very early in the novella. While the others are still sleeping off the aftereffects of the previous night's festivities, Prince Romano is already up and striving to cover up all the defects in his appearance that have resulted from a misspent youth.[58] The clearest expression of this misrelationship between appearance and reality in Romano, however, can be found in a strange episode much later in the novella. Prince Romano is riding to Count Leontin's castle by night.[59] Losing his way in the dark, he decides to wait for morning and so halts for the night and lies down to sleep in the open. During the night he dreams that he is making a nocturnal visit to his sweetheart. Making his way to where she lives, he comes to a garden gate, where he finds a

---

[57]Cornelia Nolte, *Symbol und historische Wahrheit: Eichendorffs satirische und dramatische Schriften im Zusammenhang mit dem sozialen und kulturellen Leben seiner Zeit* (Paderborn: Ferdinand Schöningh, 1986), 63.

[58]Eichendorff, *Werke* 2:662-63.

[59]Eichendorff, *Werke* 2:680-83.

servant lying on the threshold like a dead man. All the better, Romano says to himself, for he can now make his way to his lover unobserved. Entering the garden, he finds everything quiet, when suddenly he catches sight of the tall and graceful form of his sweetheart stepping seductively from out between the trees. As he pursues her, however, it seems to him as if it is his own shadow that is fleeing from him across the lawn, before disappearing among some dark bushes. At last he catches her and seizes her by the hand, only to discover to his horror that it is his own hand he has grasped. "Let me go," he cries, "you're not the one I love. This is all just a dream." "I am and have always been the one you love," replies his hideous image, adding, "You are now awake and not dreaming as usual." The ghost now begins to caress him with grinning tenderness. Horrified, Romano flees from the garden to the sound of horrible laughter.[60]

This strange story expresses Romano's discovery that the life he is leading is unreal. His life is not real life at all, but is merely the *appearance* of real life. He treats the appearance-reality he has created for himself as if this were genuine reality, but in actual fact this appearance-reality is merely an illusion, a dream. Paradoxically (and satirically), it is only in his dream that he discovers his true reality, namely that his real self is a dream reality he has created for himself. Dream-reality is the means by which Romano discovers that his existence is itself a dream-reality.

What is the significance of this portrayal of Romano? Romano represents a false understanding of poetry. He makes use of the poetic as a means of disguising, indeed creating, reality. As a result, he is guilty of confusing poetry with reality. The true poetical attitude, however, is not to employ poetry as the means of escaping reality but as the means by which the human being can penetrate to the transcendent reality that underlies all that is. Poetry must not become an end in itself but must function as the medium and mediator of transcendence.

It is possible that this episode may have influenced the scene in the *Soap-Cellars* in Willibald's study. In his study Willibald first conjures up Echo out of tobacco smoke, before the "real" Echo

---

[60]Eichendorff, *Werke* 2:682.

knocks on his door and makes his appearance. Although Willibald's confrontation with Echo is not as horrible as that of Romano with his shadow, there are some clear similarities. Alone in his room reading Chamisso's *Peter Schlemihl* Willibald compares himself to "one of Chamisso's fantasies . . . a shadow myself who therefore cannot cast any shadow" (EPW, 107). However, in *Peter Schlemihl* the eponymous character of the work is not himself a shadow but has sold his shadow for money. Willibald's description of *himself* as a shadow thus does not correspond exactly to the contents of the book he is reading. It does correspond more closely, however, to Romano's dream, in which it seems to Romano that he is chasing his own shadow. A further echo of this episode from *Viel Lärmen um Nichts* may occur in Willibald's conjuring up of Echo from tobacco smoke. Willibald describes this nubilous image of Echo as "my tormentor—my other self" (EPW, 108). Romano, when he grasps hold of what he takes to be his sweetheart, is horrified to discover that he has seized hold of himself. Like Echo with Willibald, this "other self" then torments Romano. In view of the fact that idea of being tormented by the "other self" is common to both *Viel Lärmen um Nichts* and the *Soap-Cellars*, it is possible that Kierkegaard may have been influenced by Eichendorff at this point.

The second major character in whom there exists a negative disrelationship between appearance and reality is (false) Aurora. She too appears to be more that she actually is. To all appearances she is the Countess Aurora, "whose poetic nature and enchanting beauty was celebrated by all the poets in the land."[61] It emerges in the course of the novella, however, that the reality underlying this beautiful, poetic appearance is quite different. The Countess Aurora wooed by Prince Romano, Herr Publikum, and praised by the various poets that pepper the novella is none other than the real Aurora's *chambermaid*. Throughout the novella there are hints of Aurora's true identity. The deception only becomes apparent to Romano, however, when he is on the point of being married to Countess Aurora, marriage being a bourgeois institution that is incompatible with the romantic ideal of love. The bourgeois and *eo*

---

[61]Eichendorff, *Werke* 2:660.

ipso nonpoetic nature of Aurora is made still clearer by her behavior when she is left standing at the altar by Romano, for her
reaction is far from poetic. It is one of fury at having lost the
opportunity of making a good match.[62] Her desire for marriage is
soon fulfilled, however, for she is shortly afterwards joined in holy
wedlock with Herr Publikum, who, as Nolte puts it, "is only too
willing to believe the appearances set before him."[63]

The other two leading characters in the novella are Willibald
and Florentin. The Willibald of *Viel Lärmen um Nichts* is a wanderer and, like most of the other characters in the work, a romantic
and a poet. Willibald makes his appearance approximately half
way through the novella. Prince Romano is making his way on
horseback through the forest by night, when he and his companion
run into Willibald.[64] A brief conversation reveals that both parties
have the same destination, namely the castle of Count Leontin, and
they resolve to continue the journey together. At Leontin's castle
the two travellers join a larger party for dinner, where the wine
flows freely. Leontin's cheerfulness and good wine leads the
company to decide to spend what little remains of the night each
telling a story from his or her life. It is in this context that Willibald next makes his appearance. Apparently profoundly excited by
his fairy-tale-like surroundings, he tells the following story.

In his student days Willibald once went on a trip with several
friends from Halle to the Harz mountains. In a tale permeated
with romantic descriptions and allusions, he relates how he and
his companions broke their journey one evening at an inn. Sitting
down at a table at the top of a slope, they spent the evening drinking wine and praising their sweethearts, whether they had one or
not! Willibald, elated by the wine and the rustling of the forest,
suddenly sprang to his feet, proposed a toast to his future beloved,
and, dropping his ring into the now empty wine glass, hurled both
glass and ring out into the sunset. At that very moment a beautiful
woman on horseback raced across the green plain. Catching sight
of the ring sparkling in the evening light, she looked up in

---

[62]Eichendorff, *Werke* 2:713.
[63]Nolte, *Symbol und historische Wahrheit*, 80.
[64]Eichendorff, *Werke* 2:690-91.

astonishment at Willibald, before riding on.[65] Willibald resolved to make the young lady's acquaintance. Discovering the inn where she and her companions were staying and learning that they intended to climb Mt. Rosstrapp on the following day, he managed to persuade one of her guides by means of a substantial bribe to let him take his place.[66] But that night Willibald slept too soundly and when he awoke the women had already left. Taking a short cut, Willibald eventually managed to catch up with the party and take his place as their guide. Sometime later, when the young lady's elderly companion needed to rest, the young lady left her with her two servants and "flew like a deer over the green plain."[67] Willibald pursued her as quickly as possible, but was only able to catch up with her on the pinnacle of Mt. Rosstrapp, where he found her sitting with her legs dangling over the edge of a cliff. The young lady demanded that Willibald lead her down, for "a proper guide should know every path."[68] Willibald, knowing the area well, led her down through the rocks and past the chasms and crevices all around them. At one point they had to leap over a deep chasm to a promontory on the other side. Willibald went first and then turned and held open his arms to catch the young lady. When she jumped into his arms, Willibald took advantage of this propitious moment to press her to him and plant a passionate kiss on her beautiful lips. Quickly pulling herself away, the young woman wiped her mouth with some distaste, and, complaining that Willibald had led her down the wrong path, disappeared into the undergrowth with a laugh. As she did so, Willibald was astonished to see that she was wearing the ring he had hurled from the cliff-top the day before. Nonplussed, at a loss at what to do, and with his emotions all awhirl, Willibald now stood alone in the wilderness. In vain he sought to catch the beautiful young lady. Often he believed her to be quite close but then she would somehow suddenly appear far away above the treetops, before disappearing once more into the undergrowth. Then he would hear

---

[65]Eichendorff, *Werke* 2:701.
[66]Eichendorff, *Werke* 2:702.
[67]Eichendorff, *Werke* 2:704.
[68]Eichendorff, *Werke* 2:705.

her sweet laughter waft over to him and see her waving and calling to him, constantly teasing him.

Finally, he believed he could perceive his beautiful lady far below him when suddenly he caught sight of her, laughing loudly, like an elf floating high above him from the highest peak of the mountain they had left earlier. At this scornful treatment of his love Willibald's pride was roused and he hurled his staff against the cliff, where it shattered, and full of anger he made his way down into the chasm.

The young lady did not seem to expect this. At least it seemed to Willibald when he looked up one last time that she suddenly appeared pale and frightened. Indeed, as he quickly made his way down between the rustling of the treetops and the murmuring of the brooks, it seemed to his great astonishment as if she were repeatedly calling his name, as if she were calling after him from the depths of her soul: my dear, dear Willibald!

On hearing this Willibald underwent a change of heart and once again began to climb the mountain in search of his beautiful lady, but nowhere was he able to find a trace of her and her companions. Exhausted, he eventually returned to the same isolated inn he had left that morning. Inquiring of the people there what they knew of the mysterious, beautiful lady they stared at him in astonishment: a party such as that described by Willibald had not spent the night at the inn.

Willibald concludes his story by telling his companions that he never again saw the beautiful lady of Mt. Rosstrapp, but he has never forgotten her image. Looking up he discovers that every one of his audience is fast asleep.

In his review of *Viel Lärmen um Nichts* Willibald's story is one of the episodes to which Kierkegaard points as an example of Eichendorff's exquisite irony. He writes that, "in the first place the irony lies in the fact that that angel and almost supernatural beauty, who here plays the main role, is personally present without Willibald suspecting it; in the next place the irony lies in the fact that he has safely finished his story and finds that the guests have fallen asleep just at a time when he believes that he has expressed something of the deepest reality in his existence" (Pap. I C 86, p. 240).

Willibald's final appearance takes place at the conclusion of the novella.[69] The novella's concluding scene is told from the perspective of the (anonymous) author of the novella, who, hearing of the forthcoming union of Herr Publikum and the renowned Countess Aurora, had set out for Publikum's residence in order personally to present the happy bridegroom with a novella that he had written specially for the occasion. The author, however, arrives too late and finds that the wedding celebrations are already well advanced. As he stands leaning against a tree listening to the music and thinking of the happy days of his youth, a young hunter suddenly runs through the bushes and falls breathless into his arms. Before the author knows what is happening, the young hunter pushes him along in front of him, while frequently looking back over his shoulder. "What on earth do you think you're doing," the author asks when they have gone further into the garden. At this the young hunter stops short and, looking the author up and down, asks him who he is and what he is doing here. The author introduces himself and explains the purpose of his journey. The hunter begins to laugh at this and tells the author that the latter should save his speech for him, the hunter. He, too, wishes to get married. While all this has been taking place, the two men arrive at the exit of the park, where two saddled horses stand tethered. The author and the young hunter mount their horses and ride as fast as an arrow into the night. As they ride, they hear a charming song coming from some distant bushes. The young hunter, who has in the meantime introduced himself as Florentin, then squabbles with the musicians, before continuing his ride. Behind them they hear the musicians singing the name "Wil- Wili- Willibald!"[70]

Day is beginning to dawn when, after a wild ride, they arrive at a castle in the mountains, where Florentin behaves as if he were at home. Florentin is clearly looking for someone, but when he asks at the castle whether the person he is expecting has arrived, he is told to his great consternation that no one has turned up. Entering the castle, Florentin and the author make their way

[69]Eichendorff, *Werke* 2:715-21.
[70]Eichendorff, *Werke* 2:718.

through innumerable magnificent rooms towards the garden. Sitting down at the threshold of the castle, Florentin sings a melancholy song, bursts into tears and rushes into the garden. Concerned for the young man's welfare the author searches for him in the garden. After wandering about in the garden for some time the author at last hears Florentin's cheerful chatter. As he steps out from the bushes the author is astonished to see a stranger resting against the slope of the garden. Sitting at his feet and gazing happily at him is Florentin. Suddenly the author recognizes the stranger. It is Willibald, whom the author knew from Halle and with whom he had once journeyed to the Harz mountains. "You're here too?" Willibald exclaims, "as well as my darling from Mt. Rosstrapp," pointing to Florentin. To the author's astonishment Florentin reveals himself to be Countess Aurora and that he/she has passed her maid off as herself in order to make a fool of her "mad suitor."[71] Only Romano had spotted what was up. In the course of the conversation it emerges that Aurora has bought the estate on which they find themselves in order to give it back to Willibald, its ancestral owner. Aurora then tells the author the whole story of what has happened, from the beginning to the end. The couple then set out for Italy, and in the distance the author hears them singing:

Und über die Felsenwände
Und auf dem grünen Plan
Das wirrt und jauchzt ohn Ende,
Nun geht das Wandern an![72]

How are we to interpret the figure of Willibald and his relation to Florentin/Aurora? We should probably take the two Willibald scenes together if we are to succeed in making sense of them. According to Nolte, the first episode "is an account of nothing less than the first encounter of the poet and singer Willibald with his Muse, his first contact with the world of the Eternal, his first

---

[71]Eichendorff, *Werke* 2:720.
[72]Eichendorff, *Werke* 2:721. "And over the cliff faces / And on the verdant plain / There is excitement and exultation without end / Now the roaming begins!"

experience of poetry."[73] Willibald's love, then, does not exist in the
real world, something which is indicated by the fact that no one
else has observed his beloved or is aware of her existence when he
asks after her at the end of the first episode. If Willibald is to win
her, he must abandon this world, an act which is symbolized by
his joining the party of travellers, in order to find his muse. Once
Aurora and Willibald have left behind the rest of the party, the
episode takes on a new quality. Pursuing Aurora across the rocks
and crevices of Mt. Rosstrapp, Willibald feels as if he is in a
dream.[74] According to Nolte, this is the cue for "a change in perception; [Willibald] has crossed over from the 'rational' world into
the uncertain and dangerous sphere of the dream."[75] However, this
movement from reality to dream-reality is not in itself sufficient to
win Aurora. If Willibald is to avoid Romano's fate and avoid the
dream becoming a nightmare, it is not enough to search for the
muse; he must also be "called." He thus has to undergo a rite of
initiation. Nolte claims that this test of Willibald's vocation is laid
down by Aurora, when she demands of Willibald: "A proper
guide should know every path, lead me down quickly."[76] Willibald
takes up the challenge and leads Aurora down into the abyss. He
fails the test, however, not because he is not called, but because he
treats Aurora as his earthly beloved and not as a heavenly muse.
Catching her after both have jumped over a crevice, he takes
advantage of the situation to kiss her on the lips. With this the rite
of initiation is interrupted: " 'Ugh,' she cries, hastily freeing herself
and wiping her mouth; 'look, because of your nonsense you've
failed to take the right path.'"[77] She then disappears, leaving
Willibald to pursue her in vain.

Willibald's first attempt to win his love thus ends in failure.
This, however, proves to be only a temporary setback. In the final
episode he is finally united with his muse, who reveals herself to
be the true Aurora. Also significant in this final episode is the
introduction of the personality of the author. Willibald, the

---

Nolte, *Symbol und historische Wahrheit*, 85.
Eichendorff, *Werke* 2:705.
Nolte, *Symbol und historische Wahrheit*, 85.
Eichendorff, *Werke* 2:705.
Eichendorff, *Werke* 2:705.

author's alter ego, is united with Aurora, the poetic muse. This poetic existence of Willibald's is not mere appearance without substance in the manner of Prince Romano, however, but is the acceptance and incorporation of transcendence into Willibald's existence. This is true poetic existence: existence that genuinely expresses the transcendent, the infinite, and the eternal, not merely the exploitation of poetry as a means of disguising the poverty, shallowness, and hollowness of one's existence. Florentin/Aurora and Willibald, in contrast to their false counterparts Romano and false Aurora, bring appearance and reality together into a genuine whole.

This analysis of the role of Willibald in *Viel Lärmen um Nichts* would at first sight seem to indicate that the Willibald of the *Soap-Cellars* and Eichendorff's Willibald have little in common. Eichendorff's Willibald is a cheerful individual, given over, like most of the other characters in the novella, to romantic fantasies. Kierkegaard's Willibald on the other hand is, at least in act I, a rather morose individual. However, if we turn away from detailed, direct comparison of the two works to consider what *general* impulses Kierkegaard may have gained from a reading of *Viel Lärmen um Nichts*, then a number of interesting points emerge.

One interesting feature of Eichendorff's novella is that it is a satire on developments in German literature in the late 1820's. According to the editors of the *Eichendorff-Kommentar*,[78] the target of Eichendorff's satire was the change from romanticism to bourgeois realism that took place in German literature around 1830. Eichendorff was a member of the so-called "Wednesday Society" (*Mittwochgesellschaft*), founded in 1824 by J. E. Hitzig, which included among its members Adelbert von Chamisso, Willibald Alexis, Friedrich de la Motte-Fouqué, Karl von Holtei, and Karl Schall. Opposing this society and its literature was another literary society called the "Berlin Sunday Association" (*Berliner Sonntagsverein*),[79] founded by Moritz Gottlieb Saphir in 1827. The members of this society were adherents of realism in

---

[78]Ansgar Hillach and Klaus-Dieter Krabiel, eds., *Eichendorff-Kommentar* (Munich: Winkler, 1971), 148; see also Eichendorff, *Werke* 2:969-70.

[79]The association later changed its name to "Tunnel over the Spree" ("Tunnel über der Spree").

literature. The rivalry between these two groups reached a climax in 1828, but flared up again in 1831.

Perhaps the clearest expression of this rivalry in *Viel Lärmen um Nichts* can be detected in the discussion among the "novel makers," who early in the novella get together in order to determine the plot. Rejecting romanticism, they wish to introduce realism into the proceedings. In reply to a poetess's inquiry as to what is going on, a young man replies:

> A new idea of the highest importance, the consequences for the whole of literature of which are hard to foresee. . . . Now, I know, O most honored one, that you have long shared our conviction that those extravagant, artificial inventions in poetry alienate us from nature and little by little impose a wondrous, conventional, nowhere existent, written life on the living. To put it another way, these inventions have set a Bible above tradition, so we must return to reality posthaste.[80]

A "gray man" then adds to this the comment that every novel the novel makers write, regardless of subject, will without compromise be drawn from real life. Everything, a young man adds, is to be simple and natural.[81]

Eichendorff's satire on the relationship between romanticism and realism can also be seen in the ironic and humorous conclusion of the stories and anecdotes related in the novella. On several occasions in the novella a character describes an event or tells a story full of romantic imagery, in which something extraordinary, magical, or fairy-tale-like has allegedly occurred. The true explanation for these extraordinary events, however, turns out to be quite mundane. For example, Romano describes a truly gothic experience at a castle where the living dead seem to be at work.[82] The true explanation for his astounding and horrifying experience, which initially seems to repeat itself at the gates of Count Leontin's castle, is merely that Leontin was eloping with his beloved and they had both put on masks in order not to be discovered. It was these masks that accounted for the death-like appearance of Leontin and his two companions and not, as Romano supposed,

---

[80]Eichendorff, *Werke* 2:671.

[81]Eichendorff, *Werke* 2:671.

[82]Eichendorff, *Werke* 2:691-98.

that the three of them belonged to the living dead! Many other examples of this kind could be cited. The satire consists in the fact that all the fantastic events described in *Viel Lärmen um Nichts* turn out to be mundane events with quite ordinary, everyday explanations. In other words, the romanticism of the various characters in the novella is constantly forced to give way to realism. I suggest that this satire on the rivalry between romanticism and realism may have given Kierkegaard the idea for a satire on (Hegelian) philosophy. The "direction" of the satire is "reversed," however. Whereas Eichendorff's satire is to reduce the fantastic imaginings and imagery of romanticism to the mundane, Kierkegaard translates Willibald's earthly existence into the fantastic realm of the "pure" philosophy of Hegelianism.

Conclusion

The Battle between the Old and the New Soap-Cellars marks an early stage in the development of Kierkegaard's critique of confusing thought with being, philosophy with existence. One of the impulses for this critique seems to have been Eichendorff's *Viel Lärmen um Nichts*, which is a satire on an inadequate understanding of poetry, namely the use of poetry as a means of escaping from reality rather than as the means of transfiguring reality. Kierkegaard seems to have adopted this critique and transposed it to philosophy. The *Soap-Cellars* is a satire on those who confuse philosophy with reality.

The structure of the play, especially act I, seems to be based on Goethe's *Faust*. The scene in the study is surely intended to be a parody of Faust's study and the figure of Willibald, as a number of scholars have observed, clearly bears the hallmarks of the Faustian doubter. The play can thus be said to be a loose fusion of Goethe, Eichendorff, and Hegel, viewed through the prism of contemporary intellectual trends and student life.

The *Soap-Cellars* also gives us an insight into the development of Kierkegaard's irony and its application to Hegelianism. Kierkegaard is clearly influenced by romantic irony, particularly that of Eichendorff, whose satirical skills he greatly admired. Kierkegaard, however, transposes this irony from the literary to the philosophical sphere. Nevertheless, the thrust of the irony of the two writers is similar. In *Viel Lärmen um Nichts* Eichendorff is satirizing those who employ poetry as a means of escaping life rather than using it as the means to penetrate to the infinite which underlies finite existence. Kierkegaard's use of irony is levelled first and foremost at Hegelian philosophy. It, too, constitutes an escape from life as the transition from earthly existence in act I to the ethereal existence of the prytaneum in act II makes clear.

As well as indicating the development of Kierkegaard's anti-Hegelianism, the *Soap-Cellars* also gives us an insight into Kierkegaard's misgivings concerning romanticism, for the transition from act I to act II can also be read as a satire on the romantic movement. The melancholy, Byronic figure of Willibald abandons his reading of Chamisso and his literary discussions with Echo and finds the solution to his doubt and despair not in romanticism but in Hegelian philosophy. However, on arriving in the Hegelian paradise, he discovers that it is divided into two camps and that the unity Hegelianism promises is far from being achieved. Interestingly, one of the weapons Kierkegaard uses against Hegelianism is romantic irony. Thus although the Willibald of the *Soap-Cellars* abandons romanticism for Hegelian philosophy in act I, we find a feature of romanticism being employed to undermine the philosophical system that had apparently rescued Willibald from the impasse of romanticism.

In conclusion, it should be clear that *The Battle between the Old and the New Soap-Cellars*, despite being the only play Kierkegaard ever wrote, can hardly be said to be a significant piece. It does, however, give us an insight into the development of his thought. In particular, it provides an insight into his growing critique of both romanticism and Hegelianism and his employment of the tools of the former as weapons with which to attack the latter.

Contributors

International Kierkegaard Commentary 1
Early Polemical Writings

DAVID CAIN is Distinguished Professor of Religion at Mary Washington College in Fredericksburg, Virginia.

BRUCE H. KIRMMSE is Professor of History at Connecticut College in New London, Connecticut.

GRETHE KJÆR, an independent Kierkegaard scholar, lives in Hellerup, Denmark.

DAVID R. LAW is Lecturer in Christian Thought at the University of Manchester.

GEORGE PATTISON is Dean of Chapel at King's College, Cambridge.

ROBERT L. PERKINS is Professor of Philosophy at Stetson University in DeLand, Florida.

RICHARD M. SUMMERS, an independent Kierkegaard scholar, resides in London.

JULIA WATKIN is Lecturer in Philosophy at the University of Tasmania, Australia.

Advisory Board

Index

Abraham, 141
Absolute Spirit, 173
Academic Lecture Association (*Den adademiske Læseforening*), 134, 138
Ahasverus. *See* Wandering Jew
Albeck, Gustav, 56-57
Alexis, Willibald, 174, 191
Ammundsen, Valdemar, 10n.
Andersen, Hans Christian, 3-4, 8, 17, 45-57, 64, 66, 69-88, 109, 119, 124, 124-30
Andersen, Wilhelm, 55, 56
Anderson, G. K., 110n.1
androgyny, 20
anonymity, 102
Andreasen, Uffe, 122
anti-Semitism, 111, 128-30
appropriation, 151, 153
Archimedes, Archimedean point, 132-33, 151,156
Arnim, Achim von, 112
Auber, Daniel, 162n.7

Bagger, Carl, 57
Baggesen, Jens, 60
Barfod, H. P., 8
Bertung, Birgit, 12, 16
Biel, Charlotte Dorothea, 10
Blicher, Steen Steensen, 53, 87, 163n.6
Boemer, Peter, 163n.11
Boisen, Eline, 11n.
Borup, Morten, 9n., 15n.
bourgeois realism, 191
Brandes, Georg, 51
Brandt, Frithiof, 51, 124, 159, 161n.6, 172n.35
Bredsdorff, Elias, 51, 73-74, 82-85
Bremer, Fredrika, 13-17
Brontë, Charlotte, Emily, and Anne, 10n.
Buntzen, Johan, 8, 88, 94
Bürger, Gottfried August, "Lenore," 162-64

Byron, George Gordon, 56

Cain, David, 5-6, 149, 153
Caligula, 167
Camilla Collett, 15n.
Cappelørn, Niels Jørgen, 174
caste systems, 21
Chamisso, Adelbert von, 167, 170-71, 184, 191
chauvinism, 7-25
Christ, 110-13, 116-18, 148
Christian VIII, 133
Christianity, 166
church, People's Church, 27
Claudius, Matthias, 164
Clausen, H. N., 30
Collett, Camilla, 15n.
Collin, Jonas (the Younger), 81-88
communication, 151, 153
communism, 19
Connell, George, 49
Constant, A.-L., 115
Copenhagen Post, The, (*Kjøbenhavnsposten*) 19, 30, 35, 37, 41
corporate responsibility, 37
Corsair, The, 27
Crites, Stephen, 140-41
Croxall, T. H., 10n.

Delavigne, Casimir, 167
Descartes, R., 144, 152
despair, 124-25, 130
Don Juan, 119, 130
Dostoevsky, F. M., 127-28
doubt, 150-51
Drewsen, Viggo, 82-85
Dupin, Armadine Lucile Aurore, Baronne Dudevant, 11
duty, 103
Duveyrier, Honoré, 91

earnestness, 143, 149, 151
easy/difficult, 142-43

Pattison, George, 3-4, 55, 115n., 119n., 121n.
Percy, Walker, 146-47
Perkins, Robert L., 2-3
personality, person, 49, 55
Petersen, Teddy, 9, 20, 27, 30, 34
Philip of Navarre, 110
philosophy, modern, 144, 150, 152
Plato, 35, 37, 42
Ploug, Carl, 138
poetry, 191, 193
political discourse, 35, 39, as a matter of taste, 42
politics, 27-44, 105
press, 2-3, 7, 27-44
    freedom of, 28-29, 34
    self-justification, 34
pride, spiritual, 148

Quinet, E., 114-19, 125

Rahbek, Kamma, 10
Rahbek, Knud Lyne, 10n., 90, 92
realism, 191-93
Réflecteur, 33, 38, 44
repetition, 141, 151-52
research techniques, 29-30
resignation, 66, 67
Robespierre, 31, 32
Roger of Wendover, 110
Rohde, Peter P., 56, 167
romanticism, 36, 40-41, 45, 54-56, 58, 64, 67, 180, 190-93, 194
Roos, Carl, 159n.1, 160-61n.6, 168-71, 174
Roskilde Consultative Assembly, 27, 29
Rousseau, Jean-Jacques, 59, 89, 92
Rubow, Poul, 56
Rudelbach, Andreas Gottlob, 138

Saint-Simon, Comte de (Claude-Henri de Rouvroy); St. Simonists, 12, 19-23
Sallust, 142, 166
Sand, George, 10, 11, 13
Saphir, Moritz Gottlieb, 191
Schall, Karl, 191
Schlegel, Friedrich, 56, 67
Schleiermacher, Friedrich, 152
Schopenhauer, A., 122
School of Civic Virtue (*Borgerdydskolen*), 136

Schall, Karl, 191
Schiller, Johann Christian Friedrich von, 6, 112, 175
Schlegel, Friedrich, 112
Schubart, C. F. D., 112, 113
Scribe, Augustin Eugøne, 115, 162n.7, 167, 168n.21,
"sentimental idyllic," 36, 40-41
sexism, 7-25
Shakespeare, William, 181
Shelley, P. B., 113-16, 125
Sibbern, Frederik, 11
sin, sinner, 141, 148
Slesvig-Holstein, 27, 37
social change, 32-33
Spinoza, Benedict, 152
St.-Georges, J. M. V. de, 115
Student Association, the (*Studenterforeningen*), 134
Sue, Eugène, 115
Suetonius, 167
suffering, 148

Talleyrand-Perigord, Charles Maurice de, 94
Thulstrup, Niels, 13, 33, 134, 138-39, 156, 159, 160-61n.6
Tieck, Ludwig, 67
Tjønneland, E., 130n.
Tøjner, P. E., 130n.
Topsøe-Jensen, Helge, 51, 73
Tranholm, Iben, 132
Tscherning, Anton, Frederik, 20

understanding, 147
"universally human," 2

Walsh, Sylvia, 22, 45, 46, 48
Wandering Jew, the, 3-5, 109-130
Watkin, Julia, 1-2, 24, 73, 131, 134-35, 138-39, 165, 166n.18, 168n.21, 176
Wessel, Johann Herman, 165, 166
Wieland, Christoph Martin, 176-78
Winge, Mette, 10
woman; gender issues, 1-2, 7-25
Wulff, Henriette, 17

Young Germany, 5, 47, 67, 121

Zacchaeus, 141, 165-66

Early Polemical Writings
International Kierkegaard Commentary 1

Mercer University Press, 6316 Peake Road, Macon GA 31210-3960.
Isbn 0-86554-656-8. Catalog and warehouse pick number MUP/H489.
Original (1984) text, interior, cover, and dustjacket design
    by Margaret Jordan Brown; recast (1992) by Edmon L. Rowell, Jr.
Camera-ready pages, cover, and dustjacket
    composed by Edmon L. Rowell, Jr. on a Gateway 2000
        via WordPerfect wp/5.1 and wpwin/5.1/5.2/6.1/7.0
        and printed on a LaserMaster 1000
        and a Hewlett Packard LaserJet 4/4M (Postscript).
Text font: Palatino 11/13 and 10/12. Display font: Palatino italic.
Printed and bound by Cushing-Malloy, Inc., Ann Arbor MI 48107.
    Printed via offset lithography on 50# Glatfelter Natural, B-31.
    Smyth sewn with Rainbow Pearl A endsheets tipped.
    Casebound in Kivar 9 over .088 binders boards;
        stamped on c.1, spine, and c.4 in blue foil with one hit gold foil
        on c.1 from dies supplied by Cushing-Malloy, Inc.;
        with black and white headbands and footbands;
        wrapped in dustjackets printed 2 pms colors
        (427 gray, 302 blue) and layflat film laminated.

[May 1999]

051299elr